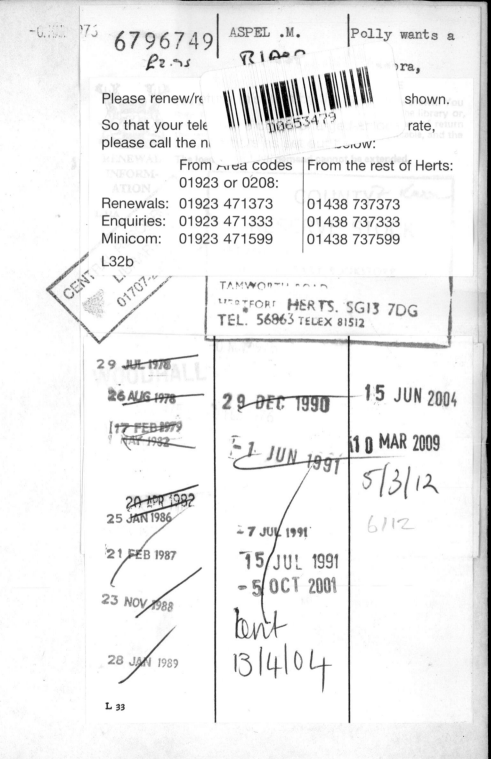

Polly wants a zebra

Polly wants a zebra

———◆———

The memoirs of Michael Aspel

Weidenfeld and Nicolson
London

Chapter two, 'The evacuees', appeared in a slightly
different form in the book,
The Evacuees, ed. B. S. Johnson, published
by Gollancz.

Weidenfeld and Nicolson
11 St John's Hill London SW11

ISBN 0 297 76835 2

Printed in Great Britain by
Butler & Tanner Ltd, Frome and London

For Gregory, Richard, Edward and Jane

Contents

Illustrations

Illustrations

16 With Elizabeth Power in *Private Lives* at the Devonshire Park Theatre, Eastbourne, February 1974 (*Reproduced by kind permission of Charles Vance of the Eastbourne Theatre Company*)

The author and publishers are grateful to the owners for permission to reproduce the pictures.

Line drawing on page 51 by Michael Aspel

Preface

Write a book, they said. What about? I said. About you, they said. But I'm only a lad, I said, I've only just begun. Nonsense, they said. You're a big boy now, and you've been in the game a long time. Go away and write about it.

So here, many blisters and ball-points later, is the book. I can't say it was easy. I can't type, and I'm now a registered sufferer of that exotic disease, writer's cramp. But apart from the stolen jokes and borrowed anecdotes, it's all my own. I hope you find it easy to read. If not, the fault is entirely mine. Thank you. And now the weather forecast.

MICHAEL ASPEL
Maida Vale,
April 1974

I

Polly wants a zebra

Question: What do you get if you cross a parrot with a lion?
Answer: A bird that says 'Polly wants a Zebra'.

Not only is that one of my favourite silly jokes, but I feel a strong affinity with Polly. I don't just mean because I too want the impossible, but because over the years, I've evolved into what might be described as a hybrid parrot spraying words out in many different directions. Certainly it's difficult to define my working role. I have a rather confused image; what can you call a person whose work ranges from current affairs to the Miss World contest – apart from greedy?

My passport describes me as a broadcaster, and that's what I've been, in various disguises, for the past twenty years. But one or two things occurred before then. Take what happened in 1933.

That was a significant year. Hitler, the Loch Ness monster, and me. The other two got bigger headlines when they emerged, but I still caused quite a stir at No. 78 Grant Road, Battersea.

Of course, not all the years that followed were quite so glorious. Being born at that time meant being old enough to be frightened when war came, being too young to be involved in the action, and being simply the wrong age immediately afterwards. Teenagers in the late forties did not count. We had no money. We weren't commercially exploitable. Our voices were seldom raised, and the girls' skirts never. Not down our street, anyway. Perhaps that's why fellows of my vintage are so often described as the oldest teenagers in the business, desperately trying to cash in on today's lively goings-on before being trendy means looking grotesque.

So I am now in my forties, and as life, I am assured, has just begun, let me offer you from the crossroads an account of those pre-natal years as a representative of a generation that wasn't lost, but wasn't quite sure of the direction either. On second thoughts I'll speak for myself.

As soon as any child gets beyond the 'gimme sweetie' stage – and sometimes before – someone starts asking him what he wants to *be*. There are children who start knocking out tunes on the violin at the age of eighteen months. But not every child wants to entertain cinema queues, and a large percentage of us are doing what we are doing now by accident, persuasion or necessity. Whoever in the mid-1930s wanted to be a TV announcer? It hadn't even occurred to me by the mid-1950s – just a couple of years before I mutated into that very animal. There are many plumbers, bus conductors, post office clerks and housewives who are pulsating with unexpressed talents – talents which they may be unaware of themselves, but leave them with a nagging feeling that there is something they could do really well given a chance. There are also a lot of people in glamorous professions who would be much better suited handing out tickets or fitting new sink units.

I read of a man who came to this country as an immigrant, with three shillings and sixpence in his pocket. Forty years later, he was an office boy. There are many heartwarming stories like that. God knows what I would be doing if I hadn't somehow landed on my feet in the broadcasting business. My father's ambition was for me to become a customs and excise officer. That was because he loves uniforms. He was in the army for many years, before and during the second world war, and afterwards he was a commissionaire at the front door of the *Sunday Times*, where they respected his work a lot more than they respect mine.

No, as a small child I never felt a deep compulsion to become a customs and excise officer. To be honest, the BBC's 'Children's Hour' and Uncle Mac represented all that was desirable in the outside world. What a thrill it was to be told by Uncle Mac that we all had shocking handwriting and that he could hardly read our postcards. I won a prize at elementary school for taking part in a little Christmas frolic. It was a book called *Wireless in Toytown*. The fabric front of our wireless was a bit tattered, and I used to trace the action of the plays we listened to on the loose tendrils of material, then in the pattern on the wallpaper. Heroes at that time? Larry the Lamb, and comic characters like those enervated gentlemen of the road, Tired Tim and Weary Willie, Bonzo the Dog (Oh – and Darkie Peters the local policeman who was afraid of nobody, and would even walk down Wardley Street alone at night).

We also enjoyed looking at photographs of Dad's early days with the mounted artillery in India. A pyramid of young men with Dad at the base, feet astride two fine stallions. He's had a lot of hernia trouble since those days.

On my birth certificate, my father's profession is listed as 'newsagent'. He ran a little shop in Knockholt, Kent, but I was born in my granny's house a few hundred yards from Clapham Junction station, where more railway lines crisscrossed than anywhere else in the world. Could it be that with my father in the business of selling news, and all that communication going on just round the corner, destiny was weaving a pattern for me, even as I filled my nappy? The answer is no – I have always found it difficult to retain anything but the most lurid of facts, and get lost on the simplest of journeys; I was never to be the James Cameron of Wandsworth.

My parents still live in the flat where we all lived after the brief sojourn at Granny's. One night when I was two years and ten months old, my father crept into the room, picked me up and whispered, 'Come and see what Father Christmas has brought us.' It was a baby brother and he did not impress me as a Christmas present. Even now I look at Alan and think wistfully of building bricks. Sister Pat was two years older than me, and that's how the family remained until the arrival, twelve years later, of brother Geoffrey. He was a surprise for one and all, as were many of the 'Bulge' babies of 1944. Apparently during the blitz of the early forties, places like Hyde Park were writhing masses of uniformed couples, hot limbs entwined in the ultimate embrace – just in case a bomb should drop and they'd never have another chance. In recent years I heard of a town in Austria which has a birth rate eleven times greater than the rest of the country. It seems that through some quirk of geography they are unable to get television pictures, and the nights are long in those parts. It gives me a small thrill of pride to know that my industry is doing its bit to ease the population problem.

3

Polly wants a zebra

So far as I remember, those prewar 'Wireless in Toytown' days were happy enough – not too deprived, lots of home-made fun, with sister Pat keeping us awake laughing, pretending to play the piano on her pillow, and keeping us awake weeping – with her rendition of 'The Little Boy That Santa Claus Forgot'.

I have a memory of my mother in a long blue dress going out for the evening, and I seem to hear at the same time the strains of 'Just the Way You Look Tonight'. But my parents never went out, except to the pictures, so where did that memory come from? Perhaps she was merely wrapped in an old army blanket, going out the back for some more coal.

My mother is very small, just under five feet, and it is very pleasing to stand next to her. 'The tallest midget in Britain,' my father would declare. She would reply, 'All good things come in small parcels, Ted,' and he would say, 'So does poison, Vi.' There was no rancour in all this. It was just a ritual they went through for our amusement.

The street we lived in was and is typical of hundreds in London's suburbs. Our flat number was 42, and the people who lived above were in number 42A. The front doors were set close together. Then came a baroque sort of arch, and then flats numbers 44 and 44A. The railings that topped the low wall in front of the flats were later sawn off to provide much-needed metal for the munitions drive. The stumps still protrude like blackened teeth.

By putting a small poster in the front room window, my parents got free trips to the local cinema. The posters advertised the latest pictures. My first taste of the cinema, a taste that developed into an obsession, was a cowboy movie. I was about five, I suppose. My mother tried to explain to me what was happening, but I couldn't understand why the men came running out of the house (saloon) and kept falling down ('biting the dust' whispered Mum). It also took me a long time to get over the fear that we were going to be drowned shortly after we took our seats in the Supershow – that, believe it or not, was the name of the local 'bug-hutch'. Why the fear of drowning? My sister had told me that most of the films we saw were American, and that between England and America was the Atlantic Ocean, and one day the screen was going to split and

4

the ocean was going to come rushing in and fill up the Super-show.

I mentioned Darkie Peters, the stalwart copper who feared no-one. He was never held up as a bogie-man and used as a threat like he was in some families. ('If you don't shut up in there, I'll send for Darkie Peters and he will take you away and lock you up!') He was one of the original Friendly Police-men, the protector, the Keeper of the Law, strong, wise, incor-ruptible. And if he really *did* walk down Wardley Street alone, you can add Flash Gordon, Buck Jones, Tarzan and Captain Marvel to that list.

That part of Garrett Lane was the darkest and toughest, and although Wardley Street had the worst reputation, the next street, Lydden Road, certainly looked the most horrific. It was occupied exclusively by the costermongers, and they had built sheds on the pavements in front of the terraced houses. These sheds were, in fact, garages or stables – the cart would be left in there and the horse led through the house to the yard at the back. So from the top of the road, and that's the closest we got, our fearful peep would reveal a menacing shanty town of lean-tos in various stages of collapse. One of my father's other enterprises at that time was a cafe. That is a euphemism for what was really a sheet of corrugated iron supported by three brick walls. It was near Lydden Road, it served the barrow-boys, and he called it with great flair 'Ted's Refreshments'. According to Dad you couldn't find a friendlier, more warm-hearted bunch of fellows in the land than his clientele. That adventure didn't last long, but although my folks never struck a really successful formula, nobody could say they weren't game. Some years before Pat was born, they took themselves off to Australia. It cost hardly a penny to emigrate, but it was a hard journey.

The men and women were separated, the weather was often rough, and conditions were like a below-decks scene from the 'Onedin Line'. And it took a very long time. However, they made it, and for four years they lived out in the bush of New South Wales, my father working as a station-hand and my mother doing the cooking. She learned at her employers' expense; she claimed to be an expert in order to get the job, but in fact hadn't quite mastered the art of boiling water. If I repeated some of the tricks she used in the early days, particularly when colouring gravy, the survivors would even now start legal proceedings. Apparently they were happy days, the memories becoming rosier as the years pass. There are some romantic sepia photographs from that time, one showing my mother silhouetted at sunset, sitting on a horse. She's facing the wrong way. She didn't, as you might suspect, take to the raw outback life quite so easily as my father, and when she saw a real live duck-billed platypus, frolicking in its own habitat, she decided that Australia had given up enough of its secrets, that the allure of foreign parts had gone, and that she wanted to go home and have her baby in England. The baby, of course, was Pat, and the family joke has always been that Pat was manufactured in Australia and produced in England.

2
The evacuees

When Pat was eight and I was six and Alan was three, war broke out. I don't remember any of the build up, any of the 'peace in our time' paper-waving of Mr Chamberlain, or anything about Poland. All I can recall is the growing air of menace and gloom, and I remember asking my father, 'Is there going to be a war?' He said of course not. My next clear memory – and of course it's been recalled in films, on radio and TV programmes a thousand times since – is Chamberlain's broadcast, the announcement that put the lie to all the brave and optimistic reassurances. We weren't too young to understand the gist of what he was saying. I can still feel the terror grow as that statement moved on inexorably to the phrase which ended all hope: 'I have to tell you that this country is now at war with Germany.'

I can't exaggerate the drama of that moment. Everyone who heard it will recall the atmosphere surrounding the broadcast, and the depth of the silence as he paused between each fateful word.

When you're six years old you can't spring to your feet and cry, 'Let's get out there, chaps, and have a crack at the Hun!' You can't weigh up the situation, calculate your chances or think in terms of a quick, clean fight and all home for Christmas. What you feel is the dread of men with sinister uniforms marching through your streets, burning everything down and dragging you away.

At school they made us try gas-masks for size. For the infants, there were masks with Mickey Mouse faces. For the rest of us, those sawn-off elephant trunks, which kept steaming up. The visor of mine was too close to my face and kept bending my eyelashes.

7

There was talk of evacuation, a word they made sound exciting and adventurous, and there were a few practice runs.

Then one day, it happened.

We marched through the streets of Wandsworth, just as we'd done several times before, with labels round our necks, heading for the railway station. Only this time people stood on their doorsteps to watch us pass, and shopkeepers gave us sweets and packets of nuts and raisins. And this time, instead of assembling on the platform at Earlsfield station then marching back to school again, they put us on a train.

I have a picture in my mind of the steps of Earlsfield station. There are short legs by the score, clambering upwards, none shorter or fatter than Alan's. He was four years old by this time, and surprisingly delicate for such a chubby little boy.

By mid-afternoon we were being re-assembled in a large dark building. Even then we were unaware that there was anything sinister in the day's developments; but we were aware an hour or so later. Then, one by one, occasionally in twos and threes, children were taken away by smiling strangers. Our numbers dwindled; my brother and sister went, and by the time I was called, there were very few left. I worked it out afterwards that my sister had to take our brother with her because he was the baby, and she, being the eldest, had to take care of him. I imagined I, being seven years old, was regarded as being practically independent.

The smiling stranger who took me explained, as we bounced along in a car which was small even to me, that we were in Chard, in the county of Somerset. My sister, brother and I, and all the other children, were evacuees. We were to spend a short, happy time in the country. The war would soon be over, and then we should be going home. The little car bumped and rattled through the town. It was late afternoon, and the brightness was going out of the day. My spirits were sinking too. I was confused; it wasn't fun any more. Where had they taken my brother and sister? Where had all the others been driven off to? Would we ever meet again? How far away was London? The man sensed how I was feeling and tried to cheer me up with assurances of what nice people I was going to stay with, and what a fine time I was going to have. I wasn't very responsive, and looked out of the window at Chard. Rows of small houses, one side higher than the other, with occasional steps leading down from the raised pavement. The doors of the houses opened straight on to the street.

The road curved a lot, and started to rise. Less houses now; long stretches of bleak wall, shutting off . . . what, a prison? No, must be a farm, or a big house belonging to someone rich. Then we passed a place which hissed and clanged and smoked – an iron foundry, I was told, where my new foster-father worked. 'Nearly there now.' The road forked; we kept to the left. A hundred yards more, and we had arrived. Park Cottages was a row of terraced houses, red coloured, not a bit like cottages really, with small front gardens. They were built on a gentle slope.

We went through the front gate with a seven on it, and along the short path. I could see a potted plant in the front room window. The man knocked at the door. There was no reply. Then, to my surprise, he turned the knob, opened the door, and pushed me into the house. A staircase led almost from the front door, but to the right of the tiny hall was the room containing the potted plant. The man murmured a few encouraging phrases, patted my shoulder, and was gone. I heard the little car buzz away.

I've often wondered why he left me standing there. I suppose he'd had a pretty hard day. I don't know how many journeys he'd made, how many pale-faced kids he'd delivered. He knew he'd brought me to the right place; my label said so.

It was incredibly quiet in that room; an almost oppressive silence, complete except for the ticking of a clock. No traffic, no voices, no footsteps. There was a strange smell, too, not unpleasant, but different from our own front room. The furniture was brown and leathery. There was an oval mirror over the fireplace, and a picture on each wall of the same old-fashioned lady in various attitudes. She was dressed the same in every picture. She wore a long white nightgown, and she seemed very fond of animals. Behind me, the window, a small table, and the aspidistra. On the table was a strange-looking wooden structure like a vice. Strands of golden wire hung from

9

it, and what looked like bits of bristle an inch or so long littered the surface of the table.

I don't know how long I waited – probably not more than a few minutes. Then I heard footsteps in the room beyond a closed door. A second later the door opened, and a middle-aged woman walked in. She was tall and heavily built.

I realized later she wasn't actually a very big woman, but compared with my mother she seemed huge.

The tall woman and I stared at each other. I saw that her hair was white, streaked with grey. She wore glasses which rested on a generous nose. I stared up two large, round nostrils. Her eyes were fierce, but her mouth was wide and smiling. She wore a cotton dress with flowers on it, an apron over this with more flowers, thick brown wrinkly stockings and black shoes which bulged painfully in several places.

What she saw was, I suppose, a round-faced little boy, with spiky hair and dark rings under his eyes; travel-stained shirt, Fair Isle pullover, short trousers above thin legs, scuffed shoes. And a label.

I was the first to speak – and what I said would have made Dickens proud, 'Please, I'm the new evacuee,' I said. Strange that I don't remember what she said, but I know she led me into the kitchen and sat me at the table. I kept the same position at that table for the next four and a half years.

I don't know how Rose Larcombe would have rated as a cook; small boys judge by quantity, and a poor cook would be someone who gave you an excess of brussels sprouts. Two features of Aunt Rose's meals were to become familiar. First, her new potatoes. They were the smallest, sweetest things imaginable. She made a good gravy, and when those delicious pebbles were sliced open and splashed around, ecstasy wasn't far off. Unfortunately it wasn't long-lived either; because no matter what we had for 'afters' Aunt Rose insisted that I took bread with it. Every mouthful of prunes, or rice-pudding, or just plain custard, had to be followed by the hateful bread and marge. Why she made this rule still baffles me. Perhaps she reasoned that if I ate more bread, I'd eat less of the other stuff, and so supplies would last longer; she may honestly have thought that it was good for me; it may have been a local custom. Or it could be that it was intended to be an early lesson in life: that too much undiluted pleasure is bad for the soul, one must take the rough with the smooth and so on.

But that first evening I found more to brood over than spoiled prunes.

The room grew more and more oppressive. Every object in it took on a strange and hostile aspect. I shrank into myself, and saw instead miles and miles of railway track, now dark, and at the end of it, home. I was completely cut off. Somewhere, not too far away, were Pat and Alan. I imagined them in a bright cheerful place. Between us, darkness, but a specially quiet and sinister darkness. Eventually the thoughts became too much to bear. Without taking my eyes off the tablecloth I said, 'I want my Mum.'

Once again it was Rose Larcombe's actions rather than her reply that I remember. She went to a cupboard and, after a few minutes' rummaging, brought out an air rifle. It belonged to her son Leonard, now in his twenties, and a soldier.

It was an interesting exchange. Small boy wants his mother; he gets a gun. Wise Aunt Rose. It had been a long time since her son was a child, but she still knew that the only swift solution to some emotional problems was a material one. How long it would have worked in my case I don't know, because a few minutes later there were heavy footsteps at the back of the house, and a large man appeared at the kitchen door. He was a good deal taller than the woman, which made him a giant in my eyes. Huge dusty boots disappeared into a vast expanse of blue dungarees, enough material in each leg to make me two overcoats. In the middle distance, a well-worn sports coat, with a bag of brown material hanging from the left shoulder. A Thermos flask protruded from the bag.

A large hand disappeared upwards and came down again holding a cloth cap. Then the whole figure bent forward, and a lean, dark, strong face came close to mine. This was George Larcombe. He smiled, put his hand on my shoulder, and said, 'Wobby dune yur? Ascum from Lunnon? Tes battur yur, snow.' It was difficult to know how to react to this. Was I expected to reply? Happily he quickly followed up this statement with the second generous gesture of the evening. From a pocket bulging with metal rulers and other instruments, he produced a two-shilling piece. As he gave it to me, he uttered some more foreign words. Again I was baffled, but his tone was gentle, and the two-bob bit was real enough, so I murmured, 'Thank you very much.'

I don't think I ever learned Uncle George's birthplace, but it was far enough to the south west of Aunt Rose's to make his accent almost twice as thick. His face was the face of a Cornishman. Photographs of his son showed the same dark looks, the long face and the splendid nose.

We listened to the wireless for a time, to hear the latest news of the war. Leonard was in the infantry, and would soon be going abroad. Then it was time for bed – for me, anyway. There was none of the noisy ritual we had at home. No 'Come on kids – B-E-D!' No groans and shouted protests. I drank up my cocoa, and followed the Larcombes up the stairs. I think my room must once have been the bridal suite, because the bed was large, and Aunt Rose's room, where I was to call in time of need, contained only a single bed. My suitcase was unpacked and my belongings were lost in a cavernous chest of drawers. My attention was drawn to an equally cavernous po which lay half under the bed. The lavatory being too far away for convenience (it was downstairs and out the back), this was a vital piece of furniture. One night some months later I was taken short but missed the po in the dark. After that the lavatory was considered to be within reasonable distance.

I scaled the sides of the bed. The floor seemed a long way off. The Larcombes told me to sleep well, and went out. I lay deep in a feather mattress, another novel experience. The oppressive silence bore in on me again. My ears began to ring. I sat up in bed. The room was dimly lit by a small lamp – a first night luxury. There were more pictures, so sombre that in that half light I couldn't make out the details. Over the foot of the bed, a sampler. I could read its message clearly. 'Blessed are the pure in heart, for they shall see the Kingdom of Heaven.' I lay back and closed my eyes. At once I saw and heard again the things that had happened that extraordinary day. Endless railway tracks, fields flashing past – 'take Alan to the lav' – the small car jolted again – 'nearly there now' – Leonard's airgun – the po far below me – 'Blessed are the pure in Heart...'

Something was touching my mouth. I woke at once and sat up, bumping my face against Rose Larcombe's. I squinted up at her through the brightness streaming into the room. Her nose was red and her eyes were watering. I don't know whether I guessed it at the time – I might have, because I didn't ask her what was the matter – but I concluded later that she was moved by what she saw. Small head on pillow where her own boy's had lain years ago; probably, too, the added poignancy of my reason for being there. It was a moment of extreme tenderness for Aunt Rose, I'm sure of that. Not surprisingly, it was never to be repeated. I didn't give her a very easy time of it, and there were many occasions over the years to come when Aunt Rose's emotions towards me were far from tender. It's remarkable, when I come to think of it, that either of us survived the experience. Oddly enough, on the one occasion when it seemed there might be a chance for me to live elsewhere, with several other children, neither of us wanted it. By then ours had become a kind of Tom and Jerry relationship – not always the best of friends, but needing each other.

The mood I awoke to that morning was one of happy anticipation. A chance to explore my surroundings, to find out what had happened to Pat and Alan. I knelt on the bed and looked out of the window. The back garden was long and narrow, and it wasn't so much a garden as an allotment. No flowers grew, but there was a profusion of vegetables. At the far end, a shed which looked as if it might hold all sorts of exciting things – more guns, perhaps; some war relics; at the very least an array of impressive tools. On either side of our garden lay other segments of land. Park Cottages consisted of only a dozen or so houses. The fences between the plots weren't high, so that if you stood midway down the garden path of Number One, you could see the boundary fence of the last house. I looked beyond the gardens. There were more houses some distance away set at an angle to ours, but between us there was an expanse of lumpy ground covered with straggling bushes. Smashing, I thought.

Over breakfast Rose Larcombe (George having gone to

work) explained to me that she had heard that my brother and sister had been taken to stay with the Dalbys. Something in her voice when she mentioned the name suggested that the Dalbys were people of substance. And so it turned out to be. After living in a flat in Wandsworth, it was a great thrill now to realize that any sounds coming from overhead would be made by one of us.

But my admiration for my new home faded when I saw 'Greenbanks', the Dalby residence. It was large and square, and stood at a discreet distance from its neighbours (it was several miles from Park Cottages). It even had a drive, with a gate on each side of the immaculate front hedge. Pat and Alan came screeching from the side of the house, and you could almost see it wince as our London accents twanged and ricocheted from its walls.

I don't know how the allocation of billets was organized, whether all foster-parents were volunteers or whether there were callers in the night who said, 'You'll take two.' Certainly some unlikely families were formed. If I was incongruous in the Larcombes' house, it was mainly because they had probably forgotten what little boys were like: there were no social problems.

My brother and sister looked definitely odd in the 'Greenbanks' setting. There the problem was not that the Dalbys had forgotten how to handle children. The problem was that they had never known; and the situation was complicated by the fact that these children were from a completely different environment. We had never been in a 'drawing room', never used a 'toilet'. Although we too used euphemisms for the basic things in life, ours sounded crude in comparison with theirs. I was never able to imagine that anyone 'posh' would make a nasty smell in the lav.

The Dalby family – at least, those living at 'Greenbanks', consisted of Mr Dalby, a widower, and to me always a remote, patriarchal figure. He seemed to be very old. He had been a businessman, a JP and was once the Mayor of Chard. Then, two of his daughters, Frances and Meg. Both were unmarried, and it was Frances who ran the house. It was Frances who now had the job of looking after two children. She tackled it with courage and firmness. She had immediately overwhelmed

Alan. She frightened me when I saw her. Even Pat – brave, imperturbable Pat – was awed into temporary submission. Frances Dalby wasn't large, she wasn't old, she wasn't beetle-browed. Her spectacles were the only remotely intimidating feature of her appearance. And yet she controlled everything around her with complete authority.

A wire-haired terrier completed the family circle. No doubt about it, it was a nice place. 'Narf smashin,' I whispered to Pat. 'Yeah,' she said, without too much conviction. And somehow I couldn't feel very envious of my brother and sister. We wanted desperately to be together, but if that wasn't possible, then it was quite a consolation to live with people like Uncle George and Aunt Rose. I would boast about them as soon as I met another kid I could boast to. 'My Lady makes tooth-brushes,' I would say nonchalantly (for that's what she did with the bits of wire and bristle I'd seen the day before), 'and Mr Larcombe has got ever such a lot of tools and things.' And their son was a soldier. I mustn't forget that. He'd be coming home on leave sometime.

Chard itself turned out to be fascinating. The main street was on a slope, and on each side little rivers ran. The gutters weren't flooded, these were permanent and intended streams which disappeared now and then under pedestrian crossings. The town hall was half-way down the High Street. This was where we had all gathered on our arrival.

An ironmonger's, just opposite the town hall, boasted a star-chamber above the shop, where the dreaded Judge Jeffreys had held his court. But the most marvellous discovery in those first few days was the reservoir – the 'rezzie'. It lay a mile or so outside the town, a great stretch of dark water, the next best thing to the sea I'd yet come across. Swimming was allowed, and I marked it high on my list.

Of course we didn't forget home just like that. An air rifle doesn't make a permanent substitute for the family life, and our foster-parents must sometimes have found it a little difficult to keep the impatience out of their voices when answering for the twentieth time that day the question, 'When shall I be going home?'

One day I tried to work out how long I'd been an evacuee. Life before that time seemed to be getting a bit hazy, so I reckoned it to be about nine months. I was out walking with Uncle George at the time. He was singing his favourite song – or the song he thought amused me most:

'A huntin' we will go,
A huntin' we will go
To catch a fox
An' put'n in a box
A huntin' we will go,'

sang Uncle George. It seemed to me that I had heard that song before so many times that I really must have been living in Chard for an age.

'Uncle George?'

'Ar?'

'How long have I been here?'

'Ooh ... well, let's see now. Well ... I s'pose 'tes gettin' on for six weeks now, snow.'

Six weeks. It was a dreadful shock, because although time moves faster or slower in relation to age, it's also relative to the situation. If I had been told we were all due to go back to London in six weeks' time, it would have been an agonizing prospect, an endless wait. But to have only a month and a half behind one was not impressive.

After a few months, our strange surroundings became familiar, and new routines were established.

Settling into the new school was exciting, sometimes a little too much so, because for us 'vaccies' there was no cordial welcome from the local kids. All they extended to us was a fast-moving fist between the eyes.

They were not to be blamed. In fact, they saw themselves as little patriots, valiantly repelling invaders. The fact that we were unwilling invaders made no difference, and we fought back as tenaciously as if our lives were dedicated to the complete domination of the town.

The most familiar sound in that divided playground, rising clearly above the shrieks and squeals was the shout of, 'Free fight! Free fight!' And there inside a circle eight deep would be one of them and one of us locked in combat. I was often our representative, being not big but quick-tempered.

A fight was only a fight if the two were fairly matched in size.

The evacuees

Fights rarely ended in a knockout. They were a combination
of punching and wrestling, and it was usually the wrestling
that decided the contest. Heads were squeezed beyond the
point of endurance, or 'secret' holds were applied – usually to
the front of the trousers.

The loser wasn't always honest enough to admit he'd been
fairly beaten. As soon as he felt the unyielding pressure of the
other boy's 'double whammy' around his throat he'd croak,
'Ah! My bad back!/ear!/ankle!' as the need dictated.

Scraps weren't confined to the opposite camps. There was
inevitably a fair amount of civil war. For a short but glorious
period I was the playground champ: my temper saw to that.
Of course I got my come-uppance. A lanky, good-looking lad
called Georgie Duckworth finally relieved me of the title. It
was an ignominious experience. Georgie specialized in a sophisticated version of the half-nelson with a bit of nostril-stretching
thrown in. Today, doctors tell me that the blockage in my right
nostril is caused by a fibroid, but I know it's because of something Georgie Duckworth did with his finger.

Just about the most unfortunate playground victims were
the contingent of Chinese children from Limehouse. They were
given the title of 'Dirty yellow Japs', and came in for merciless
hammering from our hosts, which they didn't take with any
oriental calm and a hiss of 'ah, so'. They yelled 'git orf' and
hit back.

But the most horrible and cruel irony came when an under-
sized boy with a strange, guttural voice was set upon. Whether
his tormentors were country children or evacuees, I can't
remember. They could have been either, because they were
about to beat him for being a 'dirty rotten German Nazi'.
Some of us knew the truth, that he was an Austrian refugee.
He was rescued from that particular assault.

We didn't live in perpetual strife. Amidst all the brawling
and raspberry-blowing, true friendships were born. Very soon
after we arrived, a partnership was formed between two other
Londoners and myself which made the Three Musketeers look
positively incompatible.

Albie Mallows, Ronnie Bronstein and me. Albie, with a
great laughing face, was from my part of London; Ronnie was
small and dark and came from north of the Thames. The whole

Bronstein family had come to Chard. The children were all extremely clever. I was invited into their house once or twice and was fascinated by Mr Bronstein, who had a thick, unfamiliar accent, and talked a lot about dollars.

Albie, Ronnie and I shared almost every adventure for the next four and a half years. Together we scavenged and preyed upon the American troops who were briefly stationed outside the town. We scoured their rubbish dumps for the grubby pound notes and perfect leather boots they jettisoned. They felt bad about our situation as evacuees, and we became their messenger boys and mascots.

We learned a lot about life from those men. One day I was on my way home from an afternoon down at the rezzie with Albie and Ronnie when a black soldier called to me 'Hey, boy. What you doin'? Picking flowers?' He gave me a card with his name and photograph on it and asked me if I knew of any nice lady who would like to go out with him. There was a woman who sometimes took me to the pictures. Each Tuesday night, she would take me to the Cerdic. It was usually the Cerdic, because that was bigger and posher than the Regent. I've forgotten her name, but she had black hair in ringlets on her forehead, like Oliver Hardy, and bright spots of rouge on each cheek. Anyway, I showed her the card with the soldier's name and photograph and soon afterwards, my Tuesday evening outings were finished.

There weren't only American troops stationed near us. There were Poles as well for a time. They were pretty kind too.

Not long after the troops arrived, we began to find strange objects like soggy balloons in the grass and hanging from bushes. I don't know the effect the friendly military invasion had on the population figures for Chard. Probably the additions outweighed the girls carried off as GI brides, and there are no doubt quite a few gentle Somerset lads whose paternal grandparents live in Texas or New Jersey.

One afternoon a group of us were on one of our parasitic raids of the American camp when a soldier, cleaning his rifle said, 'See this bayonet, kid? Know what that's for?' 'For sticking in Germans,' I said. 'No, kid,' he said, 'that's for rippin' up them goddamned niggers.' I didn't know that there were any black men in the German army – or the Japanese army, for that matter, but luckily no-one else pursued the subject and I put it out of my mind.

Something that wasn't so easy to forget was a photograph another GI showed me. 'Want to see a picture of my wife, boy?' he said – and he produced a photograph of a woman, stark naked, posing with a bow and arrow. I went crimson, but was fascinated. There was a dark upturned triangle between her legs. 'What's that?' I asked. He didn't answer. They all just slapped their thighs and squealed with laughter.

A GI named Philip Demopoulos wanted to know if my parents would allow me to go to the States. It was an exciting prospect.

One morning they were gone, and in the deserted barrack-room I found a box full of badges and buttons. On the lid of the box was scrawled: 'To Mike from the Boys. So long, Kid. It was swell knowing you.'

Visits from our parents were rare and wonderful. I remember one occasion when my mother came alone. I raced to meet her, straight from Sunday School, where I had just signed the pledge – at the age of eight. (I broke it three weeks later when the cider was passed around during hay-making, and afterwards walked around hunched-up, waiting for the shaft of retribution from above.) As I turned a corner, I ran into our Monday-to-Friday headmistress. When I told her I was hurrying to meet my mother, she gave me lengthy instructions on the way a gentleman should greet a lady. And she watched me as I stopped before my mother's outstretched arms and doffed my cap and said formal and polite things. My mother was quite upset. That was the time she wore her new false teeth. They had obviously been designed for someone else, and seemed to have thirty-two in the top row.

Dad was in the army, but in the memory I have of him he is wearing civilian clothes, springing towards us, looking every inch the warrior back from the front that I claimed him to be. Actually he was an instructor in the RAOC. His subject – preservation and packing of army equipment. Not quite so exciting as those prewar days in India – but less chance of a hernia.

After two years, my sister went back to London. She'd not

settled, and was determined to rejoin my mother, who was secretly glad to have her with her.

Pat had refused to allow herself to be moulded into a 'little lady'. Deceptively gentle, she had a strong personality and a will of her own. And yet she is probably the least spiteful and most unselfish person I know. I ground my teeth and wept on her behalf when, one Christmas in Chard, the school hall was filled with two huge piles of gifts – one for the boys, one for the girls. As our names were picked from a hat, we were allowed to come forward and choose a present. Pat's name was the very last. She had seen big dolls, pretty dresses, books, games, all disappear. I hated those happy, lucky, greedy kids who'd gone before. Pat was left with a small glass-fronted box containing tiny marbles which you had to roll into holes. Her smile of pleasure convinced almost everybody.

One night the whole town was awakened by the sound of falling bombs. We knew the noise bombs made – we'd all been to the pictures.

A crippled German plane had jettisoned its load. None of the bombs exploded, and the most exciting part of the war for us was to hear the boom and see the black smoke when the Sappers came and detonated them. The craters were magnificent.

That was the nearest war came. To us it meant occasional incomprehensible newspaper headlines and stern voices on the wireless. I did caper about when we were told that Italy had capitulated, but only because I thought it meant we should be going home the next day. For the rest of the time there was school (where I studied Miss Guppy's legs), afternoons down at the rezzie with Albie and Ronnie, and the 'Happidrome' on the wireless on Sunday nights. (We three, we're not highbrow, working for the BBC . . . Ramsbotham and Enoch and me . . .)

But it was the cinema I enjoyed most. Every Saturday afternoon, it was down to the Cerdic.

The authorities were very lax about children and films.

They were categorized U, A, and later, H. If a film was U, anybody, adult or child, could see it. If it was an A, you had to be sixteen, or you could go in with an adult. When the H (for Horror) certificate arrived, then a child couldn't see the film in any circumstances.

That was the system – except in Chard.

There, everybody could see everything.

When a very popular film was shown, like Disney's *Dumbo*, or one of Abbott and Costello's, or the Bowery Boys, the management would put wooden benches in front of the front seats, so that the screen was almost behind us, and our heads rolled back so far that only the whites of our eyes were visible. But for tuppence a go there were no complaints, except when the manager came round with a flit-spray to combat the diseases we'd obviously brought in with us. If you were sitting at the end of the row you got an earful of the sticky disinfectant.

After the show came the re-enactment. I would be the director and, of course, star, and Albie and Ronnie the rest of the cast. Puzzled grown-ups would pause and watch as we re-created Hopalong Cassidy's recent triumph. (He always seemed to get wounded in the left shoulder, but still managed to beat hell out of half a dozen king-sized layabouts.) 'The Lone Ranger' was another favourite. 'Hi-o Silver, Awaay!' I would shout, and canter up the high street, just like he did, with Ronnie and Albie doubling as Lucky and California, trotting behind. My enthusiasm for re-enacting the most dramatic scenes almost proved fatal on one occasion. We all poured out of the Cerdic one Saturday afternoon after seeing some terrific film about the history of the Great American Struggle. Raymond Massey was playing the part of John Brown – he whose body lies a-moulderin'. He made a noble speech from the Scaffold, which impressed those of us who weren't still trying to scrape the disinfectant out of our ears. When I got back to the cottage I went into the kitchen, stuck my head through the roller towel on the back of the door, and did what almost turned out to be positively my last performance, as John Brown about to take the drop. It was a bit too realistic, because I woke up on the floor some time later with a big lump on the back of my head, and with Aunt Rose standing over me saying irritably, 'Do thee get up and stop this yur messin' about!' I must have pressed the towel against a vein, I suppose, and lost consciousness. That's the trouble with being a Billy Liar, you see. Too often I'd spreadeagled myself on the carpet when I'd heard her coming and hoped for a bit of drama. But she'd always ignored me – even the first time.

The only time I got any strong reaction out of Aunt Rose was when I came back from morning service at the Congregational and told her that the vicar had asked me why she never came to church. 'What did you say?' she snapped. 'Well, I told him you were too busy making your toothbrushes.' 'You little bugger,' she shrieked. And she fetched me such a whack around the ear.

Knowing how much I enjoyed the pictures, Uncle Cyril had a few laughs at my expense. 'Do you know,' he said one Tuesday, 'they was queueing up all along the High Street at 'alf-past nine yesterday mornin' to see thick there new film *Gone with the Wind*. Fightin' to get in they was.' This was a film I had to see, and at nine o'clock the next day I was outside the Cerdic with two pennies at the ready. At two o'clock they opened the doors. I was first at the pay box, prising the coppers from my green hand. Behind me two old ladies. No-one else. I put Uncle Cyril down for a long session of my Peter Lorre impressions. To be fair, I don't think he ever thought I'd be so daft as to go and stand outside the Cerdic, all morning.

He was invariably kind. After months of badgering he at last agreed to take me with him when he delivered the Sunday papers to some nearby farms. He did it every week as a favour to the delivery boy, and because he enjoyed the walk. In fact he seemed to enjoy it so much that I was determined to go with him. I did – once. It was a very long and quite adventurous journey. I disturbed an adder with my squeaky new Sunday boots, and then broke them in properly in a mad dash across a field when the 'harmless old cow' Uncle Cyril pointed out turned out to be a bull – a four-legged Ena Sharples, only faster. The great attraction of the weekly tour transpired to be the hospitality at each of the farms. Out came the apples, the bottles of pop – and then, the visit to the great barn where barrels of cider lay sweetly side by side. That's why I only went once, because Aunt Rose, ever suspicious after the haymaking incident, smelled my breath and knew I'd broken the pledge again.

I had my own paper round eventually. When the local shop stopped delivering, I offered my services privately, at threepence per customer per week. My business acumen didn't last, I'm sorry to say. I drive a very soft bargain now, but by the end of my brief career in the newspaper industry, I'd saved £12 10s 0d in threepenny bits.

In the autumn of 1944 I won a scholarship to a London school which had transferred to Hampshire. Accordingly, one morning I stood by my suitcase in the parlour which had seemed so strange four and a half years before, and waited for Aunt Rose to put the finishing touches to her hat. Then she took me to Chard Junction and the train to Waterloo.

Arrival at the new school was an anti-climax. I was a week early. The other boys had been sent telegrams to tell them not to come for another eight days. That night, I slept alone in a dormitory and cried for Aunt Rose and Uncle George, for Albie and Ronnie, Alan – even for the odious Georgie Duckworth.

Although I'd travelled to the new school via London, Waterloo station was the nearest I'd got to home, and it was several more months before I at last saw the streets of Wandsworth.

The time spent in Hampshire with the new school was short and not quite painless. We were assembled from all over the country although we were all London boys originally, and a student of dialect would have been in raptures. Our host school was Churchers College in Petersfield, and our new digs were in a graceful old building called Lyndum House. It was presided over by the Hyde family.

Bill Hyde was my form- as well as dorm-master. He had two pretty daughters, Erith and Hilary. I tried to ingratiate myself with them by doing my impressions of Abbott and Costello or Johnny Weissmuller (an early Tarzan) or the mock gangster who snarlingly slides his hand into his inside pocket and pulls out his hankie. The trouble was I always chose to do this at mealtimes, and the giggles and chatter would spread around the room until Bill Hyde, after several gentle appeals for quiet, would suddenly scream and smash his fist on to the table. The silence was instant and complete, even when once his fist bounced a blob of semolina on to the eyelid of the boy opposite me. It dangled there while he did his best to keep his mouth shut and stare straight ahead.

What wasn't funny was the awareness of one's social ignorance.

At the first meal, I was offered a dish of what I thought were those sweets with sherbet inside. I reached forward and took a few. The sweets were pats of butter, which slithered between my fingers.

After my first term with the new school, I went back to London at last. Everything was bigger. The buildings seemed immensely tall. The only disappointment was our flat. It was much smaller than I remembered. All the same it was wonderful to be there, and to realize that the long-dreamed-of day had arrived. I was home! The war wasn't yet over, but at the end of the holiday, my mother got permission for me to stay at home and attend local tutorials. We weren't yet a complete family. Dad and Alan were still away, but there was Mum and Pat and myself – and baby Geoff, four and a half months old.

My mother was in a poor state. She jumped at every sound. Later her hair came out in great handfuls, but by a happy chance it grew again as soft and brown and wavy as it had been years before.

Pat was now in her teens, a plump girl with the elastic of her school hat deeply embedded in her jowls. My mother once disturbed her when she was practising some elephantine ballet steps in the kitchen, and had to stop her before she wrecked the place.

The strangest thing, after the peace of life in the country, was to see the devastation caused by the bombing. You'd walk down a street of solid old buildings, and find that the terrace would suddenly end in a pile of rubble and gaping craters. Whole new vistas were opened up, as the backs of houses in the next street became visible. Today's children aren't dismayed by demolition, but to us, London had seemed unchanging and indestructible.

By the time I got home, the bombs had stopped – almost. One day I heard a motorbike going by, and Pat said, 'That's one.' It was a buzz-bomb passing overhead. If you could hear them, you were reasonably safe. They only became dangerous when their engines cut out and they came whistling down. All the same, we went into the passage and sat under the stairs of the Sewells' flat. Pat looked at me and smiled. 'You're scared, aren't you?' Actually, I was more fascinated than frightened, but she was, after all, a veteran and entitled to feel superior, so I just gave her a non-committal look.

The evacuees

A few V2s – the dreaded rockets which fell without warning
– still came over. One Saturday afternoon we went to the
Savoy cinema in Battersea. The next weekend it was demolished
by a V2.

The war ended in two stages. We celebrated VE and VJ
days (Victory in Europe and Victory over Japan). The headlines in the *Daily Express* read PEACE IN OUR TIME, and there
were celebrations in the streets. We capered around bonfires
and listened to emotional speeches. The feelings of comrade-
ship and togetherness had never been stronger. Old Mrs
Stewart kept shouting 'Praise the Lord for our victory', and
had to be restrained from doing the Dance of the Seven Veils.
Everyone toasted everyone else, and linked arms for the
Lambeth Walk. The rapture faded after a while, and looking
at the same faces today, it's difficult to believe it ever happened.

Alan stayed in Chard for almost another year. He'd left
home when he was four years old. When he came home he was
nine. He emerged from the genteel seclusion of his middle-
class foster-home and found himself in a place he didn't
remember and didn't like. Our flat was small and noisy; there
was no lawn to play on, no stairs to climb to the quiet room
he'd known. It took him a long time to readjust. I mean years.
He was sometimes a very haughty little boy, at other times he
would snap and bicker like the old wire-haired terrier he'd left
behind. And he was no longer the baby.

I went back to Chard about a year after I'd left it. It wasn't
much fun. Then there was a gap of thirteen years. This time
Aunt Rose was much smaller. We had our photographs taken
in the back garden, then I went up to the allotment to see
Uncle George. He hadn't changed at all. He was still bigger
than me, and as warm-hearted as ever.

Aunt Rose died some years ago, and I'm ashamed to say
I don't know where or how Uncle George is. I saw their son,
Leonard, some years ago. He came along to a cricket match
at Luton, and he waited while I went in to bat. I wasn't gone
long, and then we talked, a bit self-consciously, about the times
he'd come home on leave and given me the occasional souvenir
and let me fit the bayonet to his rifle and taken a bullet apart
to show me how it worked. He'd put the little sticks of cordite
in a line and set light to them so that they'd flare up like a fuse.

Now he was a quiet, middle-aged man, smaller of course than I'd remembered him, and I haven't seen him since.

There was a marvellous first line to the film *The Go-Between*. As the car sweeps through the country which he knew so well as a boy, Michael Redgrave says 'The past is another country. They do things differently there.' That's how wartime Chard was. They'll never do things like that again there. For us evacuees it was an agonizing, exciting, endless wait to get back to something we'd begun to suspect no longer existed.

3
Home again

Once we were all back at our own parent school, Emanuel, in
London, the West Country and mid-Welsh and Yorkshire
accents ground back into cockney. The school was on Wandsworth Common, very near Clapham Junction and not a mile
from Wandsworth Prison.

I wasn't the greatest academic success of the twentieth
century, and I didn't exactly tear up the sports field either –
well, I did, but only when I tried to bat. But I wasn't bad at
English and Art and languages. 'What will you do, Aspel –
German or Greek?' I was asked when the time of decision
came at the third year. 'German please,' I said. 'Right, you'll
do Greek,' they said. And so I did, for a year, and then gave
it up, to their relief and mine. Our Latin master, Taffy Neath,
never took to me much, and was fond of saying, as he tapped me
on the head with the cricket bat he always carried, 'Dreary day
after dreary day! Weary week after weary week! Monotonous
month after monotonous month! Tedious term after tedious
term! – and you still don't know. Engrave it on your behind in
your blood, boy, or you will be felled by the Pelian shaft and
be sent on a journey to a place from whose bourne there is no
return!'

Then I'd say 'Pardon?' and the bat would fall again. Like all
schools of its type and time, it had its share of the unchanged,
unchanging scholarly masters who'd existed for ever in the
rarefied academic atmosphere, there were the progressives, the
eccentrics, the sadists, the perverts, the ineffectuals. Particularly brutal was the geography master who would grasp the
hair of an ignorant or recalcitrant boy and yank him savagely
to the floor. The music master was a tyrant, always ready with

27

the punishing gym shoe. How one of the classics staff kept himself out of the Sunday papers and prison, I'll never know. He molested, groped and did his best to seduce and deprave every boy who passed through his nasty hands. I suppose he was protected by the boys' fear. How ironic that years later I read that one of the other teachers, who had never shown anything but the healthiest interest in his pupils' minds and bodies, and was certainly one of the most popular, had been arrested for importuning at a public lavatory.

I seem, perhaps, to have given the impression that the whole place was a riot of unbridled and misguided lust. No, as I've said, the vast majority of the staff were of high calibre in every way, and all the normal activities went on – including nipping up to the tower for a quick Woodbine during lunch-break. The staff enjoyed a smoke, too.

I think the school had a pretty good academic record. It was certainly very different from the quality of tuition I'd been used to down in Chard. Wartime classes were sometimes held by young and inexperienced people. I remember Miss Wyler, who filled her blouse as prettily as Miss Guppy filled her stockings, once went around the class checking whether our top teeth overlapped our bottom teeth. She'd just realized hers did. It never occurred to her that if they didn't, we'd all have protruding, Neanderthal jaws.

Few children rush eagerly back to school after holidays, but for me the approach of each new term was a time of gloom and dread. I was only going a tuppenny bus ride up the road and was home every afternoon but after uninterrupted weeks of being back in the family fold, the wrench was almost unbearable. The need to get home as soon and as often as possible, and the bitter disappointment if the flat was empty on my return, stayed with me right through school.

Tottering in one day from a cross-country run (I'd come fourth), I collapsed next to, and coughed up particles of lung alongside a tallish, lean boy called Jim Healy. Actually he came in after me, which stands out in my mind because Jim's always been a keen and skilful sportsman, and I never compared well with him again. But we did become close friends, and still are. Jim's speed has been cut down a little in the intervening years, though I've never seen anything quite so subtle and cobra-like as his wrist movement when a gin and tonic appears.

If he could have done that with a Colt ·45, they'd be telling the story of Wild Bill Healy out west – or Buffalo Jim. As it was, we were the Butch Cassidy and the Sundance Kid of Emanuel School. We spoke a great deal in cowboy language, and were once apprehended by 'Boozer' Ginn, our French Master, while exchanging notes. Jim's read, 'Ah'm a-headin'' back to th' ol' Bar X to whup up some chow.' Mine said, 'Ah'm gonna blast yore guts all over Texas.' 'Boozer' Ginn said, 'The pair of you will report to my corral after this lesson.' He was a popular man, and a good example of the esteem he was held in – and the standard of fourth-form repartee – was when he announced that he was going to leave teaching but stay in the system as an inspector. 'What route?' we shouted. 'Seventy-seven,' shot back 'Boozer', quick as a flash, and quicker still, we topped it: 'We said route, not age!'

We knew just how far we could go with Boozer. Like all the experienced teachers, he gave us a certain amount of rope and not an inch more. I still wince with shame at the memory of our treatment of some of the student teachers – particularly the foreign ones. A young French master driven out after a mere couple of weeks; an Indian with exquisite manners being pelted with books and gym shoes as he cried 'Gentlemen, marvel at the board!'; and an Austrian who constantly begged 'Please boys – do not fighting!' Where are they now? Safely tucked away in industry, I imagine.

As I've hinted, I was never able to master any game of skill. I was healthy, agile, good at gymnastics, had sharp eyesight and quick reflexes, but I couldn't hit or catch a ball to save my life. I tried athletics, but discovered that invisible weights were attached to my feet. Oddly enough, years later I discovered how to co-ordinate my movements, and was able to put one foot in front of the other quite quickly, especially when I was holding a rugby ball and somebody three times my size was reaching for my intestines. One summer the school boats club was opened up, and there at last was something I could do – grab hold of a lump of wood and pull. Rowing is a strange sport. Eight fellows sitting behind one another, sliding up and down on little seats and beating at the water. There's no chance in that context to show individual flair or skill unless you're particularly masochistic and want to be the one who sits in front and regulates the rate of strike.

It gives you big muscles, calloused hands and blisters on your behind. After a hard, long race, your lips have foam on them and you want to die. But it's good to see your opponents' craft slipping behind, and a well co-ordinated crew splashing and rippling smoothly under a bridge is a pleasing sound.

The Schools Head of the River race is a fine sight: lines of boats chasing each other between Barnes and Putney; lots of purple faces and wild eyes and much splashing. We were never very successful. I remember one year when we were late getting to the start. We dropped the boat heavily into the water and somebody stuck his foot through it. Chewing-gum and sticking-plaster were applied (to the boat) and we headed for the start line, a sharp breeze ruffling the water and sending arcs of spray from the tips of our oars. On the way we hit a dead horse, and Number Six got something nasty stuck to his blade. None of this augured well for the race.

Now when a rowing race is started the procedure is that cox says 'Come forward!' and you slide up the rollers until your arms are stretched and the blade poised to strike hard at the water. Then the starter, from a launch, cries, 'I shall only ask you once! Are you ready? Row!' And all hell breaks loose. On this occasion something else was released. Our stroke – the leader of the crew – heaved so ferociously at the water that when he came rushing up his slide for the second stroke, his shorts split open and his genitals spilled out onto the seat. Not a pleasant sensation (and not a pretty sight for the coxswain, facing him). But worse, much worse, was to come. As he pulled back on the oar, his legs, naturally, closed and acted like nutcrackers on his unprotected parts. The agony made him rush even faster up his slide, which inevitably meant his balls were back in the vice two seconds later. It was the fastest race I've ever been in. We really tore up the Thames, inspired by what we thought were cries of enthusiasm from the other end of the boat.

Emanuel has since become one of the finest rowing schools in the country. I joined a Putney club after I left school, but was never very interested in the sport, and learned hardly

anything about rivercraft. I've never been one for over-dedica-
tion, for changing-room post-mortems or for esoteric jargon –
sporting or otherwise. I care more for simply keeping fit. I
have a rowing machine, which I've put in the most conspicuous
and awkward place so that I'm constantly falling over it and
being reminded that I should have a pull. One day, old and
flaccid, I shall give one final heave back on the springs, and
then my legs will give out and I'll be projected through the
air like a bullet, a little black dot, high over Maida Vale.

I do envy my sport-orientated friends sometimes. It seems
so important to them, and I would dearly love to have found
something to hold my interest, something I didn't tire of after
a little while. Apart from sex, laughter, a good movie and a
bottle of wine I don't have many enthusiasms, but as you so
rightly say, who needs any others? I'm not sure I'm quite so
blithe and cynical as all that. Perhaps I shall find out as this
exercise continues.

One thing I really could do well when I was young was sing.
I was blessed with one of those pure, bell-like voices which
never wavered from the true note, except in terror. I was soloist
with the school choir, which was formed and nurtured by our
music master with dedication, talent, and a lot of flailing
around with the gym shoe.

I even took the lead in a school opera. Snegourochka, the
Snow Maiden was my role, and ravishing I was too. The House
Rugby team dropped me from their list of possibles. During
one scene I had to be transformed from a fire-bird into the
aforesaid snow maiden, and bloody hot it was under all those
feathers. Conscripted members of the fourth form had to gather
round, howling and moaning, while I did a quick-change act
– on stage.

They invariably drew back too soon, and I was left hopping
around, pulling on a snow-maiden boot and spitting out
feathers.

My sweetheart in this epic was a tough boy from Tooting
called Walter Anderson, who played Lell, the shepherd boy.
When I last heard of Andy, he was a police sergeant – no
doubt still on the look-out for people doing quick-change acts
in public view.

The dramatic society once produced Auden and Isherwood's

The Ascent of F.6 in which I appeared, significantly, as the Radio Announcer. Someone afterwards suggested that I should think about taking it up as a living. By that time I was well into my teens, and the dulcet singing voice had gone, never to return. The nightingale had become a crow. Nowadays, I can still hold a note, but not for long and with no power. Naturally, I gave the broadcasting idea no thought. I knew I'd never be allowed in the same building as Frank Phillips or Uncle Mac. Indeed, in the days of Lord Reith's director-generalship, they wouldn't have allowed me in the building, for a variety of reasons, all of them social. Did you know that before the war radio announcers had to wear dinner-suits to read the news, and, if there was a particularly illustrious guest in the studio, tails? No, I would never have passed Lord Reith's fierce scrutiny.

But I continued to appear in school plays, once as Dr Caiaus in *The Merry Wives of Windsor*. Our headmaster used to censor the texts of our productions, his guiding principle being 'No references to any parts of the human body'. So Dr Caiaus's enraged lines, 'By gar, I will cut out his two stones: he will not have a stone to throw at 'is dog' had to go. But if I couldn't draw sniggers I could certainly draw blood. In the swordfight scene between Dr Caiaus and Simple (or was it Rugby? Caiaus pulled his rapier on both of them), the other character was played by an amazingly thin lad called Bob Bray. Bob was a fine long-distance runner, having so little weight to carry about. He had even less after our encounter.

He got a bit carried away during the duelling sequence and his foil swished dangerously near the tip of my nose. I reacted with a few flamboyant thwacks of my own. Suddenly Bob Bray dropped his foil, wrapped his arms around himself and rushed off; he left a blob of blood behind on the stage. 'By gar,' I thought, 'he will not 'ave a stone to throw at 'is dog after all.' As it turned out I'd only nicked his little finger, but it gave an edge to the performance.

My father at that time regarded my theatrical activities as a bit 'pouffy' for a working-class boy to be involved in.

From the distance of the years, I can understand and forgive a lot of the things that happened during those early postwar days. Any man returning from service life, with a few stripes on his arm, a well-ordered existence and no responsibilities

beyond the daily routine would have found a large, boisterous
and undisciplined family difficult to handle. And when he finds
he can't, he gets tough. So, I wouldn't describe home life
during that period as idyllic: there was, to say the least, a lack
of rapport. Now I see the situation in its context, and realize
that adolescence isn't the best time for a person to get to know
his parents, particularly when the preceding years – which
should have been valuable and formative for both sides – have
been traumatic for everyone involved.

There were lulls in hostilities, and happy evenings spent
listening to radio serials like 'The Lost World', 'Journey into
Space', and 'Dick Barton, Special Agent'. Can anyone under
the age of thirty imagine a family planning their week around
a radio programme? 'Monday Night at Eight' kept us all
indoors, with Ronnie Waldman's 'Puzzle Corner' and 'Dr
Morell Investigates'.

Valentine Dyall kept us not only indoors but with every light
in the place blazing when his sinister 'Man in Black' told tales
of the macabre. And when Muir and Norden's 'Take It from
Here' arrived, the pubs were deserted.

Snatches of dialogue from the Glum family saga remain:
Jimmy Edwards the loathsome Mr Glum, advising his daft
son (played by Dick Bentley) about marriage: 'Best to do it
in the morning, Ron, so that if it doesn't work out you haven't
wasted the whole day.' Ron's doomed sweetheart, Eth (originally Joy Nicholls, then June Whitfield), 'Ooh, Ron, it's so
romantic snuggling my cheek into the rough manly tweed of
your jacket.' 'Mind you don't get my fountain pen up your
nose, Eth.' Or something like that.

When there was no favourite programme to listen to, we'd
sit around the kitchen table, my father trying to get one of us
to play cribbage, and the rest doing word-games – or, in my
case, drawing funny faces. 'Very nice, dear,' said my mother.
'Who's it supposed to be?'

Or I'd get someone to sit still and I'd draw their likeness, or
copy a photograph, or do dramatic sea scenes with captions
like 'He clang on desperately': Pat used to write stories, usually
about he-men confronting each other in log-cabins. The
dialogue was strong meat, too. ('Karlson,' said Carruthers
quietly, 'you're a beast.')

Christmasses were riotously happy times in our home. Nowadays they tend to be itinerant affairs for me: a round of Yuletide programmes and calls on friends and family. But in the late 1940s no-one left our place. Everyone came to us. A fire was built in the front room, and it gradually lost its dankness. Balloons in vulgar clusters festooned the multi-patterned walls, and crates of brown ale were stacked in the passage.

I was in charge of the radiogram. I wish we had been able to salvage our rich stock of 78 records; some of them were vintage even then. There were lots of fun and novelty records like 'Sandy's (Macpherson) Own Broadcasting Station'; 'Kitten on the Keys'; 'Tiger Rag'; a favourite was a number by 'The Two Leslies' which went: 'I Live Down on a Country Farm – and I like it I must say – where the ducks go quack and the sheep go baah and pigs go (enormous raspberry) all the day.' The more raucous the better.

I get confused over dates and names; but then and into the early 1950s we seemed always to be playing stuff by Dick Haymes, Jo Stafford, Al Martino, and of course, Bing and Frankie – including the one the BBC banned, 'Paradise' 'And then you dim the light . . . and then you hold me tight . . . one kiss, one soft caress, can lead the way to happiness . . . you take me to Paradise.' Christopher Stone wasn't going to play anything like that, and 'Housewives' Choice' chose to ignore it too. The sales were enormous and we all knew the words by heart.

For our Christmas knees-up, livelier stuff was required. Both sides of the family were very strong on impromptu comedy. My mother's brothers, Ern and Albert, did all sorts of eccentric routines with balloons and Uncle Albert always ended the night being tearful about his 'Old Mum', who'd died a year or two earlier. Then he'd sing 'Bye-Bye Blackbird' apropos of nothing at all, and that would make everyone else tearful. My father's brother, Arthur, went in for straight-faced humour – but at one am always announced, quite seriously, that he had to walk to Brighton, although he could hardly stand. Through it all, Auntie Phoebe's husband, Eddie, sat and smiled. Mum and Auntie Ethel rarely left the kitchen.

When the party finally wound down, those who could made their way to the mattresses that had been strewn, Mafia-like around the flat. The others lay where they had fallen. We kids, hollow-eyed but still game, were herded, en masse, into the spare bedroom. My fingers would be sore from changing gramophone needles.

The only personalities missing from the later of these festive occasions were grandparents. We'd never had a full set. My mother's father died just before I was born, and none of us ever knew my father's mother. Grannie Robinson was the one whose house I'd been born in. She died not long after the war. I remember my mother coming home one day and saying simply 'she's gone'. We loved her, not just for the gifts she always bore, nor in my case for the use of the room, but for her odd, endearing little ways. She was always fierce in the defence of dumb beasts, and I'm told she once wrote to the BBC saying how cruel it was that those poor horses should be tethered in the snow while Big Bill Campbell and his Rocky Mountain Rhythm were playing their music in the warmth of their old log cabin.

My father's father was one of the Boys of the Old Brigade, a Chelsea pensioner at the Royal Hospital, heavy with medals and mystery. The mystery was his name. He was listed as Sergeant Nugent. 'Why, Dad?' we'd ask. 'Why is Grandad's name Nugent? Are we Nugents or is he an Aspel?' 'Never mind about that,' Dad would say, although he vaguely hinted that one day all would be revealed. The old boy was certainly a colourful character, and I don't just mean the splendid uniform. He'd blame his poor eyesight as he groped his affectionate way towards the females of the family. The chink of his medals always gave warning of his approach. There are photographs of his diminutive figure (he took size four in boots) being presented to Queen Elizabeth (the Queen Mother) and he even appeared in a film called, I think, *Old Soldiers never Die*. There was Grandad at Chelsea, pointing out the rolls of honour to visiting Americans. By the way, it turned out that his name *was* Aspel. I believe the name change came during a furtive period a war or two earlier, when he'd decided to leave one regiment and join another, more convenient, one. Yes, he was certainly an Aspel.

Two highlights of those stay-at-home, do-it-yourself evenings were my successes in newspaper competitions. One was in the children's section of the *Daily Mirror*. Readers were invited to suggest the best and safest way to learn to dive. The neatest and most succinct entry would win. Uncle Mac would have been proud of me. If small, neat, handwriting denotes intelligence, as some say, then my postcard bore the mark of genius. My suggestion was certainly simple: start at the shallow end on the bottom step and work your way up. My reward was £1 and, more important, my name in print.

The second triumph was a few years later. This contest was in the *Sunday People*, the same newspaper which recently printed a photograph of me at the age of nine in their 'Guess Who?' feature. My hair was slicked down with water, and I was on my way to Sunday School in Chard. 'Just as smooth in those days,' chortled the *People*. Anyway, no hard feelings, because I did after all win their £1,000 'Guess Who' competition about twenty-five years ago. You had to identify the various features of film stars – Clark Gable's left ear – a Spencer Tracy nostril, that sort of thing. As I practically lived in the cinema, I knew I'd got all the answers right. A few weeks later, a letter arrived from the *People*. 'Congratulations,' it said, 'you have won first prize in our one thousand pound competition and you share it with one thousand and seventy-two other people.' Enclosed was a postal order for 18s 3d.

My love for the cinema was a bit one sided. One cinema in particular, the Granada, Tooting, didn't seem to welcome my company at all; at least the commissionaire didn't. He was a vast, military man who had a job to do and by God, he was going to do it. He picked me out of the 1s 9d queue so often that I began to get a persecution complex. I wasn't a troublemaker and I wasn't trying to get in for nothing. It was simply that I was too young to see most of the films I queued for. I looked even younger than I was. At fourteen, I appeared to be no older than twelve, and that, in the uniformed monster's eyes, made me four years too young to see *The Big Sleep* no matter how much I loved Dorothy Malone. I used to long for the time when *he* would go for 'The Big Sleep', but he looked invincible and I began to dread that when I was thirty-seven he'd still stop me going in. Once, when I was furtively queueing for another forbidden film aptly titled *A Matter of Life and Death*, the familiar hairy hand whisked me out of the line. 'How old are you, sonny?' he boomed, from a great height. 'Sixteen,' I squeaked. 'Oh, yes – and when was you born?' The swine. I was never good at sums. '1921,' I said, and forty seconds later was queueing for a bus home.

One thrilling evening Dad lent me his identity card. Adults (eighteen and over) had white cards; children had blue. I was ready for the Granada Gargantua and boarded the 612 trolley bus with bright anticipation. That night he wasn't on duty. I hoped he was down with an acute attack of leprosy. Seeing the film, however, was more important than my victory over oppression, and I sauntered up to the pay-box, an unlit cigarette dangling from my lips. 'How old are you, sonny?' asked the cashier. I blanched at the well-known words, but I flashed the identity card. The white symbol of maturity wasn't enough. She snatched it from me and looked at it closely. Then she smiled. 'According to this,' she said, 'you've just done six years in the army. Hop it.' I hated that bus queue.

An affectionate word in passing about the Granada, Tooting. I did eventually manage to get in, and thereafter never went there less than once a week. For students of nostalgia, architecture and the bizarre I recommend it.

The man who designed it also designed the Bolshoi Ballet. It's a massive, ornate, wildly exotic building, with huge pillars, marble halls, soaring balustrades, sections of moorish castles – you name it, the Granada's got it. The seats were featured before the war in *Encyclopaedia Britannica*. Honestly. When last I heard, a preservation order had been put on the place and I hope it sticks. When one day the Great Director calls me to that film-set in the sky, I hope the entrance looks just like the Granada, Tooting – minus commissionaire.

My sense of timing has never been good, and it was probably about the most unattractive period of the twentieth century to choose to be a teenager. We didn't count. We weren't commercially important, we weren't artistically precocious, and so far as fashion was concerned, we were simply small replicas of our elders. At that time, of course, clothes rationing was still in effect. For each garment, the draper's scissors snipped away at your little brown booklet. I still remember – and so does most of Isis Street, I expect – my first pair of long trousers. I've never been exactly mighty in the thigh, so that to get a pair of trousers to fit around the middle *and* reach the ankle was a problem. They only seemed to make them for people who were built to standard proportions. I tried on many pairs, all of dreadful quality, a cheap coarse flannel – we couldn't afford worsted, even with my school grant. If they reached my shoes, the crutch was just above my knee. If they fitted around the loins, then you could see the tops of my socks.

Eventually we compromised, and settled for a pair that didn't fit anywhere. The backside went into a huge point of excess material, like an erection in reverse, and the turnups never shone my shoes. But I was thrilled. They were my first pair of long trousers, a sign of manhood, and if I stuck my bottom out and bent my knees slightly, they wouldn't look too bad. I was always able to rationalize in this way. Some time later I bought a jacket in a sale. It had survived several sales, I think. It was double-breasted and sky blue. People covered their eyes and reeled back when I approached. I wore it for the Boat Race that year and it never occurred to me to feel incongruous shouting, 'Come on, Oxford,' in my coat of shimmering pale blue. Oddly enough, the BBC commentator there must have been colour-blind, too, because he came up to me and asked if I was an Oxford supporter. I said of course, and he said would I like to come along after the race and talk into his microphone. Unfortunately, I was swept away by the crowd and so missed my chance of a broadcasting debut at the age of fourteen.

The Boat Race used to attract massive crowds in those days. The rosette-hawkers made a mint, Putney came to a standstill, and Boat Race Night in the West End was as festive as New Year's Eve.

Apart from the grotesque trousers and the heavenly jacket, my teenage taste in clothes was very reserved. I did in a fit of self-indulgence buy a pair of suède shoes. At that time, suède shoes were only worn by consenting adults in private, but I didn't care. Not only were they suède, they had extremely thick crêpe rubber soles, thereby qualifying as 'brothel-creepers'. Much good did they do me. There were no brothels in Earlsfield to creep into. The girls I knew were divided into the ready, the willing, and the majority. I exaggerate.

Most of the girls I knew were untouchable, a few were ready, but none was willing. So far as I know, all the girls down our street went into marriage untouched by human hand – except for the occasional furtive grasp when they weren't looking. We spent a lot of time talking about it. 'Why don't you let me?' 'I would if I could – I will when I'm older.' 'How much older? What about tomorrow?'

I was in love, deep honourable love, three times during that period. Once with Margaret Parnell, who played with my emotions and nothing else, and who was secretly in love with Jim Healy. Once with Jean Francis, a lovely dark-eyed girl whose mother told me off for cycling ceaselessly past their front room window. And once with a girl whose name I've forgotten. I followed her home from the library one afternoon. Then I dropped a note through the letter-box, explaining that I was the handsome stranger and how about meeting me outside the Granada (of course) on Tuesday? She came, we met, and I got pins and needles from keeping my arm around the back of her seat.

It was a short-lived romance. Perhaps she tired of my flamboyant goodnight kisses (one arm around the neck, one around the waist, and bend sharply to the left). But I never touched her. She wouldn't let me. None of them would ever let any of us touch their lovely, inhibited postwar young bodies.

Jim and I were keen, for a time, on a pair of twins. Luckily he liked one, I the other. We all played tennis together, and sauntered over the common, the girls chattering gaily, and Jim and I exchanging sympathetic looks of frustration. The girls determined to keep the whole thing platonic. Gentlemen to the last, and incapable of a straightforward grapple – we resorted to subtle hints like fixing them with burning eyes and singing 'A Fine Romance, with no kisses' . . . But nothing. Not even a friendly hug.

So we found consolation in the *Sunday Pictorial*'s pin-ups and waited. And waited. Occasionally, at a party, there would be a joyful scuffle, but the evening normally ended with the girls going home with a few loose buttons and the boys nursing aching scrotums.

I blush to confess this to the world of the seventies, but I even emerged from National Service a virgin. It was not through lack of opportunity, but ironically enough, I wouldn't let any of the camp-followers touch *my* lovely young body. Not with the proverbial barge pole.

Sex was not, of course, an obsession with us. It was the lack of it. To read now of lads who are clocking up their three hundredth conquest at the age of seventeen strikes hard at someone whose score until the age of twenty was nil. Do I mean it when I say I really wouldn't have wanted to be that promiscuous? I think I do. Unscrupulous, indiscriminate, non-discerning and non-stop screwing is bound to diminish the potential enjoyment, if not the appetite. Although in attitude and way of life I'm now much more of a teenager than I was twenty-odd years ago, I've come to know what I like, and it isn't to be found in tearing the pants off everything that moves. When I describe myself as a 'teenager' I don't mean that I'm a raver; I don't, except slowly, adapt my language to the latest catch-phrases; I've never tasted pot, and I don't clamber into beads and moody unisex gear every evening. But I enjoy the freer atmosphere, and the vitality of today, and I don't feel out of it. My hair is longer than it used to be, and my trouser bottoms are wider. Where is the advantage in sticking to the fashions of ration-book days? A few years ago I sported a brutally short 'Italian' haircut. It was the fashion of the day, but nobody complained. To many people, long hair signifies dirt and degradation, and a short back and sides is next to godliness. I remember meeting a man I'd been at school with at a dinner some years ago. We chatted in a desultory way, and I asked him if his work involved him in much travel. 'No, no, no,' he said, 'I leave it to the younger chaps now – the younger chaps, yes, yes, yes.' He was thirty-two, and desperate to be middle aged and out of it all.

Nowadays there might be some justification for that attitude. People run businesses, design furniture and dresses, and produce shows when they're barely out of their teens. Their aim is to be free while still young enough to enjoy the fruits, and if to retire at thirty-two means to be able to live life to the full and concentrate on what you really get pleasure and satisfaction from, then I'm all for 'leaving it to the younger chaps'.

But that, of course, is not what my complacent friend, patting his paunch earned at the bar of the Old Boys' Club, had in mind. I watched a lot of fellow teenagers make an early disappearance into adulthood. The girls became matrons overnight. Their lips tightened and their arms became permanently folded. I'd see them, girls who only months before, it seemed, were bright, desirable (if unattainable) young things, now standing at the greengrocer's with finger on cheek. The men/boys would start talking about 'the wife'. 'The wife?' – that lovely Brenda he'd been sending love letters to via a friend only a year before – 'the wife?' And I'd see them a few years later, deeper into their mutual gloom, replying to every request from their small child with a mindless 'No'. 'Can I?' – 'No'. 'Will you?' – 'No'. 'What's this?' – 'Shh.'

The reason so many of my generation abhor today's teenagers, the reason we loathe, hate and fear each long-haired, carefree individual, is not because we really believe they're all doomed and depraved and leading us to destruction, but because we are, quite simply, jealous. We're eating our hearts out, because they've got it all and we had nothing.

There will always be a gap between the generations, based partly on the fallacy that what happened 'in my day' was either more desirable or so bloody awful that it's not fair you shouldn't suffer too. But we all suffer. The bleak outlook for today's teenagers wasn't caused by the length of their hair. Thank God most of them have more energy, ambition and self-confidence than their parents ever had. If we let them, they may save us yet.

They're attractive people, what you can see of them, and you have to admit that today's styles have meant the rejuvenation of many a poor old duffer in his late thirties, and even beyond, because we can join if we want to.

Most of us middle-aged moodies only go to the middle of the road and stop short of the grotesque (we hope) but it's surprising how many mental years can be knocked off by a discreet widening of the lapels. If a man dresses in an up-to-date way, he's likely to think that way too, and I'm all for reappraisal of one's ideas at regular intervals. It doesn't mean discarding old virtues, but opening your eyes and mind to new ideas and fresh possibilities. There's a lot of it about.

Anyway, when not commiserating with each other about our lack of carnal prowess, and expressing amazement at the sort of creeps who did succeed, Jim and I spent a lot of time at concerts. Although he wasn't musically gifted, Jim had an intense interest in the subject and quickly became encyclopaedic in his knowledge.

I, on the other hand, never learned the titles or composers of more than a very few pieces. This in spite of the fact that I'd been a star warbler in the school choir, and able to read music in my own way by guessing at what would sound euphonic when the black dots went up or down. I've never been good at absorbing facts or figures, except of the useless kind. A lack of empathy occurs, particularly when I'm faced with something which I know will benefit me. 'Twenty lines from now I shall be a better man,' I tell myself, and immediately the veil comes down.

One of the first concerts we went to was during the promenade season at the Albert Hall. Our attention was split between Cyril Smith's playing of Rachmaninoff, and the size of the timpanist's ears, which trembled with every blow. Jim had a comprehensive selection of classical records, and would conduct his favourite pieces with a knitting needle. I was the orchestra – switching from 'cello to french horn at a flick of his wrist. They were exhausting sessions for both of us.

The time rapidly approached for big decisions. Was I to stay on at school, take School Certificate, then attempt matriculation and go on to university? Or leave and get a job? My parents were guided by my own self-doubts and eagerness for the rattle of silver in my pocket. University seemed quite unattainable. It simply wasn't for the likes of me.

My form-master, Bill Hyde – the same Bill Hyde who had been driven barmy by our dining-room antics, tried to persuade me that I could get through. My last school report contained a classic phrase by Bill. 'Possesses a certain maturity,' he wrote, 'whether this is a superficial maturity, or indeed a mature superficiality, remains to be seen.'

The English master, after my triumphs with the school opera and dramatic society, thought I could make a go of it on the stage. The headmaster, an endearing, popular and perfect example of the owl-like academic with a twinkle in the eye, asked me what I *really* wanted to do. I had no idea, but muttered something about working with cameras. It was an odd thing to say, because I'd never owned a camera in my life, and the idea of a career in television had never entered my consciousness.

Home again

'Would it not be better, Aspel,' suggested Mr Broome 'to specialize in languages – Russian perhaps? You could become a spy – a brief but colourful career. . . .'

All suggestions, frivolous and otherwise, were disregarded. Well, not quite all. I did stay long enough to sit the School Certificate examination (now GCE). I knew I'd do all right in English and art and modern languages, but as for history, maths and Latin . . . no chance. Our history master had once played tennis at Wimbledon, and this and other entertaining topics filled our history periods. In the dying moments he'd say, 'Now go away and read pages 79–91.' That's how we learned, or in my case, didn't learn. On the day of the history exam for School Certificate, I lay out in the playing field and boned up on Chartism, the Industrial Revolution and something else. The next day every detail had fled my mind, but that afternoon my pen fairly whizzed over the paper, because every topic I'd studied came up in the exam. Result – a few marks short of a Distinction. How ludicrous the exam system is.

Maths and Latin went the predicted way. At the beginning of every question in the Latin paper I wrote '*discipuli, pictorem spectate*' which was the exhortation in our textbooks to 'study the picture'. The picture, I remember, was usually of a Roman family. One showed a slave who'd transgressed and had been lashed to the back of a horse and sent galloping off into the forest to be torn to pieces by the wild animals. Underneath this picture in my book, somebody had written 'Nice rides, sixpence each'.

In the geometry paper I wrote, in answer to every question, 'The angles of a triangle add up to 180°.' That probably earned me two marks – not quite enough to satisfy the examiners. I failed in both subjects. To matriculate, it would have been necessary to sit the maths exam again, and again, until I passed. I'd still be there now.

4
A change of uniform

In July 1949 I left school. I was sixteen. The schools Employment Exchange, or Careers Bureau, or whatever the body was called, had fixed me up with a job with a publishing house – a prospect that at once elated and terrified me. The eagerness to throw off the childish world of school and get out amongst the big boys began to dwindle as the summer holidays passed.

The day came. I walked down St James's Street one autumn morning, bitterly regretting the greed and impetuosity that had made me throw away my chances of improvement and the company of my friends. For years afterwards, I swore that if I won the pools, or earned enough money, I would give up whatever I was doing and get myself a degree. I'm not sure if I wanted academic qualifications, the experience of wandering, gown-clad, amongst the dreaming spires, or simply to be able to drop into conversations the phrase 'When I was at Oxford . . .'. The need passed long ago, and although I occasionally feel the pang of envy, I must say that I don't notice a breadth of horizons or a depth of perception in every varsity man I meet.

Life at William Collins & Co. wasn't hard. I was the office boy, destined it seemed to become a member of the sales team. I packed the parcels, and made the tea. The packing involved returning manuscripts to would-be authors, complete with rejection slips, or, if the work merited it, a consoling letter. If the letter said 'too much sex' I would add a few thumbprints to the manuscript before packing it.

One of the firm's most illustrious authors was Peter Cheyney, the writer of thrillers. One day I was sitting at the switchboard in reception while the girl took her lunch. The doors swung open, and my eyes slowly panned up a flamboyant figure. Loud

44

check suit, monocle, bucolic features. Mr Cheyney had called to see Billy Collins.

Later that afternoon, as I carried the tea around, I passed Peter Cheyney sitting on the stairs. He was looking up the skirts of the typists as they trotted past. I offered him tea. 'What's your name, boy?' he asked. 'Michael,' I simpered. 'Irish, eh?' he said. 'My forebears were Irish – they were landlords. They were all shot, and their bodies thrown down deep wells, the water of which has never been drunk since.' Before I had a chance to reply, a door was opened, and he was hauled away.

There was another office boy called Colin Miller, who became a firm friend, and who subsequently became an actor. Publishing is a wonderful training ground for show-business. My immediate boss was a man called Sydney Goldsack, who was very patient with me. Once I got over my initial fear of working for a living, I became a rather cocky youth, always ready to answer back and over-estimate my own importance. It did me no good with the one I most wanted to impress. She was one of the secretaries, a haughty girl with enormous breasts. There was a theory that she often went sick because they were sapping her strength. They certainly sapped mine. I've since decided that neatness and style are preferable to abundance, but in the autumn and winter of 1949–50 I dreamed of nothing but diving into, wallowing in, and frolicking amongst those massive mounds. I was tempted to grasp once – no, twice – and then run for my life; it would almost have been worth it. But it was not to be. I was transferred from headquarters to the warehouse at Bow Street. The Bosom and I did come face to face once more, at an idyllic office outing to Marlow, where we swam and sunbathed and drove launches up and down the river. Then it was goodbye. I believe the move was part of the training scheme, and not due to the fact that I got drunk at the Christmas party. It was on gin and orange, and I was very ill indeed. I don't remember getting home. The family, with one exception was either sympathetic or amused.

Brother Alan wasn't, but I don't blame him. I was sick down his back. For years afterwards I couldn't stand the smell of gin. He's never touched it since.

I don't think the move was due to my ignominious performance as Buyer of Carbon Paper, either. I was given the job of seeing the carbon paper representative when he called, and ordering what was necessary. Unfortunately, nobody told me how much we needed. The salesman was a charming man, and I bought enough carbon paper to last the firm for the next fifteen years.

At Bow Street, we wore casual clothes, and had to clock in each morning. The warehouse was a fascinating place. There were rows and rows of books, all ready to be dispatched to any part of the world. I soon became adept with brown paper and string. If friends were after the latest book, I would arrange for them to get a 'job' copy. This was a book which had been damaged in some way, and was available to staff for next to nothing. If there were no 'job' copies available, I would solve the problem by holding a perfect copy between finger and thumb five feet from the floor, and releasing it.

There was a much freer atmosphere at Bow Street. We were away from head office, manning an outpost of the empire. Most people there were, of course, doing much more basic jobs than at Park Place. Ours was not to make editorial decisions, or to arrange publicity, or even to order the carbon paper. Ours was simply to pack 'em up and send 'em off. Several edges were knocked off me during my stay there, except, needless to say, the chafing edge of virginity. There was one tempting girl there, a tiny, snub-nosed thing with rudimentary swellings around the diaphragm. We called her 'Duchess', and we all lusted after her. She allowed me occasionally to press her affectionately against the clocking-in machine, but that was all.

Apart from the Duchess, there was one other colourful character who paid periodical visits to the warehouse. His first name was Irwin, and he had a romantic set of continental family names. His hair was very blond and he wore gay little scarves carelessly thrown over his shoulder. I can't remember his precise designation – I mean I don't know what his job was – but he was almost as popular as the Duchess. Irwin was good company. He was chatty, sympathetic, and amusing. I once told him of the great rats we'd seen at the warehouse. He squealed and put his hands between his legs. 'Don't!' he cried. 'You make me shudder.'

Two years seems to be a significant period of time in my life. I've seldom lived anywhere more than two years. Interests change, new attractions beckon, moves are made. I'd been in the publishing business for almost a year and a half when a brown envelope arrived, containing a suggestion that I might like to spend the next two years in the uniform of His Majesty's Armed Forces. National Service! I was thrilled. It was the confirmation of manhood. As I said to the Duchess, 'If I'm old enough to be a soldier, I'm old enough to—', but she skipped away. Then came the medical, and the reassurance that I was A1, fighting fit, and ready for anything. I indulged in a bout of Walter Mitty fantasy. As yet I didn't known which arm of HM Forces would win me, so I could imagine myself in heroic circumstances on land, sea, or in the air. Actually, it was difficult to get into the navy unless you had some family connection. The air force had by then lost its dashing wartime image and was considered a bit soft. Most lads went into the army.

My father was pleased. It would, of course, do me the world of good. Predictably, my own enthusiasm waned as the date of induction approached. Apprehension took over, which then deepened into gloom and despondency. The most important thing in life was, after all, freedom. I'd proved I *could* be a soldier – why bother to put it to the test?

On 5 April 1951, I reported to Winchester. Winchester is a garrison town, and far too gentle a place to be blighted by the military. Our camp was some way out of town and had a pleasant rural name like Hollybush or Meadowcroft. The name was in stark contrast to the uncompromising row of huts which stood bleakly in the pale spring sun.

We spilled out of the trucks in scores; a dazed, bewildered assortment of youths, clutching suitcases and uneaten sandwiches, and clinging to what we suspected were the last vestiges of our individuality and self-respect. We were right. Within hours we were shaven-headed and kitted out with uniforms that didn't even fit where they touched. 'You are now a rifleman in the King's Royal Rifle Corps,' barked a corporal, handing me my documents. There was a brief flickering of pride. I stood on the verandah of the reception hut, the evening breeze ruffling the tuft of hair that still remained on the top of my head. By the time that barber had finished, I thought we were in the First Royal Mohican Regiment. I looked around that forlorn landscape. There were distant sounds, and every sound was harsh. Boots crashed against stone, metal utensils clanked as people marched to the cookhouse, a bugle rasped.

'My God,' I thought, 'two years of this!'

The homesickness and despair were soon swept aside by good honest fear. Every situation contained a threat. We didn't leap from our beds, or blanco our equipment, or shave our hairless, bleeding baby faces because we wanted to be smart, efficient soldiers; we did it because if we didn't, we'd be on a charge. 'There's a bloody spider in this rifle – put this man on a charge.' 'Take this man's name – there's a stud missing from his boot.' 'How close did you stand to the razor this morning, sonny – stand up straight.'

They were, of course, making men of us – identical men who sprang into concerted action at the merest hiss of instruction, men with interesting names like 22473170. Like all ex-National Servicemen, I can still rip that number off like a machine-gun.

The corporal who saw us through our initial six-week training period advised us on our first day that there would soon be a third world war, and that as we were all going to be in the army for the rest of our lives anyway, why not sign on at once and get a regular soldier's pay (which was considerably more than the four shillings a day conscripts were paid)? Most of us declined, but one or two gullible lads signed on.

The terror receded as time passed, but I didn't grow to love the army. The only time I enjoyed was between eleven at night and six in the morning. Then my head was safely tucked under my blanket. In spite of this somebody got the idea that Aspel, the reluctant warrior, was officer material. I knew they were wrong, but at least I could have a comparatively cushy time before they found out. Life in the OR 1 platoon (Other Ranks Class One) was very different. Everyone was called Julian or Greville. They sorted themselves into chummy little groups, depending on which school they went to. I'm afraid Emanuel School didn't qualify for membership to any of them, and I watched from my unprivileged bunk as the select few roared off for the evening in the old Lagonda. Those who remained preferred not to engage in conversation. The boy on the bunk above me was particularly uncommunicative. 'What's the time?' I'd ask, and his reply was to pick reflectively at his nose.

A change of uniform

The War Office Selection Board series of tests was, for me, consistent in one respect. I failed the lot. I didn't do too badly in the impromptu two-minute talks we were made to give, but for the rest, it was a repeat of the exams of two years before. I could swing on ropes and shin up poles with the best of them, but given a situation involving equipment, a number of men and an obstacle to be crossed, I'd just shrug and say, 'I'm afraid it's every man for himself, gents. Good luck.' One of the written exams – or projects, as they were called, was entitled 'Catching Burglar Bill'. B.B. was, I read, the scourge of the neighbourhood. I had about eighty yards of rope, a handbell, a box of matches, one earring and an old copy of the *Tatler* – useful props like that – with which to trap the bounder. Given that sort of tackle, there was only one thing I could do. I wrote what I thought was a highly entertaining comedy routine. It might have worked well on 'Crackerjack', but it didn't impress the military. I was not recommended for officer training. The next day I was returned to my unit.

Now if there's one thing the ordinary soldier detests more than an officer, it's a failed officer. I could see that I was not going to be in for a very easy ride. But rescue was on the way, and it came in the form of Hank Jansen. Hank Jansen, as every well-read person will know, was a literary giant at that time. His books gave solace to many a lonely serviceman. Titles like *You Took Me*, *Keep Me* were to be found in every self-respecting barrack-room library. And I found the key to instant popularity. I read the works of Jansen, aloud, to the lads. This was particularly helpful to those who couldn't read themselves, and seemed to be appreciated by all. The secret was to read the books with a very affected upper-class accent. I remember sitting on the top of a mound during a break in target practice, holding a tattered paperback. 'His knees turned to water and he hit the sidewalk,' I drawled languidly. 'She felt the weight of his body on her, his hands tearing at the flimsy material of her shirtwaister. "Baby," he gasped, "I just gotta have you." ' I glanced at the rows of upturned glowing faces around me. 'That's all for today, boys.' They reacted as one man. 'Go on, you daft bugger!' I did. Who could resist such a wonderful audience?

Once we were considered presentable enough to be seen in

49

the King's Uniform in public, we were allowed to leave camp. We had to pause at the guardhouse for a final check-up, which involved pirouetting before the NCO in charge. He checked on angle of beret, baldness around the ears, and spotlessness of belt and boots. For the first few evenings I was turned back by a sadistic character who screamed that no part of my person was in a fit state to pass those gates. Later I discovered he was the duty bugler, with no rank or authority at all.

Our standard of cleanliness and turn-out at that time was beyond reproach. We were impeccable, immaculate, and extremely uncomfortable. The knife-edge creases and gleaming boots and buckles had to be preserved at all times. To do this, it was necessary to move with extreme care. We walked with arms and legs stiff, like Frankenstein's monster. The relief as we climbed out of it all at the end of the evening was enormous. Amazing sights were seen as berets were removed. We all complied with the maxim 'Everything under your beret is your own'. As long as all areas below the band were hairless, you could keep chickens in your hat if you wanted to and some of the lads very nearly did. As the little green circle of wool came off, great thickets of hair were released. They sprang up to enormous heights – made even more bizarre by the fact that they started so suddenly. But those fenced-off copses were of great psychological value. They were our own, to be nurtured and admired in our own time. Paradoxically, our daytime wear was shapeless in the extreme. We collected fresh denims every morning. Size and shape didn't come into it. Each man collected one jacket, one pair of trousers. Then we swopped around. I once found myself with a pair of trousers so huge that the waistband was level with my shoulders.

Luckily, big Ginger Markham's trousers were making his eyes water, so we swopped.

One of my favourite characters in the early days was Corporal Moriarty. His job was to organize the sanitary arrangements – and he was taunted daily by the cry, 'How many buckets of shit are you short today, Moriarty?' He was grey and grizzled and ground his gums with venom at all us National Servicemen, particularly 'smart-arses' like myself. But we found him pretty repulsive, too, so it was a nicely balanced relationship.

One of the more reasonable 'regulars' was Corporal Koorlander. He was a noisy, amusing character who only got tough when we pushed our luck. A few years ago, in the basement of Broadcasting House, a young man well over six feet tall came up to me and said, 'I think you knew my father in the army.' I was afraid I wouldn't have a clue, but he turned out to be none

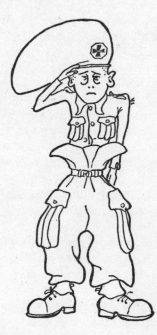

5 April 1951.   Rifleman Aspel reporting for duty.

other than Corporal Koorlander's son – the baby boy I'd seen in his mother's arms in the photographs the corporal had shown around. It was a severe shock.

Training continued. There was fun, and there were nasty moments. Like the time we were throwing hand-grenades from a dug-out. I didn't need to be taught – I'd seen Sergeant John Wayne do it a hundred times. I pulled out the pin, and hurled the grenade in what was meant to be a delicate but far-reaching arc. Just before I let go, my thumb caught in the sacking around one of the sandbags. The grenade went spinning, bounced a few times, and lay in the grass a few yards away. The instructors, fellow pupils, and watching officers couldn't have moved more quickly if they'd been blown up. The air was filled with diving bodies, and then with bits of flying metal. No-one was hurt, but no-one spoke to me afterwards. Until they got their breath back.

We at last qualified for weekend leave. For me, it was a mistake. I rushed home whenever possible, thumbing lifts along the Winchester bypass. The roadsides were dotted with figures in khaki every weekend, and people were generous with their lifts.

Nobody wanted to come back. Some didn't. When they were caught and brought in, the time they were absent and the length of their punishment was added to the time they'd had left to serve, so that for habitual deserters, two years' National Service stretched into many months more. I always went back on time, but it was agony. Sunday nights at Waterloo station. I felt again that sense of isolation and surrounding menace that I'd felt in the early days at Chard. There was a genuine menace on those occasions. Amongst the returning troops and other bona fide travellers, there were the queers and perverts, out to pick up a likely lad.

Some were outrageous and quite amusing, others a lot more sinister, and difficult to spot. I was waiting for my train one Sunday when a well-dressed character stopped at the bench. 'Hello,' he said, in a bluff and hearty way, 'the old Sixtieth Rifles, eh? My old mob.' I wasn't encouraging. I didn't mind comparing military reminiscences with my father every weekend, but I didn't want to spend the dying hours of my precious leave nattering about the glorious old days of the King's Royal Rifle Corps with a stranger. But he sat down and chatted on. It soon became apparent that he didn't know very much about the Sixtieth Rifles or any other branch of the army. My suspicions about his real interests in life were confirmed when he surreptitiously touched my leg and suggested we went back to his place for a drink. I explained that I wasn't feeling thirsty and that to avoid a punch in the throat he might like to move on. I've met a lot of homosexuals since then, most of them charming and amusing, and some of them good friends, but they are perceptive enough to know how far a relationship can go, and they stick to the caution offered by some pub-owners to seekers of credit: 'Please don't ask – a refusal might offend.'

A change of uniform

So, in spite of the temptation to stay at home and barricade myself in the bathroom, I always went back, and was never late. In fact, during all my time in uniform, I never did a day's 'jankers' (a punishment for minor offences, involving extra duties and parades in full equipment). It was the avoidance of this punishment that exhausted me. A man in the forces will spend a lot of energy in avoiding work. For example, he'll walk up and down all day with a bit of paper in his hand, pretending to be delivering a message. It's known as 'skiving', and it's very tiring. Only old hands have sufficient stamina.

I was comparing notes with a friend of mine, Michael Forrest. Mike, a lazy, untidy man told me that when he was on parade one day the company sergeant-major said to him, 'Get your hair cut! Stand up straight! You're like a fuckin' actor!'

'I *am* a fucking actor, sir,' replied Mike with dignity. They put him in the guardhouse for insubordination. Being an actor, he had a finely developed sense of melodrama – which was stimulated by the fact that all military prisoners have their bootlaces removed (in case of attempted suicide). Mike had a mouth-organ smuggled into him. He couldn't play the mouth-organ, but in the best prison scenes, somebody's always got one, so he sat on his bunk and made mournful sounds. Better still – the muster parade was held right outside the guardroom each morning. When Mike Forrest knew that all his mates were lined up facing his prison, he'd haul himself up to the bars and gasp, 'Water! Water!' He was the Cool Hand Luke of his day.

The time came for me to decide on a trade. I was no good at anything technical, so they sent me on a clerical course. I was taught how to type and understand army forms. At the end of the course we were each given sealed envelopes containing our assignments and destinations. It was a rare, exciting moment. 'Washington!', shouted one happy conscript. 'Fontainebleau!' cried another. I opened mine with trembling hands. Tidworth. Tidworth, Hampshire.

At least, the barracks were new and reasonably comfortable, and we weren't destined to stay there long. In February 1952, the King, George vi, died, and we, the Second Battalion KRRC and hundreds of others, were detailed to line the route of the funeral procession through London.

We were hastily instructed in the ritual of street-lining. This

c 53

involved some pretty tricky manœuvres with our rifles, but we eventually got the hang of it, and were taken up to Woolwich Barracks the night before the procession.

There was no time for sleep that night. Reveille was at two am, and we went off in bus-loads to Hyde Park Corner. Our part of the route was along Piccadilly, by the side of Green Park. As dawn broke, the crowds began to assemble. We stamped our feet and adjusted our bayonet-scabbards and generally tried to attract the attention of any likely-looking females in the crowd. One or two sympathetic mums offered us bits of chocolate, but there was no response from the young ladies. Eventually, a fearless lad called Donk (his real name was Arnold Senior, but we called him Donk because he came from Doncaster) said to me, "Ere, Mike, lad, let's chat up these little darlin's over 'ere, like.' 'Go on, then,' I said. 'Will you back me up, like?' said Donk. 'Of course I will,' I said, edging away.

Donk strolled casually over to two very pretty girls, and put on his smoothest voice. ' 'Ullo, loves,' he said. ' 'Ow are you fixed, like?' 'What do you mean?' they said, coldly. They were very cut-glass. 'Well,' said Donk, ' 'Ow are you fixed, like – generally?' They turned away, and Donk turned to me for support, but I'd melted into the mass of greatcoats.

Then we were called to order, and put in our official places in the Piccadilly gutter. From the direction of the West End, came faint sounds of music. The procession slowly approached. We watched as resplendent horsemen trotted past. The cavalry officers looked magnificent, unreal in their perfection. Several bands moved past, pouring out mournful music. It was very emotional. We all agreed that the police band was best. As the coffin itself came by, our instructions were to 'reverse rifles', that is, to turn them slowly until the end of the barrel rested on the instep of our left boot; then both hands were to be laid over the butt and the head lowered with eyes downcast. It was very irritating to have to do this and be robbed of the most impressive spectacle in the whole parade, but orders were orders and we had to be content to squint under our eyebrows. I said our training in this routine had been a bit perfunctory, and I'm ashamed to say that one or two of us lost control of our rifles half-way through. I made it safely, but along the line there was the occasional clatter, and groan of 'Oh balls'. Then there would be a ripple of dismay through the crowd. I distinctly heard someone murmur, 'What a shower,' which was very unfair. We might not like the army, but we were doing our best to give our King a respectful send-off.

5
Foreign correspondent

A month or two later, we went to Germany. I rate this as one of the most significant events of my life, because it released me, once and for all, from the crippling homesickness I'd always suffered from, whether three miles from home at the beginning of school term, or a hundred miles down the railway line after a weekend's leave.

The excitement of seeing another country swept away all such pusillanimous feelings, and I was never bothered by them again.

Conversely, the pleasure of foreign travel has never dimmed. I'm at my happiest when packing a suitcase. That's something the army taught me – have bag, will travel, and fast. I can be packed and on my way ten minutes after the phone rings. Sometime I'm a little too fast. I decide to rush off for a few days to forget things, and when I open my case I find I have.

Soldiers have very little chance to forget anything, and in the spring of 1952 we sailed from Harwich, complete to the last button.

We stood on deck, the troopship (or was it simply a ferry?) feeling its way through the mist surrounding the Hook of Holland. I strained my eyes for the first glimpse of foreign soil. Gradually the outline of buildings emerged. They were different, surely? Yes, they definitely were a different shape from English buildings. And the writing on the sheds – I couldn't understand a word. I was abroad!

As the train carried us into Germany, the faces staring at us from the level crossings became hard and sullen. This was only seven years after the war. Germany's economic miracle hadn't yet begun, and the country was still in a mess. And for a people still smarting from defeat and disillusion there was nothing endearing about trainloads of pimply young Britishers giving the V-sign as they rattled past.

However, if the people of Münster, the Westphalian town we were stationed near, felt resentful, they didn't show it.

They were polite and friendly and seemed to realize that it wasn't our idea to be there, and that as soon as possible we'd pack our little bags and be on our way. (I felt a lot more menace on a holiday trip to Jamaica just two years ago.)

The countryside was pretty, the food and wine were good. But the girls. . . . Germany at that time seemed to specialize in women with flat chests and massive legs. I say at that time, because subsequent visits (and close scrutiny of the German entrants in the Miss World contest), show that there has been a great improvement. Perhaps it was the food – or lack of it. Pale girls with consumptive coughs would sidle up to us, brandishing tobacco tins full of contraceptives. I always refused the offers.

One night, after a meal of *Bratwurst mit Kartoffelsalat* (similar to bangers and mash) I innocently asked the waitress, who was not young and looked a bit like Dr Goebbels, what time the place closed. She misunderstood, and gave us all a leer. 'We close at one,' she whispered 'but at twelve I can come and sit at your table.' I hurt my leg in the 11.55 pm stampede for the exit. And so my life of celibacy continued.

There was a thriving black market in coffee. '*Haben-sie Nescafé?*' was a regular question from the locals. The profit rate was approximately two hundred per cent, and the same with cigarettes. Occasionally, through encounters with American troops, we would get hold of nylon stockings – at that time something new, as luxurious as oysters. We'd send these home, singly, in thick envelopes, hoping to beat the customs man. Eventually I smuggled a wrist-watch home as a present for my mother. The customs man made no search – perhaps he knew my father's ambition for me. I'd cunningly wrapped the watch in greaseproof paper and I hid it in a tin of foot-powder. During the journey the paper worked loose, and the watch was full of powder. They couldn't even clean the black suède strap. But my mother was delighted. She has it still. It's never worked.

I sent the stockings, and regular love letters, to a sweet girl called Anne, who lived in London, and worked for William

Collins. I used to sit in the NAAFI in dirty denims, with my great boots resting on the next chair, and puff on a Woodbine as I scribbled. My speciality was the long, romantic postscript – usually something by Rupert Brooke which I hoped she'd think was my own work. 'PS', I'd write, 'If I should die, think only this of me: that there's some corner of a foreign field that is forever England.' Once I wrote the payoff in German: 'Darling, *haben sie auch das licht ausgeschaltet?*' which Anne thought was pretty sexy, and I suppose it was. It means, 'Have you remembered to turn the light out?' – and it was printed on our barrack-room wall.

Once established in Germany, and with my new-found independence of spirit, I decided to change my job. In Tidworth I'd been a clerk in the quartermaster's office. He was a benign old chap, a Major who'd come up from the ranks, and life had been fairly easy. But now I was over there, it seemed a bit feeble to sit at a typewriter when most of the others were dashing around the countryside. I applied to go on a signals course, and with a confidence that surprised me, I not only got through it, but came out with top marks. I became a radio-operator, and so, unconsciously, moved closer to the finger of fate beckoning from Broadcasting House.

I crouched over my No. 19 radio set, making every message sound like a Richard Dimbleby report from the front line. On the next set of manœuvres, they gave me the job of being the CO's operator. It was almost a disaster. We bounced along in his jeep, with me in the back passing on instructions to the rest of the battalion. At least that's what I meant to do. But the radio wouldn't work. I disconnected and replugged and changed earphones and rechecked frequencies and finally changed the valves. The CO was impressed and irritated at the same time. Eventually I saw the trouble. 'I think I've got it sir,' I cried and within seconds, the vital information was crackling through the microphone. The trouble was simple. I'd forgotten to switch on.

I was also taught to drive, in a fashion. 'Remember, lads,' said our instructor, 'if you're coming along the road behind a woman driver, and she gives a hand-signal, the only thing you can reasonably assume is that the window is open.' It's a well-established prejudice. Manœuvres were, if not the most enjoyable part of army life, certainly the most memorable. Although we were peacetime amateurs, there were dangers. People were killed, mostly through their own mistakes; they slept under tanks when the ground was soft, and died when the tanks settled on them: or they didn't keep their heads down when live ammunition was being used. Once I came back to our tent after being delayed on a trip, to find that everyone thought I was a ghost. Apparently one of our number had been found dead on a nearby railway line, the victim of a mysterious accident or a local farmer harbouring a grudge. The victim's name hadn't been revealed. By the time I got back, my comrades were composing a letter to my parents.

On one outing involving troops of various nations, we came across a group who were all Red Indians – a whole company of them. During the war, we were told, the enemy could break any code, given time. There were two 'codes' they couldn't break: when the wireless operator was a Red Indian, and spoke in his tribal tongue, or when the operator was Welsh. *Cymru am byth*!

Working a field telephone could be fun as well as a chore. I sat there one day, passing messages back and forth from company to company. As one company commander, a captain, was waiting to be put through, he started to hum a well-known tune. After a few seconds I joined in, and the two of us carried on a duet. When the last note died away, he gave a baritone chuckle and said, 'Splendid! Is that you, Mathew?' I chuckled back and said, 'No, it's Michael here,' and Rifleman Aspel pulled the plugs out.

We had the most extraordinary bunch of officers you can imagine. The Sixtieth Rifles was one of the 'smart' regiments, so you could rely on getting a fascinating cross-section of the cream of society commissioned into it. I overheard one saying to the other, 'You know, Gervase, my chaps get terribly naughty sometimes. I really get quite cross with them.' And at a briefing before a dawn attack, we were told, 'Now if you get captured by the enemy, chaps, *do* destroy all your papers and things, won't you? – because I for one shall be running like fury.' Very entertaining, and many of them regular soldiers, with war records of amazing valour.

After one six-week series of exercises, during which we had never returned to barracks, we packed up our gear, struck camp and headed for home, leaving behind us the imprint of many bodies on the grass.

After all that time in the open, occasionally sleeping in barns or kindly farmers' houses (where we hung our socks out of the window to avoid the fumes) the return to a real bed and a proper bath was a pleasant prospect. Seeing ourselves in large mirrors was a shock: our faces were burnt black, our hair bleached by weeks of sun and open air. That first night back I dreamed that we were still under canvas, but our tent was being wrapped up until the next training season with me inside it. In my dream I ran to the window-hole in the side of the tent and tried to clamber out. Our room was on the first floor of the barracks, and one of the boys woke up to see me about to throw myself out of the window. He grabbed my leg, and I woke up. Nobody slept easily for a few nights after that. I've always suffered from claustrophobia, and my dreams have always been profuse and lurid. But that was the only time I've walked in my sleep.

Something that struck me – struck us all – with recurring force, was the great gulf between officers and men. I've heard of the old army announcement of a regimental dance which invited 'Officers and their ladies, NCOs and their wives, other ranks and their women'. You can imagine them all striving for promotion, so that their women could at last be recognized officially as their wives – never, alas, to be ladies. That was too much to hope for. That was many years ago, but the social divisions have always been deep. I found the difference at its most ludicrous not socially but in so-called 'active' conditions. One dreadful day, a troop of us squaddies were tramping through the mire and looking for a dry place to flop down and scrape the mud from our corned-beef sandwiches, when we happened upon a clearing which looked as if it had been prepared for a fairies' banquet. A trestle table with a pretty embroidered cloth on it was laid with silver and glass. Bottles of Liebfraumilch stood in rows, and scattered languidly around, their bottoms and feet far from the nasty wet grass, were our beloved leaders. One or two of them looked slightly embarrassed, but only, I suspect, because we reminded them of the sordidness of real life.

When not actively engaged in operating wirelesses, I worked

in the signals office. The man in charge was a captain, named Michael Walsh, a gentle and sympathetic character who occasionally let the barriers down. He went back to England to get married, and when he brought his bride back, he told me about some of the shows they'd seen. 'There was a sketch in one revue, Aspel,' he said, 'where two secretaries were talking. One said, "Doesn't the new boss dress well?" The other one said, "Yes – and so quickly." ' We both roared with laughter. 'And then there was—' but he suddenly stopped, realizing that he was becoming too familiar. The smile faded. 'Yes, well, just finish typing those forms, will you?' he said. (I met him years later, coming out of a cinema in Chelsea. Without the social restrictions, he was totally relaxed and very good company.) He was rare. Most of the officers maintained an austere remoteness, and were obviously developing into replicas of that well-known military leader who was so convinced of his own infallibility that when reading the lesson during church-parade, intoned, 'And Jesus Christ said – and I'm inclined to agree. . . .'

The lads in my platoon were as mixed a bunch as you'll get anywhere. Put a few dozen young men together from all kinds of backgrounds and you'll find a comedian, an eccentric, a troublemaker and a philosopher amongst them. I remember Allen Dawson, a likeable and irrepressible Londoner who never stopped laughing. Allen was a period piece. When he went out on the town, he wore the long drape jacket, the drainpipe trousers, and the brothel-creepers. He also sported the D A haircut. (Duck's Arse. The hair's spikey on top, the sides curve around and meet at the back.) His laugh was something special. His mouth would open wide, there would be a long silence, and finally a short, quacking sound. It was very tiring for him, and he used to grasp his trouser leg to take the strain. Laugh and grow fat they say: Allen's as thin as a rake. He now runs a flower shop in Stoke Newington, and hasn't changed at all.

'Hawkeye' (his name was Hawkes, and he had a big nose) was another character. He was blond, tall and well built. He wore a shining windcheater with the name of an ice-hockey team across the back, and always spoke with an American accent when girls were near.

There was another whose name I forget. He'd been brought up in India, and had obviously been used to ordering people about. I don't know why he wasn't an officer. One day he fell out with an easy-going boy from Cornwall, who listened calmly while the other raved and cursed and insulted him. We all cringed. They were both powerfully built and there was obviously going to be a clash of dinosaurs. It went on for about six minutes; when he finally finished, the Cornish boy smiled gently and said 'Bollocks'. Ah, the gift of repartee.

I remember, with affection, a windswept character from Liverpool called Nicholas Leo Benedict St John. He always looked as if he was walking backwards. And Eddie Powick, a cheerful prototype of Private Walker from 'Dad's Army', complete with pencil-line moustache and knowing wink.

I was, I suppose, an almost faceless observer. My own style at that time was the conventional, approved short-back-and-sides image. I had a favourite jacket – a blue-green cord affair – which was too big for me. I used to keep one hand in my pocket to break up the voluminous flow of material.

If you're good at sport, the army is the place for you. You will be excused almost all military duties if you can defend the honour of the regiment on the field or in the ring. I was a keen gymnast, but predictably, not clever at team games. Our PT instructor suggested I enter for the inter-battalion boxing tournament. 'No thanks,' I said. My nose is much too sharp and unyielding for that sort of thing. 'If you get hurt, I'll give you a pound,' he said. 'No thanks,' I replied. I went to the tournament. The fellow who took my place left most of his teeth on the canvas, and the next bout was delayed while they mopped up his blood.

I did enter for the pole vault in a three-cornered athletics match. (I'd once cleared four feet six inches at school.) Unfortunately, a week before the event, I cut my foot while swimming in a river. We were coming to the end of another of our open-air adventures at the time, and the medical officer had no anaesthetic. This was a pity because the gash required six stitches. 'You've got skin like a fucking elephant, Aspel,' gasped the MO, as he forced the needle into my toe and out at the other side of the wound. I didn't say much. I was too busy burying my teeth into the tent-pole.

Anyway, no athletics match for me. My place was taken by a room-mate, who claimed a lot of vaulting experience. I wasn't able to attend the match, but I heard reports. Apparently he went dashing down the track, put the pole deftly into the box, and did a superb leap – under the bar. He never managed to get over the bar, but our team won the match, and every member got a little silver cup. He used to polish it every day and stand it on his bedside locker.

I also remember a photograph which appeared in an army magazine of a sergeant breasting the tape at the end of a gruelling race. The look of agony and triumph on his face was compelling. It wasn't quite the focal point of the picture though – that was further down. He had forgotten to wear his athletic support – and through the gaping leg of his shorts his entire genitals were on view, flowing back in the slip-stream. He deserved his medal.

Although I was an agile gymnast, my physique was slightly unbalanced due to my years of rowing. My shoulders and arms were heavy, but I'd done nothing to develop the notorious family legs. Hence the cry from our witty PT instructor: 'Aspel! What are them two white pieces of string hanging from your shorts?' They were strong enough to bear my weight, however, and because I could move swiftly it was taken for granted that I'd be a natural for the rugby team. Now I've always liked the game, and if I'd had the weight I think I might have made a useful forward, but I have unreliable hands. Like my legs, they're long, rather thin affairs, not made for plucking a spinning ball from the air. Still, I was offered a place in the battalion rugby team by the desperate captain. He was a gigantic lieutenant with a squawky voice. At one point in the game I got the ball and ran a good ten paces before I was felled. 'Oh, Aspel!' he shrilled, 'are you delirious with success?' Moments later someone threw me an easy pass, which I dropped. 'Oh, you leprous animal,' cried the captain. I only played in that one match.

I tend to be accident prone. I survived my rugby-playing career with no more than a few lacerations, but I've taken heavier knocks at other sports. My last public appearance for an army team was when they were one man short in the hockey team. 'No thanks,' I said. I was going on leave the next day, and didn't want to risk anything. After all, I wouldn't be able to get into the ultimate embrace with plaster all up my leg.

'How can you get hurt?' they said. 'Come on – just to make up the numbers.' So I played. After three minutes, the puck flew from the ground and scored a friction burn across my chin. In the second half, somebody swung his stick over his shoulder – a quite illegal move – and cracked me across the nose. I went on leave swollen, blue and bandaged.

Time went by slowly, stretched by our yearning for it to pass. We made wall-charts, with each remaining day to serve clearly marked. Mine took the form of a circle. Each morning, another segment of the circle was inked in, and the black road to freedom grew ever so slowly.

I spent Christmas 1952 in Düsseldorf, a pretty town even then, or so it seemed. There's a beautiful street there called *Koenigsallee* (King's Road, I suppose). A canal runs through the centre of the street. There are some lovely bridges and very fine statues and fountains. We found a night club there and with our last remaining marks bought a bottle of wine. The lights went out, a voice cried '*Kabaret!*' and half a dozen near-naked girls sprang on to the floor. They must have scoured the country for such perfect specimens. I knocked over the bottle of wine, and we were asked to leave. It wasn't a very merry Christmas. We met a group of American soldiers who were intrigued by our green berets and forage caps and black buttons. They also liked the way we spoke. 'Say some more, fellas,' begged one, 'I get a kick outa the way you talk.' 'Aw, you got rocks in your head,' said his friend. 'Whaddya mean?' said the first. 'These guys are talkin' the mother tongue, stupid!'

I spent my last few weeks in Germany drawing cartoons for the signals section, on how not to operate a wireless set – something I was an expert on. The circle on the wall was now almost blocked in. I remember one moment of supreme elation. I was walking at the rear of the barracks, by the petrol pumps. It was a clear, early spring day. I respond very easily to weather and atmosphere, and suddenly I had a tremendous uplift in spirit. The world was my oyster! I would soon be free and could do anything – literally anything I wanted to. A future of happiness and success shone ahead. I tried to leap in the air to bang my heels together, but the weight of my boots defeated me.

In March 1953 I was back in Winchester, recognizing a few

faces from the days of initial training two years before. Our release date was 27 March. On the evening of 26 March we all went down to the town to drink it dry. Several of the group drank themselves under the table and back up again, and one or two went on the rampage. This cost them another three months in the army. 'I told 'em to swallow,' said Ginger Abel sadly, 'but they 'ad to put the boot in, didn't they?'

There was a last-minute scare which took years off my life. We had been given our release papers, but had to wait until a certain hour before we were allowed to leave. (Officially the two weeks following release were classed as terminal leave, and you were still a soldier until that time was up.)

There was nothing for us to do, and I knew there was an early train to London, so I gathered my gear and started to tiptoe behind the buildings along a well-known escape route for smart soldiers. Suddenly there was an ear-splitting yell. 'That man there – yes, you! Come 'ere!' It was the voice of the dreaded 'Solly' Silver, the provost sergeant. Solly was one of the most feared men in the British army, enshrined in legend and song. With his band of military policemen, he ruled over the garrison like Papa Doc and the Tons Tons Macoute. Rumour had it that his body was pitted with scars – signs of the vengeance wreaked on dark nights by many a man whose spirit had been broken by Solly.

I was worried. Not to put too fine a point on it, I felt a certain tightening around the anal sphincter. This could mean the chain gang, or at least a thousand lashes.

'And where do you think you're going, laddie?' breathed Solly. His eyes glittered under the black brows.

'Well, I ... I ... I ... I ... pardon?' 'Pardon Sergeant!' hissed Solly. 'I suppose you was thinking of creeping out the back way, was you?' There was no denying it. I felt my blood, life and future drain away.

'Well, git out the proper way – left, right, left right!'

Could it be? Solly was human! I hovered in mid-air for a few seconds, then shot out of the barracks, and the army, like something from a Mack Sennett comedy. And that sums up my life as a full-time soldier: on the whole, a pretty undignified performance. I did very little for the army. And what did the army do for me and all the other boys who served their two years? Did it make men of us, as everyone said? We were two years older and would have grown anyway. At the time, and for years afterwards, I considered the whole experience tedious, unpleasant, and a waste of time. But no experience can be a complete waste of time. There were things I did, and saw and felt that must have been of some value in terms of a developing awareness of life. I had been to places I would not otherwise have seen, and a little iron had entered the soul. At the same time, I don't agree with the currently popular idea of forcing every long-haired malcontent into uniform on the assumption that a bit of discipline will sort him out. I saw perfectly well-adjusted boys come into the army and develop into thugs whose idea of fun was to wander around the Naafi knocking the teeth from the mouths of the musicians. On the whole, I think I should refuse the invitation if it came again.

On the 'Today' radio programme one morning before Remembrance Sunday I referred to the phrases carved into war memorials – phrases like 'made the supreme sacrifice' and 'gave their lives'. Those men didn't give their lives. They were taken from them, and I thought 'lost their lives' or simply 'died' were better ways of expressing what really happened. War is not glorious. It is shameful and horrific. Of course, I was attacked by people who considered my attitude to be typical of the callow, unthinking parasites of my age. I replied that I imagined most of the fallen would rather have lived, and that I was against heroics, not heroism.

The Korean war was on while I was a National Serviceman. Another battalion of Greenjackets was sent there instead of us, and I must admit I didn't feel in any way deprived.

Perhaps the most important thing the army did for me, and for which I should be grateful, is that it gave me a chance to reappraise my life, to look again at the direction I was to take. In fact, all I did was decide which direction I *didn't* want to take. I didn't want to go back into the publishing business. Their plans for me, I knew, followed a time-honoured pattern. I would go to Glasgow where the books were produced, to learn the practical side of the business, and after two years would return and prepare to take my place in the sales team.

I have almost always been extremely lucky in my choice of employers. William Collins accepted that I didn't want to be a representative, and they patiently asked what I *did* want to do. 'There's the rub,' I said – 'I just don't know. I think perhaps I'd like to be a cartoonist.' I produced some very crude examples of my work and when she stopped shuddering, the art editor prepared a list of magazines for me to visit, with letters of introduction. No-one was remotely interested. I thanked the publishers for their patience and help, and for the happy memories; I touched my forelock, and stepped out, once again, into the big wide world.

Something I could not have predicted was the feeling of anti-climax. The anticipation of the joys of civilian life had obsessed me for so long that when it came, it was strangely dull and tasteless.

I missed the companionship and the foul language. I even lost weight. A month or two after Solly Silver had chased me out of the army I went to Liverpool to celebrate ex-Rifleman Nicholas Leo Benedict St John's twenty-first birthday. We watched the local rugby league team Widnes get thrashed, saw Queen Elizabeth crowned on the St Johns' tiny black and white telly, and heard the news of the conquest of Everest – cleverly held back to coincide with the coronation. ('All this and Everest Too!' declared the headlines.)

Nick also very kindly arranged a partner for me to join him and his girlfriend for a gay night out at the local steak-house. I would have preferred Nick's girl, but my partner was attractive and friendly and a good time was had by all. A thoroughly respectable time, too. On the way home, Nick stopped his father's Sunbeam Talbot at a dark and lonely spot and in his delicate way shouted, 'Time for a snog! Where's the bloody passion-blanket?' The ends of a heavy blanket were then jammed into the windows on each side of the car, this dividing it neatly in two and deadening the expected sound-effects. There were no muffled love-cries, just ten minutes of giggles from the front and in the back a rather strained conversation about the merits of Rugby Union versus Rugby League. To relieve the tension, I yelled to Nick and asked him if he'd heard the one about the fellow who stopped his car in a dark lane and told his girl to get in the back and she said no, and he said why not and she said she'd rather stay in the front with him. Well, a joke session will always break up any emotion-charged atmosphere, and in no time the passion-blanket came down, the air was cleared, and we were on our way.

I took the young lady home and was invited in for tea. Lots of polite conversation, handshakes all round, and good night.

Imagine my dismay when the girl phoned me the next day to say that her parents had forbidden her to see me again. Why? She wasn't sure. So I stormed up to the house to secure justice. Her mother was horrified to see me, but her father invited me in. I asked politely for an explanation of their decision. Had I offended them in some way? Indeed I had, said the lady. They were God-fearing people and would not tolerate hearing the Lord's name taken in vain. 'Pardon?' I said. And then it came out. Twice in our conversation the night before, I had said 'Good God' in reaction to some statement or other. They had been too horrified to comment, but had vowed afterwards that I should never darken their doorstep or sully their daughter again.

When I could speak, I pointed out that as I had left the army only a matter of weeks before, they were very lucky that my language hadn't been a great deal livelier. But there was no point in embarrassing the girl, so I left – but without touching my forelock.

During the weeks following my farewell to the book business I tried, reasonably hard, to get a job. There were plenty of jobs as clerks or trainee telephonists. I could have joined the fire service, but I somehow didn't feel the required leap of the heart at any of those prospects. My father suggested customs and excise. I thought of Australia, but had enough imagination to realize that I wasn't the pioneer my father was, and that life in the outback would pall after ten minutes or so.

Eventually Dad's patience wore out, and he suggested I get a job – 'any job, just get one'. I saw his point of view, and I found an advertisement for a trainee in the bedding industry. A trainee what? I thought. But I found a certain allure in the idea. I answered the advertisement, had an interview, and got the job. If this story were being told on radio, there would now be a fanfare or a roll of drums, because getting that job was another of those well-known significant events. It led to me going to Cardiff, which led to – but I'm anticipating again.

My new employers made comfortable beds. That was their

1 Aged nine and slicked
down ready for Chard
Congregational Sunday
School. Brother Alan, then
six, is the one on the right
in the empty jacket.

2 Aged thirteen: this
photograph was taken to
impress my pen-friend. She
never wrote again.

3 Marlow, 1950. A day by the river for the office staff, and a half-hearted smile to disguise the pain of un-requited love for the lady on the left.

4 Cardiff, 1954. Victory at the firm's sports day.

5 Television newsreaders' Rule Number 1 – never show emotion; England wins the World Cup.

6 April 1968. The remains of my Morris 1800.

7 May 1968. Edward and Jane have just thought of a jolly game. It's called Pulling Away Daddy's Sticks.

8 Chatting up Violet Rose Robinson, Miss Slender Ankles of 1926. My mother. One of the more mature beauties whose language I *can* speak.

9 Christmas 1973. A rare family group. My sons Gregory and Richard on a visit from Australia, meet the twins, Jane and Edward, for the first time in eight years.

claim, and although I never slept on one, I had no reason to doubt it. It was a family concern run by three cousins. The idea of being a junior clerk evoked thoughts of Dickens. I rather expected us to be supervised by a beady-eyed old man on a high stool, wiping his nose on his mittens. In fact our office chief was a jolly man whose main concern was to be first in the nearest pub at opening time. My time at Vauxhall was completely happy. The work was undemanding, the company convivial. One of the despatch clerks was a great fantasist. He described Friday evening in the bosses' office. They all stripped naked, he said, and wallowed in the week's takings. 'Pour another bag of half-crowns over me!' they all cried.

We went on a firm's outing to Southend. Brown ale in the charabanc, the communal nosh-up (I have a photograph ot nothing but open mouths and sweat-stained waitresses), 'Kiss-me-quick' hats, and many stops on the way home. It was idyllic, and I think of it every time I read the Dylan Thomas story of *The Outing* (' "Twenty-six minutes to opening time!" shouted an old man in a panama hat, not looking at a watch.')

The only tiny speck on the sparkling surface of the day was an encounter with a gypsy. She was selling pegs, or whatever, on the beach, and we ragged her before wc bought. I must have bcen particularly loud, because she turned to me and spat, 'You'll never come to anything, you won't!' That shut me up. I had a nasty feeling that she would be right. Nothing seemed to lie ahead, and I knew that in time, I must do *something* that would satisfy me.

The present was too enjoyable for me to get really depressed, however, and the months passed with only occasional frets about the future.

6

The land of song

One day the three cousins sent for me. They wanted me to go to Cardiff for a while to work in one of their retail outlets. When I came back I would become – a representative. Oh God. I didn't want to represent anybody. I didn't want to sell any-thing. I wanted to stay nice and cosy and unnoticed until the flash of lightning arrived and lit up the road to my destiny. But I said all right, I'll go to Cardiff. The cousins bought me a new suit, and off I went.

Cardiff is a fine city. It has a magnificent civic centre, a castle, the Arms Park, and very pretty girls. It was a revelation to me. Like all ignorant Englishmen I had believed it to have coal-mines in the main street.

If I was lucky with employers, I was less fortunate with landladies – at first. The company had arranged for me to stay with the local rep. His wife had obviously accepted the idea under duress, and threw me out at the first opportunity. One night I went to the pictures after work and forgot to tell her I wouldn't be back for a meal.

The next morning I was asked to leave.

Much later I learned that she'd told my employers in London that I'd been wild and carrying on with women at all hours. If only it had been true! I'd spent most evenings writing letters – until the night I went berserk and took one of the girls from Leather Goods to see *An American in Paris*. I was luckier, much luckier, with landlady number two. Gladys Adams lived in a pleasant part of Cardiff off the Newport Road, called Roath (the district on the other side of the Newport Road is called Splott; many people who live in Splott claim to live in Roath). Gladys was plump, dark and attractive, a cheerful divorcee with a teenage daughter and two younger sons. Granny lived there too. She was a beetle-browed original of the Giles cartoon character, and her bark was not quite as bad as her bite; but she often mellowed.

I was taken into the family at once. It seemed too good to be true. A few days after I'd moved in, I thought I'd ruined everything. I spent an evening with some new friends in Pontypridd, about twelve miles away, and missed the last bus home. I caught the first bus the next morning, I tiptoed up the stairs, hoping the household was still asleep. The kitchen door was flung open. There stood Gladys with her hands on her hips. 'There you are, you old stop-out!' she laughed. 'What do you want for breakfast?' Gladys Adams rates as one of the world's great landladies – a warm, understanding, generous friend. I only ever met two others to compare with her. One was Kitty Cox who ran a house in Canton. (Canton's another part of Cardiff.) I joined Kitty after Gladys and family had moved out of the city. Kitty and her husband Stan were a fun-loving couple. She always wore a grey curl fixed to her red hair, and stockings with birds in flight up the thigh. She sang a lot, and whatever the song, she always included the line 'true lovers meet again'. Stan's hair was cut in the Kirk Douglas style, and he wore a blazer with the pioneer corps badge worked in gold braid. In fun and hospitality, they gave me far more than I paid for. Top landlady number three, and still a good friend, is Carole Thomson, who, with her husband Mel, welcomed me into their north London home some years ago while I looked for a place of my own. I came for a month, and stayed for nearly two years.

Carole is a musician, and used to do an act with the other members of her family, Cammie and Marie. They called themselves the Calores Sisters. They're warm-hearted Italians. Carole sees evil in nobody. Everyone is a nice boy or girl or, at worst, 'a bit silly'. And to her they remain boys and girls, even if they're seventy-five years old. Carole used to call up to me every morning, 'Are you alone, dear?' If I said yes, she would bring me a cup of coffee. If I said no, she would bring up two cups of coffee.

Life in digs is often a lonely and miserable business, but Gladys, Kitty and Carole made up for the other hard-faced old harridans I met.

Polly wants a zebra

In Cardiff, I was put to work in the furniture department at one of the local stores. It was a large, fairly old fashioned place, run, like my parent company in London, by a group of relatives. Being only a temporary member of staff, I was in a very fortunate position. The others, particularly the older members of the staff, were naturally committed to producing good sales figures. I was more of an observer. If I made a sale, I was pleased, but if I didn't, the disappointment was by no means unbearable. I was really there to observe, and learn, and as I had no intention of making a career in the furniture business I wasn't too diligent about that either.

One salesman, a peppery character in late middle age, once revealed his insecurity by accusing me of trying to steal one of his customers. Nothing could have been further from the truth, but he demanded that I go to the stockroom with him to settle the matter. He was very small and thin, but to my amazement he started dancing about amongst the carpets and wardrobes, working his arms furiously and calling on me to 'put 'em up'. I couldn't put anything up – I was too busy rolling on a four foot six inch spring interior mattress, helpless with laughter. Eventually he saw the joke too, and we went off to the staff canteen for a conciliatory cuppa.

It took me a little time to get used to the Cardiff accent and the Welsh phraseology generally. The Cardiff accent's a sort of Welsh cockney, spoken out of the corner of the mouth. It's difficult to reproduce in print, but it's a very flat sound. The vowels are drawn out in a harsher way than the beautiful, round cadences of the Welsh hinterland. Now a southern Englishman – well, let's say, a BBC man – will say 'pahty' and 'dahnce'. In Cardiff, they'll talk about going to a 'paaatee'. The first part of the word is like the sound a person would make when falling off a cliff – 'aaaagh!'

The first Welsh phrase I heard was when someone said, 'I'll take my coat in case it rains, isn't it?' 'Isn't it what?' I asked. 'Well – isn't it . . . I'll take my coat?' It was the first time anyone had questioned what was a perfectly natural statement. The second phrase I heard was, 'There's cold your hands are.' I can't quite recall the circumstances, but it's an interesting juxtaposition of words.

The shop had various sporting and social clubs. On sports

72

day I entered for every race. The opposition wasn't exactly ferocious, and the cups were handsome. I trained quite intensely, usually in heavy brogues, so that when the big day came and I put on my running shoes I would fly over the grass like the proverbial winged messenger. It worked, and by the time the last race was due, I had swept the board. I was ready to clinch matters with the 440, and so claim the Victor of the Day prize, a massive goblet, to go with my other trophies.

We got on our marks and the whole arena fell silent. Every group, from Soft Furnishings to Novelty Goods, waited to see if I would do it again. Even the lads from Despatch were quiet. Most of them were unconscious. It had been a long, thirsty day.

'On your marks, get set – oh, hang on, this bloody gun's stuck.' A fault on the starting pistol! Three of the runners sped away. 'Call them back, you great fool!' I cried in anguish. But the starter had lost interest, and the rest of us had to set off in pursuit. It was a hopeless task. I forced my way to second place and was bearing down on the leader, but ran out of track. The race was over, and with it, my chance of being Supremo. Still, it was a talking point for months afterwards – until people told me to shut up and forget about it.

There was also a thriving dramatic society, the Hayes Players. (The Hayes was the name of the street the store stood in.) The producer was a wonderful theatrical who occasionally wept. I auditioned for the next play. It was *The Paragon*, the story of a blind man who worships the memory of his dead son, killed in action. The boy turns up, alive, but no hero. He's an absolute rotter, detested by all but Dad. Until . . . anyway, I got the part of Max, the frightfully decent chap who loves the son's supposed widow. I wanted to play the rotten son, but the producer wanted that part for himself.

We had the use of furniture from the store's own department, so the set was quite impressive. I suppose it would have looked even more so, if they'd taken all the price-tags off, but it still looked pretty good. Our make-up was heavy ('Ugh! You're wearing lipstick!' shrieked Miss Westlake of Accounts, when she came backstage), and the acting was a bit ponderous too. At one point I had to seize the caddish son and hurl him on to a couch – with rage, not desire. One emotion I can simulate fairly convincingly is anger, and I slightly over-acted. I noticed that the producer's face was turning black (he wasn't very robust) so I cut the seizing bit short and hurled him on to the couch. Unfortunately the only couch the furniture department could lend us was a low-backed affair, and he hit it so hard that it toppled backwards. All that could be seen of him was his feet, waving feebly in the air. The audience enjoyed it very much.

At the end of the play, the curtain came down with us standing over the corpse of the son, whose heart had given out in a struggle with his disillusioned Dad. We had a couple of curtain calls, and assumed that that was it. Unfortunately the girl on curtains thought she could squeeze a bit more applause out of the patrons, so she raised it once more. There was the corpse leaning on one elbow, saying, 'Well, it didn't go badly, did it? I just couldn't go through that again . . .'

Shortly after the second-night run of *The Paragon*, our producer came to me, trembling with excitement. 'Expect a phone call,' he gasped, and would say no more. The call came, and it was as if I had been summoned to a command performance. 'Cardiff Little Theatre,' said the voice, 'would be willing to offer you an audition.' Of course I was pleased, and flattered. I knew that the Little Theatre groups around the country were as near to professional companies as most would-be actors were likely to get, and I was keen to do more. I joined them, but before I had a chance to do anything else, it was decision time again. London had decided that it was time I returned and took my rightful place at the wheel of the firm's car, order book by my side.

I went home, started a driving course at the company's expense (the army course being unofficial) and brooded. It was obvious to the most myopic person that I wasn't happy in my work, and eventually I was called to the main office. We had a long talk. As a result, hands were shaken, farewells were made, and I stepped out, yet again, into the big wide world.

I'm still astounded at the generosity of those people. I'd wasted their time and money, and yet now they were wishing me luck, and giving me a silver handshake. They even paid for me to finish the driving course in my own time. You see what I mean by my luck with employers. Thanks, bed-business. It was nice while it lasted.

* * *

This time I was no burden to my parents. I'd left friends and various interests in Cardiff, so why stay in London? The finger of fate would find me in the land of song just as easily.

I returned to Cardiff, and surprised my old friends by going back to work in the store where I'd previously been a visitor. It suited me. The work wasn't strenuous, and it was pleasant to be in familiar surroundings while I tried to sort myself out.

I had an enjoyable, if slightly dangerous, relationship with a couple of sisters from Treforest, both of whom worked in the store. It was one at a time, of course, and predictably non-carnal.

One day I discovered that there was a lady in Household Goods whose father was a writer and broadcaster. She suggested that I tried for an audition with the BBC. I wrote at once, not to the local studios, but to London, offering to take over from Frank Phillips or Alvar Liddell as soon as a vacancy arose. They wrote back very swiftly and explained that it wasn't enough simply to have a melodious voice, and that there were no vacancies for trainee announcers then or in the foreseeable future. They would, of course, make a note of my name. The speed of their rejection made me suspect that my name was forgotten even before they licked the stamp.

'No,' said my friend, 'I didn't mean London – try Cardiff, mun, the *Welsh* BBC just up the road in Park Place.' 'Who do I write to?' I asked. Well, she knew the First Lady of Welsh Drama. Her name was Rachel Howell Thomas. I decided to try the direct approach. I looked up the lady's address, and the next Sunday afternoon, I got on a bus and presented myself at her front door. Mr Howell Thomas answered, and although slightly wary of this brash youth (English, too) kindly invited me in. I was introduced to his wife, a gentle person with dark Celtic looks, her hair parted in the centre and drawn back into a bun. She looked every inch the classical actress. I described my hopes, and asked her what I should do. She listened sympathetically, and explained that although she couldn't personally arrange an audition with the BBC, she could certainly give me the name of the man to whom I should apply.

As I left she said, 'By the way, I think you have the right sort of voice. Good luck.'

Who could have asked for more? I wrote at once to the producer and quite soon received a reply, offering me a date to appear at the studios, complete with the material I intended to read for them. My ecstasy almost immediately gave way to fear. What material? I didn't know any plays, except *The Paragon*, and I'd sound like a lunatic just reading odd lines from that. I knew that my main asset was the ability to reproduce almost any accent, once heard (another link with Polly), so I scoured the local library for all works in dialect. It would, I suppose, have been enough to read random pieces in various accents, but I wanted it to be authentic.

On the fateful day, in the spring of 1954, I arrived at the BBC's headquarters in Park Place, laden with books. Pieces of paper protruded at the passages I had chosen to read. American, Italian, German – even Chinese characters were all ready to be brought to life.

The studio was fairly large, and empty except for a microphone which dangled from the ceiling and was surrounded by a series of sound-deadening screens. Between the studio and the control room was a glass panel, but a blind had been drawn down so that the listeners couldn't see the speaker, and vice versa. The reason for this was two-fold, I imagine; they would be able to concentrate on the voice, and the performer wouldn't be able to see them jeering or clapping their hands to their forehead.

'Would you like to begin, Mr – er – Aspel?' said a soft female voice. 'We'll give you a green light to start.'

There was a pause. A green light flashed. I opened my mouth. Silence. I swallowed, coughed, and started to introduce the first piece, explaining, in case of confusion, what the accent was going to be.

After six words the same voice said, 'Sorry, Mr – er – Aspel would you turn round a little?' Eager to please, I turned and started to read again, this time with a little more confidence. Ten seconds later, the door opened and a man came in and turned me round 135 degrees. I'd been speaking with my back to the microphone.

I read each piece, pausing only to apologize in advance. There was no reaction at all from behind the drawn blind. Eventually I said, 'That's all I've got,' and the voice said,

'Thank you, Mr – er – Aspel, that was very nice. We shall be in touch with you in due course.'

As I was leaving the building, there were hurried footsteps behind me, and someone called, 'Mr – er – Aspel! I wonder if you could do an Irish accent for us?' I'd omitted that one from my performance. Back I went and did a reasonable impersonation of someone who'd been born in Tralee and brought up in Worcester. It wouldn't have pleased any listeners from the Emerald Isle, but this was Cardiff. Again I was thanked and shown the door.

The days that followed were spent in an agony of anticipation. The atmosphere of the studios had excited me, and I made up my mind that that was to be the life for me. A broadcaster, a radio actor, working for the BBC!

My friends at the store were eager to know what had happened and how soon my photograph was going to be on the front of Radio Times. I was non-committal. It was safer that way.

Within a week, two marvellous things happened. I received a letter from the BBC, telling me that my audition had been successful, and that they would be offering me an engagement as soon as the opportunity arose. Sadly for me, I misunderstood the meaning of the phrase 'offering an engagement'. I thought they meant a permanent life at the microphone with breaks for meals and counting the money. In fact, it was to be very much on an *ad hoc* basis. I would be a casual labourer, getting work as the jobs came up.

But the first job followed on almost immediately after the letter. The same producer who had asked me to try an Irish accent, phoned to offer me a part in a 'Children's Hour' serial play, starting in only a week's time. Captain O'Hagarty was the character, and a right snarling black-hearted villain he was too. I was overwhelmed. Lorraine Davies, the producer, got a lot out of her performers. She bullied, cajoled and gently drew the best from them. She was plump, dark, attractive and a bit frightening. One episode of a later play ended with a woman character saying, 'I just saw somebody driving away in the doctor's car.' The actress wasn't putting enough drama into the line for Lorraine's liking. She rehearsed it again and again, her voice rising an octave at a time. In the end the rest of us were sent off to have our lunch. As we climbed the stairs we could hear the distant shriek, almost supersonic now: 'Somebody's driving off in the doctor's car! Somebody's driving off ...' Radio plays were live in those days, and it was difficult not to laugh when that line came up during the actual transmission. We weren't always able to stifle our giggles.

But back to 'Captain O'Hagarty'. I was booked for five episodes of the six-episode serial (in the penultimate episode, the evil Captain got his come-uppance). Like every other member of the cast, I also played several minor roles, so that it was possible at times, to have a conversation with oneself: Captain O'Hagarty (snarling): 'Pass me that belaying-pin, Dawkins!' Dawkins (falsetto): 'Aye, aye, Cap'n!' Not only did we disguise our voices, but we did a different accent for every character, so that a discussion between six people (ostensibly) would sound like a meeting of the United Nations at Battersea Dog's Home.

I soon learned the basic techniques of radio acting, such as pointing my mouth in the right direction, turning the pages quietly and helping with the sound-effects. They were fascinating. Apart from the hundreds of sounds available on records, there's a lot of equipment in the studio for 'live' use during a broadcast. Cups and saucers are rattled, doors are opened and slammed – there's even a box of gravel. There are few more amusing sights than a couple of men in shirtsleeves and old slacks, jumping up and down in a box of gravel and shouting, 'Hurry Sir Geoffrey! The Roundheads are coming!' Or a love scene, with the happy couple on either side of the microphone, breathing heavily and kissing the backs of their own hands. This is particularly effective when the lady is fat and middle aged but has a young girl's voice, as often happens.

The interesting thing is that you believe in it while you're doing it. You may be standing there in jeans with a tatty script in your hands, but you can *see* the car coming at you, or the trap-door that engulfs you – and that fat little old lady is, for the duration of the scene, the lovely Esmeralda.

During one violent scene in that first 'Children's Hour' serial, as Captain O'Hagarty and his band of rotters are struggling with the goodies, one actor, a burly ex-miner called Prysor Williams lashed out and sent the sound-effects man staggering across the studio. 'What the hell was that for, mun?' he asked when it was all over. His nose was bleeding slightly. 'Sorry, boyo,' said Prysor 'got carried away.'

My employers at the local emporium were reasonably co-operative in allowing me time off for my broadcasting debut, in the 'Captain O'Hagarty' series. Reasonable, but only up to a point. They allowed me Friday afternoons off for four episodes, but not for the fifth. 'You must choose,' said Mr Geoffrey (being a family concern, each director was known by his Christian name, with the respectful prefix). 'You must choose between this establishment and the BBC.' I tried to explain that I only had one more episode of the series left to go and that I didn't expect him to pay me in my absence, but he was adamant. Enough was enough. So, on the final Friday, I took the afternoon off, and Soft Furnishings had to manage without me. (I would be no great loss: my cutting of material invariably favoured the customer, and I'd once sold many yards of ex-pensive velvet for a fraction of its value. I'd misread the ticket, and mistaken the yardage for the price.)

'Captain O'Hagarty' rode again, and for the last time, that fateful Friday. 'Thank you, Michael. I'm sure we'll be using you again very soon,' said Lorraine Davies, and there were emo-tional farewells with the rest of the cast. Most of the emotion was on my part.

By this time I was totally committed to a broadcasting career. The others might be part-timers, doctors' wives, or ex-miners earning a few bob on the side, but I wanted to devote my life to it, to be a full-time BBC man.

On the following Monday afternoon I was called before Mr Geoffrey. He glowered at me from his desk. I smiled cheerfully back.

'Where were you last Friday afternoon, Aspel?' he asked, sounding like the prosecuting counsel in a court-room drama. I half expected him to rise from his seat and clutch his lapels. 'I was at the BBC,' I said calmly. He sighed, and put the tips of his fingers together. 'You'll remember,' he said, the veins in his neck swelling, 'that I told you that you would have to choose between your work here and the BBC.' 'Yes,' I said, 'and I've chosen the BBC. I'm handing in my notice.' The reaction was violent. 'I do not accept your resignation,' he barked, slamming his hand down on the desk. 'I am giving *you* notice!'

It must have been profoundly irritating for a man of his stature, a man accustomed to the respect and unquestioning subservience of each of his several hundred employees to be faced with this insolent young whippersnapper.

'OK,' I said. 'Does this mean you don't want me to go to the furniture department?' – a move that had been imminent B.O. – before O'Hagarty. It did. It meant that Mr Geoffrey and the old-established firm wished me to rush away at once. My co-workers had a whipround and gave me several pounds to see me through what were obviously going to be difficult days. Even Miss Bradshaw, tweed-suited, moustachioed and disdainful of 'pretty-boy' shop assistants, threw in the odd half-crown.

My career in the world of commerce had finally foundered, and I've never felt more relieved in my life.

The 'engagements' offered by the BBC were regular but infrequent, and even the most sympathetic of landladies has to make a living, so until a place became available in the BBC's Welsh Drama Repertory Company, which would mean a full-time job and a weekly wage, I would have to supplement my income.

My landlady's uncle was a landscape gardener. She managed to persuade him that he had need of a strong and healthy lad to help him scape the land. He took me on at two shillings and six-pence an hour. I earned the equivalent of twelve and a half new pence for every back-breaking sixty minutes, and he was a man who was very aware of the ratios involved in time, labour and rewards for same. If, at ten-thirty in the morning, he would discover me refuelling some piece of earth-moving machinery, he'd look at his watch and say, 'Ah – taking your lunch break early, are you?'

One of my workmates in this exercise was a marvellous man who had chosen the outdoor life because he suffered from epilepsy. He was a keenly intelligent and well-read person, a specialist in Victorian literature. He knew every volume of Dickens by heart, and the name of every character. Did you know that there was a Mr Sweedlepipes? I didn't and I still haven't traced him, but to my Dickensian workmate, he was a dear friend. He knew all there was to know about that prolific writer, and all his creations. I recall that he was a handsome rascal and well built, the only blemishes being the occasional scar or missing tooth – souvenirs of his impact with the pavement during his epileptic attacks, which, he told me, usually struck while he was waiting for a bus.

After my usefulness on that job had expired, I worked for several weeks on a building-site, helping to lay drainpipes. Months after the job was completed, I sauntered into a news-agents which had been built on the site; I wore my best (and only) suit, and after buying a quality paper and twenty Players, casually enquired how the drains were working.

'Why do you ask?' said the lady. 'Because I happened to lay them,' I said, expecting her to sway with disbelief. 'Fancy that,' she said, 'and what would you like, love?' to the next customer.

All this time I was gradually consolidating my position with the BBC, accepting everything they offered. More than once I rushed straight from the muddy trenches of the building-site to the studios, scraping my boots free of cement before entering. I once played the Duke of Buckingham in a historical drama with a group of actors from London, headed by one of my radio heroes James McKechnie. He was in fine voice, if a bit delicate physically. He explained that over the weekend he'd been to the Arms Park to watch Wales play England. Being a Scot he was quite impartial, and when the visitors scored a skilful try, he shouted, 'Well done, England!' at which point he was struck from behind by one of the Sospan Fach boys from Llanelly and missed the second half.

When I was laid off by the building trade, and the producers at Park Place could find nothing for me to do, I cast around for other ways of earning a crust. One was with the *Western Mail*, as an advertising representative, creeping around local garages, begging them to take space in the paper. Another was as a re-movals man. I humped many a wardrobe up many a staircase and accepted the occasional shilling tip with a 'God bless you, guv'nor'.

Gradually, I was offered more broadcasts, and the parts grew bigger. Sometimes there were more words to say than there were listeners to hear them. After one mammoth documentary programme on some obscure aspect of Welsh history, research revealed that less than half of one per cent of the potential audience had actually heard it – and that meant we'd been broadcasting to minus seven people. But it was all good experience, and the credits in *Radio Times* made me a valuable property in the eyes of the Little Theatre. On the strength of my performance as narrator in a ninety-minute account of the travels through Wales of an eighteenth-century botanist, the Little Theatre offered me the part of the twin brothers in their forthcoming production of Anouilh's *Ring Round the Moon*. I accepted at once, but explained that, due to my many broadcasting commitments, I might not be available for every performance. In fact, I had no professional work on the horizon – other than delivering a three-piece suite to an address in Splott but, by chance, I was offered a couple of dates by the BBC right in the middle of the run of *Ring Round the Moon*. 'Don't worry about that, boy,' said the Little Theatre producer, 'I'll understudy you for those nights, all right?'

Ring Round the Moon is a delightful play, full of clever language, delicate nuances, and with plenty of rich characters. It wasn't easy to play two parts, one a self-satisfied ass, the other self-deprecating (but equally twit-like). It meant going off one side of the stage as brother number one, and reappearing at the other side, a few seconds later, as brother number two, changing hairstyle, buttonhole and character on the way. However, nobody expected too much, and it was a successful production, mainly due to an experienced producer and some enthusiastic performances. On the two nights I was unable to take part because of the broadcasts, I crept into the theatre towards the end of the play. The producer, you'll remember, was playing my part, or parts, and with all his other responsibilities, he hadn't had time to become absolutely word-perfect. During one performance, brother number one, had to respond to another character's announcement of his financial ruin with a sparkling torrent of Anouilh's brittle irony. When the time came, he forgot his lines and said 'So what?'

The next night I crept in again in time to see him exit, stage left, wrapped in a blanket, as brother number one, who has just rescued a would-be suicide from a lake. As he reached the door he tripped over the corner of the blanket and crashed to the floor. His footsteps clearly thudded around the back of the set, and when he reappeared, ten seconds later, as the other brother, he was limping and rubbing his knee. That's when the audience had to indulge in what's known in the theatre as suspension of disbelief.

Stardom went to my head. I bought a Kangol cap. Success in those days – at least in the concentric circles I moved in – didn't mean dark glasses and beads. No – if you were the all-round sports-loving, sophisticated man about town, you wore a duffel coat, a Kangol cap, and you chewed on a pipe. One day I caught sight of myself in the window of the Fifty Shilling Tailors (you got a better view than in Marks and Spencers) and suddenly realized what I'd become. There I was – the perfect replica of thirty-five fellows I'd just passed, each of us purposefully striding along with our hands deep in our ex-naval pockets, the briar jutting from manly jaw.

I tore the Kangol from my Jack Hawkins coiffure, threw away the pipe (which had rarely tasted tobacco anyway) and adapted the duffel coat into a seat cover for my newly-acquired status symbol, Scumpy Foo. Scumpy Foo was my first motor car, a 1932 Morris Minor which I'd bought for twenty pounds from the bloke who'd played the butler in the Anouilh play. Spiders nested in the hood, it rarely started, and I loved it dearly. I was also a little afraid of it. It was a machine, and machines and I don't get on. But as it was mostly non-operable, I was able to overcome my awe. Once started, it would only stop when the handbrake was heaved upon, which meant abandoning the steering wheel. At speeds over twenty miles per hour, the hood flew up. This was before the days of the MOT test, of course, otherwise Scumpy would have been consigned to a life as a hen coop. But she was, bless her, a year older than I, and could be excused a few imperfections. Eventually every once-working part ground to a halt, and I sold her to an enthusiast for ten pounds.

I saw her again once after that. The enthusiast had done a magnificent job on her. Her face had been lifted, her insides over-hauled. People stopped and watched her go by. She's probably in a showroom window somewhere, admired but not for sale.

The broadcasts were becoming frequent enough for me to be able to replace the duffel coat and eat, although I still had to have a part-time job. Most of the programmes were fairly tedious documentaries, though I was given the occasional 'Morning Story' to read, and small parts in mid-week plays.

We sometimes broadcast from Swansea, which meant as many of us as possible squeezing into the largest car available. It's about a forty-mile trip, so we usually did the broadcast bent double. The worst part was the hanging about, waiting for your line to come up. The documentaries were long, with a cast of thousands – well, the entire Welsh Drama Repertory Company and as many part-timers as would make the effort for three guineas. Rehearsals went on for days.

One of the producers was a dark, intense man with black eyebrows and piercing eyes. He would stride about the studio, puffing menacingly on his pipe and destroying the actors' self-confidence with scathing comments. Once the broadcast was over, he became gentle and good humoured, so no-one minded what went before. He was a better actor than most of us. One day he was dissatisfied with the narrator of the epic we were yawning our way through. He strode among us, muttering, 'He's got to be changed, he's got to be changed.' We all stood demurely by, hoping – those of us who only had one line in the whole two hours – to be the new choice. The air filled with smoke, still he strode. Still we waited. Eventually I broke under the strain and clutched at the leather edges of his hacking-jacket. 'I'll do it, John. I'll do it,' I cried. He stopped and fixed me with that burning look. Seconds passed, the only sound the pop-popping of lips on pipe stem. Then he spoke. 'Piss off,' he said, and strode away.

One day it happened. The big part came my way. An actor, playwright and law student named John Darran wrote a six-part serial called 'Counterspy'. It was, as you might suppose, an espionage thriller, ostensibly for children, but to be broadcast on the national network every Friday. The two main characters were Lieutenant-Commander Gregory Vaughan, of Naval Intelligence and James ('Rocky' to you) Mountain of the FBI. John was to play Greg Vaughan, and I was offered the part of Rocky. It was an exciting series, well written, with real characters and a cliff-hanger at the end of each episode. John Darran had once auditioned for the part of Dick Barton, Special Agent, beloved radio hero of the late forties, and had very nearly got the part. He'd certainly got the taste for fast-moving action stories, and 'Counterspy' was a great success. John was also an immensely popular man, patient, helpful, sympathetic. He'd once studied for the Church, and although he'd eventually decided against the clerical life, he still had the sort of qualities that made people seek him out for advice or simply to bend his ear. He was also good for a laugh, and in my eyes could do no wrong. John got his law degree eventually, but is still a regular broadcaster from the Welsh studios.

'Rocky' was the fall guy, the one who needs to have the situation explained to him, the one who drinks the drugged coffee or falls down the lift-shaft. But he had guts and was a good man in a tight spot. Each week would end with Greg Vaughan shouting, 'Come on, Rocky – come on!!!' and the music would crash in – or I would say, 'This looks like the way out, Greg, through this – aaaaaargh!!!' and music, etc. The kids, plus a few million grown-ups, loved it.

One day the producer brought two small boys into the studio. It was my first taste of public reaction. 'These are "Counterspy" fans,' said Lorraine, 'and this is Rocky.' Their jaws fell to their knees. 'Oh,' they said, 'we thought you'd be ever such a big fellow.'

I drew myself up to my full 5 ft 9½ ins, tried to look rugged, but said nothing. If they'd discovered I wasn't a real American – or even Welsh – we'd have lost two listeners.

Another visitor was more impressed. 'Are you on the wireless?' he asked. I told him I was sometimes, and he said, 'I thought I'd heard someone who looks like you.'

Even as a leading player in the series, I still had to take other parts – the odd postman or lorry-driver. In one scene it was necessary to have a conversation in German going on in the background. 'Can any of you speak German?' asked the producer. 'Yes, I can, love,' said a voice. 'Right, then, on a green light, just say something in German, all right?' 'Righto, love.' 'Standby, then. Quiet in the studio, please.' The green light flashed, and the actor spoke: 'Up periscope, down periscope.' I think they used one of Hitler's old speeches in the end.

7
Head in the clouds

———◆———

Around this time, a little genuine drama entered my life. Now although I'd completed my two years full-time military service, I still had, like every other conscript, to be a member of the Territorial Army, which meant attending a certain number of evenings at the local drill hall, plus a fortnight's camp every year. When I moved to Cardiff, my commitment moved with me, so that I was transferred from my London infantry TA regiment to the nearest equivalent in Wales. As it happened, the nearest Territorial outfit was the Parachute Regiment. This presented me with a challenge. I had always been afraid of heights, and when more than thirty feet from the ground suffered from vertigo, and weakness of the bladder. Was this my chance to conquer that fear, or was the thought of jumping from an aeroplane just a masochistic dream? Eventually I decided to do it. There was no obligation to do so, but I made up my mind for three reasons; one, to try to beat that fear; two, because anyone who wore the red beret but didn't make the jumps was known as a penguin; and three, I needed the money. There were bounties to be earned if you got your wings. I saw that, literally, my reward could be in the heavens.

The parachute course lasted six weeks for regular soldiers, but they rushed us part-timers through in a fortnight. It was a fortnight to remember. There was a group photograph taken when we arrived, presumably so that they could point out the ones who didn't survive. Unfortunately, I've lost my copy, otherwise you might have had the fun of picking me out. I was the gaunt face with the frightened eyes, second from the right, back row.

Head in the clouds

There was a man called Hoskins on the course. Like the rest of us, he had never worn a parachute in his life. Like most of us, he had never flown before. But unlike most of us, he showed no fear; he appeared to relish the thought of whistling through the air. Naturally there were others who were not apprehensive. We were, after all, volunteers; but most of us had the grace, modesty, or forethought to pass only speculative comment about what the experience would be like. Not so Hoskins. To listen to him, you'd have thought he'd been with the airborne forces at Arnhem and did a high-wire act in his spare time. He used to lie on his bunk at night, singing all the old Red Devils' songs: 'Oh, they scraped him off the tarmac like a pound of strawberry jam . . .' (to the tune of 'John Brown's Body'). Then he'd sleep like a baby while the rest of us stared red-eyed at the ceiling.

We were taught how to get into the harness, how to use the supporting straps to steer us during the descent – pull down on the front left strap, and you'll move forward and left, and so on; how to land and roll to absorb the impact. It's the equivalent of jumping off a ten-foot wall, they told us, and if you just landed on your heels and tried to walk away, your head might fall off. The smaller and lighter the man, the easier his landing is likely to be. (I met a veteran paratrooper, a tiny man, who told me that he'd once jumped in the Middle East. The air was so warm that he'd float down two feet and then up three; it took a very long time, and in the end he was hovering above the sand, stretching his legs out and scrabbling for a touch-down.)

We were taught to adjust the cross-straps between the legs so that when the parachute opened, there was no chance of a dreadful accident. ('Don't want to damage the old crown jewels, do we, lads?')

The first descent was made indoors, in a hangar. We had to climb to a platform forty or so feet above the floor, wearing our harness which was attached by a line to a revolving drum, which would allow us to fall at the equivalent rate of an actual jump. We would hit the matting at the same speed as we could expect to hit the grass – wind and other circumstances allowing. Forty feet is a long way from the ground, especially indoors, and when I cast myself from the platform, I made a note to

go back for my stomach. But there was no parachute to mal-
function, and everyone had landed comfortably before me, so
I didn't hesitate. In fact it was the sort of experience that
people now pay ten pence to enjoy at Battersea funfair.

Came the day of the first real jump. We had to do eight
jumps altogether during the course – two from a balloon, six
from an aeroplane – to qualify. Conditions were perfect. The
sun shone, there was no more than a gentle breeze. The silver
barrage balloon hung in a blue sky a thousand feet above us.
A metal cage hung from the balloon, and as we watched, a
small black figure fell from the cage. A few seconds later, there
was a flapping snake of white material, which blossomed into
a round and beautiful silk canopy, beneath which the figure
dangled – now a clearly defined human shape, arms raised
to the webbing above, and legs bent in the correct position
for landing.

He was followed by another, and another, until half a dozen
parachutes were floating earthwards. It was a pretty sight –
particularly thrilling, I thought, for bloody Hoskins, who'd
gone through his mind-bending repertoire exceptionally
loudly the night before. Did he not know the meaning of the
word fear – had he no compassion for his weaker comrades?

The balloon descended, and it was our turn. We sauntered,
no, we trudged, legs forced slightly apart by the carefully-
arranged straps, towards the cage which had settled on the
grass in the shadow of the monstrous balloon. The parachutes
bounced gently on our backs.

'One despatcher, six men jumping!' called the RAF instructor who was to send us to our doom. I suppose he was checking
with the ground crew, who would then count the number
coming down. We clamped the end of our lines to the wire
running across the roof of the cage. When we jumped, this line
would wrench the cover from our parachutes, which would
then, in theory, open. This would occur a few seconds and
approximately one hundred and twenty feet after we had left.
If it didn't open, well, we'd have about six seconds to heave
a last sigh of regret.

'Righto, lads!' cried the RAF man, 'let's have a little song,
then, shall we? "They scraped him off the tarmac—"', and
seven voices bravely rang out, none louder than Hoskins's. Of

everyone on that course, he would have to be with me on *my* first jump.

At five hundred feet, the singing had lost a little of its spontaneous verve, and at one thousand feet, there was only one voice left – and that belonged, not to Hoskins, but to the despatcher.

The cage stopped rising. It swayed gently, and at a slight angle, sloping towards the exit. The despatcher looked around. 'All right, boys?' he said. 'There's nothing to worry about.' Then he did something which made my heart and tonsils change places. He unhooked my line and put the end between his teeth. 'Ready, Aspel?' he chortled. No matter how old I am when I die, I shall blame him for making it several years too soon. I managed a green smile. Then it was down to business – and who should be the first man to go but our dear old friend, Hoskins. But something seemed to be happening to him. He'd become immobile, frozen to the spot, carved in stone. The unbelievable had happened. His poison had finally worked on himself. The rest of us had screwed ourselves up to the task ahead, and had lived in fear long enough for the actuality to be an anticlimax. Poor old Hoskins had saved all his terror for this moment.

The RAF man gently took his hands and placed them in the exit position. Left hand at the side of the door, right hand to grip the trouser leg (left hand to grip right wrist during the initial fall). Then he pushed him out. 'Aieeeeee,' said Hoskins as he left. The RAF man looked out of the exit. 'He's all right,' he said. 'Next.' That was me.

Hoskins had done the rest of us the world of good. His show of fear made us all determined to hide ours. I took up my position, boots slipping on the metal floor. Sounds floated up from the ground. Vehicles, voices. 'Go!' shouted the despatcher, and slapped my shoulder. I went.

I dropped through the air, feeling virtually no sensation. Then I saw my legs moving upwards, and as my boots drew level with my face I was seized as if by a giant pair of braces – a tugging, elastic sort of sensation. I looked up, and saw a tangle of webbing and silk resolve itself into a vast umbrella. The size of it frightened me, and I looked down. The ground didn't seem so far away, and its distance was less awe-inspiring than the floor of the hangar had been from forty feet. I had a fine vista of the surrounding countryside. A shout from below reminded me that I wasn't there to enjoy the bloody view. I hastily judged the speed and direction I was moving in, and pulled gently on the front right support. The ground approached rapidly. I twisted my legs to the left, knees bent, feet together, and – thump, I was down. A gentle roll from knee to shoulder, and I lay still. The grass smelled very sweet. I was overwhelmed with a euphoric glow. The world was really a very fine place. I stood up, slapped at the harness lock, and struggled free.

I rolled up the chute, giving it a silent vote of thanks, and wondered how the hell the packers could possibly get all that material into such a comparatively small package. I gave them a vote of thanks, too.

Back at the control point we returned our parachutes and compared notes. 'There's nothing to it, boys, nothing to it.' It was Hoskins, exultant with relief and happiness.

I heard an instructor remonstrating gently with a young lieutenant who'd just come in but not brought his parachute back. 'You had one on the way down, sir, I saw you.'

One down, seven to go. The next balloon jump was straightforward, in a vertical sense, and then came the time to jump from an aeroplane. This would be different. There would be a slip-stream to contend with, and we'd be moving sideways as well as downwards for part of the drop.

Paratroopers, for the purpose of organizing the order of exit from the aeroplane, are arranged into 'sticks'. There's a starboard 'stick' and a port 'stick', depending on which side you leave from. I was on the starboard stick for the first aeroplane drop, which, as I discovered, suited me very well. I found I could get more purchase from the doorway.

The two rows of men faced each other and tried to look nonchalant. Once again there was a winking and a thumbs-up routine from the RAF men. They meant well, but it was difficult for them to hit the right attitude. A priest has the same problem. Does he play it straight or pretend to be one of the lads? The message is: 'I'm here to help and reassure, and I'd like you to believe me.' Not easy.

The red light went on and we struggled to our feet and faced the rear of the aircraft. Each man checked that the line of the man in front of him was securely fastened to the wire running along the plane. Then some twit with two pips on his shoulder yelled 'Don't forget – a refusal to jump means five years detention.' That was definitely the wrong psychology. It was also the wrong information. A regular soldier who has qualified as a parachutist may not, under threat of court-martial and imprisonment, refuse to jump, but that wasn't our situation.

'Stupid bastard,' snorted the man behind me. 'We're only here for a bloody fortnight.'

The pilot throttled back, the green light flashed. Before the main body of men started jumping, an experienced Red Devil went out as a sort of guinea-pig to check that conditions were right. Men with something like five hundred descents behind them don't bother to do things the official way. This man retreated to the far side of the plane, then projected himself like a charging bull towards the exit. There was a flash of limbs, and with a shout of 'Geronimo!' he disappeared through the door. I swear he went upwards. Apparently all was well, and we began to take our leave, one at a time, from each side of the plane. 'Go! Go! Go!' shouted the despatchers. Suddenly I was in the doorway. 'Go!' roared a voice, a hand slapped my shoulder, and I pushed myself out of the aeroplane.

The slip-stream snatched me immediately, and I was swept away, sideways and downwards. Once again I saw the tangle of lines, only much sooner this time. There was no sedate lying back in the air and studying one's boots. One moment I'd been standing upright, the next I was dangling in space. The most extraordinary thing was the silence. The aeroplane and its din, had vanished. The sky was full of canopies and suspended figures, drifting silently towards the ground.

Nowadays parachuting is a popular sport with both sexes. They dance and swim through the air, performing graceful and colourful ballets as the orange and blue smoke pours from the flares on their heels. They have time to enjoy the air, to use it. They also carry a secondary parachute, which is something we military skymen had to do without in those days.

When the fortnight was over, and I had completed the course with not so much as a sprained ankle, I returned to Cardiff. On the Saturday night I went, as usual, to the City

Hall for the weekly hop. I remember that evening for two reasons, both embarrassing. After a strenuous Valeta, I sat nonchalantly sipping a ginger beer shandy (shaken, not stirred) when my partner said, 'What's that white stuff all over your knee, love?' I looked down. My trousers appeared to be dusted with powder. My first reaction was that someone had been careless with her compact; either that or I was suffering from dandruff of the upper thigh. Then the truth dawned on me. My trousers were threadbare. The white powder was my skin. I did no more fish-tails or romantic swoops on the dance floor that night.

The second mortifying experience was when I was leaning against the wall close by the entrance to the ladies' room, watching for any emerging talent. A familiar voice said, 'Hello, Mike, where've you been the last few weeks?' It was one of the regular Saturday nighters, a fair, pretty girl with whom I'd done many a Dashing White Sergeant, and I was delighted to see her. 'Where have I been?' I said, lips twitching roguishly. 'I've been down to Abingdon, that's where I've been.' 'What for?' I told her of my daring exploits, and watched her face for signs of awe, amazement, admiration. It remained a pretty blank. 'Were you frightened?' she asked in an uninterested way. I thought a touch of humility might do the trick. 'Yes,' I said. 'You coward,' she said, and danced away. So much for impressing the women.

The most annoying thing about going on that course was that it did nothing at all to conquer my fear of heights.

My head still swam – on the upper decks of buses. When, much later, I made my first flight as an airline passenger, I was very nervous. (I'd taken off half a dozen times before, but never landed in a plane, if you see what I mean.) When people left their seats I'd will them to sit down again, in case they put their feet through the plane; and when another passenger leaned to look out of a window, I'd lean the other way to restore the balance. Even today, many thousands of air miles later, the same irrational fear occasionally returns.

My palms grow damp and on these occasions I drink a lot of whisky. Not being technically minded, it makes no sense to me that all that metal can leave the ground. It's reassuring to be invited to join the crew for a look around the flight deck and to see them so calm and able. At least from the sharp end you have a forward view and you're able to see where you're going. To sit in the body of the craft with no sensation of movement, and to look out of one window and see the sky and to see the ground out of the opposite window makes me wonder quite seriously why the bloody thing doesn't fall down. But so very few of them do – hijackers and saboteurs allowing. A few hours at London airport, watching them land and take off, land and take off all the time does wonders for a nervous traveller. So do several pills and a large helping of amber fluid.

8

Commitments

Cardiff Corporation buses were my daily form of transport in those post-Abingdon days. I moved steadily from job to job, longing for the letter that would tell me that the BBC had room for me as a full-time, glued-to-the-mike radio actor. I knew that one member of the BBC Welsh Drama Repertory Company, Arthur Williams, had dreams of grandeur and wanted to move on to production. I harassed Arthur daily with enquiries about his future. 'Any news, Arthur?' I would say, 'have you heard anything yet?' Eventually he'd snarl as soon as he saw me – and before I'd have a chance to get my mouth open – 'The answer is no! I'll tell you as soon as I know for God's sake!' I would contrive to stand Arthur in draughts and considered lacing his coffee, so keen was I to get his job and give up my itinerant life.

Although I still made only occasional broadcasts, I felt myself to be a BBC man who took other part-time work.

Then, while I was working a five-day, forty-hour week spare-time job as an advertising representative for the local newspaper between my bi-monthly broadcasts, it happened. Arthur got his job in production, and I was offered a place in the radio repertory company. It was 1955, my salary was ten pounds a week, and I knew I would want no more from life.

At the end of every week we would receive an envelope containing a list of programmes we'd have to do in the next seven days. I was desperate to get into the studio and hoped for a juicy narration or character part in almost every production. I was bitterly disappointed. Week after week my sheet would contain one phrase: 'No commitments.' I made hardly any more broadcasts than I had done as an outsider. Admittedly,

I was paid every week, but that didn't fully compensate for the frustration.

Still, there I was, a professional broadcaster, twenty-two years old, with a second-hand motor bike – lacking the personality of Scumpy Foo, but cheaper to run – and the world at my feet. Not only that, but I had at last fulfilled that other basic desire, the one that had eluded me, and that I had pursued into early manhood. It all happened through the Little Theatre, and the way it happened was certainly an amateur drama. There were no wild theatrical parties, or pioneer gang bangs. One young lady simply said yes. My joy was so unconfined that it was all over so far as I was concerned long before the act was consummated. But she was patient, kind, and extremely lustful, and guided me cheerfully into the way of all flesh. Which is not to say that she'd given herself to all comers. She was as new to the game as I was, but instinctively a champion, and I shall always be grateful for the way she played.

My newly-acquired status enabled me to open a bank account. Now this is a story I've told many times, at fêtes and WI meetings and dinner parties and even on the air – so many times, in fact, that a lady who kindly signed herself 'No. 1 Fan' wrote to me not long ago to say that fond though she was of me, she'd go right off the whole idea if I mentioned my bank story again. The last time I told it was when a TV awards show I was compering under-ran severely because no acceptance speech lasted more than eight seconds ('I don't deserve this – but thanks very much'). So I worked my way through the forty-seven pages of ad lib remarks I'd brought with me, and eventually had to turn to old favourites. Hence the re-telling of my Bank Story, and the protest from No. 1 Fan.

After all that, if you *haven't* heard the story, it's going to be a hell of an anti-climax. The fact of the matter is that when I opened my bank account in Cardiff, the manager said to me, 'Well, Mr Aspinwall – and what do you do for a living?' 'I am a radio actor,' I said proudly. 'Oh,' he said, 'you work at Harwell, do you?'

That's all. It may not be funny, but it's certainly true.

My parents were delighted at my new job. 'Just what you've always wanted, dear,' said my mother, although it had never been really clear what my ambitions were. Dad was very tolerant in the circumstances. I suppose he imagined that the acting lark was a phase that would pass, and then I would find my true place with HM Customs and Excise.

In fact, his conviction that I had some rapport with the customs game has proved to have some basis in truth. I seldom pass through an airport without a cheery invitation from the men in uniform to join them for a chat about the contraband I'm carrying. I suppose it's because I usually wear dark glasses and carry a briefcase. The dark glasses are worn for two reasons – neither of them to do with a wish to disguise myself. I don't mind how many people want to know what the Miss World contestants are really like, or how many want to shake my hand because I have touched an Osmond. The shades are worn because I'm usually very tired and they serve to keep my eyeballs in, and because I find light generally rather troublesome – particularly of the supermarket and airport variety. But I look so obviously an international criminal that the customs and excise boys rarely fail to stop me. The encounter usually ends with them doing one of four things: they ask me what the Osmonds were like, they enquire if I have any spare 'Crackerjack' pencils, or they want to shake my hand because I've touched the Miss World contestants. Or they ask me to open my suitcase. Meanwhile, the little old lady with her handbag full of diamonds slips by.

I know, I know. They have a job to do. But there is sometimes a quality about people in uniform that I do not admire. I often think that BBC commissionaires are sent on a special course, where they are shown photographs of everyone who appears regularly on television. Then they are brainwashed so that all those faces are obliterated from their memory. Most of them fail the course, and in spite of their training greet familiar faces with warmth and courtesy. But there remains a hard core of shaven-headed Pavlovian graduates who not only don't recognize anybody, but are pleased about it.

It would be pompous and arrogant to expect a great clicking of heels and saluting, but it is a bit disheartening when you've just come from addressing a luncheon party about the joys of working on TV, you've signed a couple of dozen autographs, acknowledged the ribald shouts of passing taxi drivers, promised tickets for shows to the groups of young people hanging around the studio gates, and then have to explain who you are to the commissionaire so that you can get into the place where you've been working for seventeen years. And it happens all the time – usually when you have visitors with you so that the embarrassment is at its most extreme. Even Morecambe and Wise have had to get somebody to identify them. It's like being rejected by your own family. Many of my colleagues will know well the phrases: 'Can't come in here – this is only for people who work for the BBC.' 'The name means nothing to me, mate.' Or even (after a miraculous recognition), 'Good morning, Mr Aspel. You're looking well. Can I see your pass, please?'

But, as I admit with a sigh, orders is orders; and I know that most of the gentlemen who guard Auntie's various portals will realize that I'm not talking about *them*.

Back in those radio days in Cardiff there was no one, in or out of uniform, who cared to give my features a second glance, except to say, 'Good God, boyo, why don't you get some sleep? Your eyes look like pee-holes in the snow.' And I, anticipating Lee Marvin's lines in *Cat Ballou* would groan, 'You should see them from this side.'

The trouble was that I couldn't, and still can't sleep well. I usually sleep lightly, and in short, dream-filled bursts. Strangely enough, I feel better after a restless night than one spent in deep slumber. I have slightly wonky kidneys, and without a good deal of nocturnal movement the sludge collects and I wake with an ache in the abdominal cavities and the familiar depraved look.

The months passed pleasantly, if unspectacularly, with the occasional meaty part to play. I gradually learned my trade. Occasionally a cast of distinguished voices would come down from London for a major production. On one of these visits I was told that my voice was very similar to that of a London actor called Manning Wilson. I heard Manning Wilson in a 'Saturday Night Theatre' play a little later, and had to agree that we did sound a bit alike.

On a trip home I went up to the Old School to watch Jim Healy play cricket. The assistant headmaster, the unchanged

'Pump' Hipkins, said to me, 'And what are you doing for a living now, Aspel?' 'I'm a radio actor,' I said, bracing myself for the Harwell crack. 'Really?' drawled 'Pump'. 'Another Old Boy does that – his name is Manning Wilson.' It must be something to do with the air on Wandsworth Common.

It has been marvellous to meet my broadcasting heroes and to hear their voices in conversation instead of in declamatory tones. One of my greatest thrills was when I found myself in the bar of the BBC Club, having a drink with the Mayor of Toytown, Felix Felton. I felt six years old again, but didn't say so for fear of depressing him. I never met Uncle Mac or Stuart Hibberd, but I have stood ear to larynx with the voices of Norman Shelley (Winnie the Pooh), Duncan MacIntyre, Howard Marion Crawford, Grizelda Hervey, Alvar Liddell, Frank Phillips, John Snagge, and many other broadcasters whose names are as familiar as their own to millions of people.

Away from the studios, life was full and happy and without any of the responsibilities which now come crowding in from all directions. I had an ignominious season with the humblest of the many teams fielded by the Glamorgan Wanderers' Rugby Football Club, and I joined Llandaff Rowing Club. Unfortunately, there's not much rowing to be had in Wales – apart from on Bala Lake in Merioneth, and that was too far away to pop off to on a fine summer evening. A few of us used to paddle up and down the few hundred yards of the Taff that were clear and smooth enough, but it was a bit desultory. I decided to join a tennis club. My girlfriend was good at games – in fact, most of the ladies I've known have been. I've been trounced by delicate creatures at most sports known to man – from tennis, to snooker, scrabble, horse-riding and swimming. And I do try to win. My athletic partner got me into the tennis club, and I started to learn. I noticed that a lot of the most hairy, bronzed and muscular players served the ball with a gentle forward stroke – and the men weren't much better either; so I determined to develop the killer instinct and do things the Lew Hoad way. I'd toss the ball up, pivot on my toes, bring the racket flashing over my head and send over an unbeatable ace. That was the intention, and indeed after several months of concentrated effort, I was able to perform a weak facsimile of what I've just described. Unfortunately, if the other player returned the ball, I lost the point. In fact I never won a game, let alone a set, and I believe my name is enshrined there in legend and song for that reason alone.

I knew the frustration Hoad must have felt when I watched him do his second double fault at a crucial point in a Wimbledon final. The camera zoomed into a close-up of his face as he paced the base line. Being an Australian, he was used to expressing himself colourfully, and you could see his teeth making regular contact with his lower lip.

The commentator noticed it too, and said excitedly, 'He's not happy! He's saying to himself "My word, that was an unfortunate thing to have done." '

Those summers in the early fifties were golden, idyllic times. We all used to go to a beach called Monk Nash, which was long and wide and backed by a platform of smooth rock. We used to watch the porpoises frolic and we stayed there until it was dusk and the pubs were open.

On Saturday afternoons I would go to the Arms Park and watch beautiful, open rugby. On Saturday nights we'd play Sinatra and Ella Fitzgerald records, plus a touch of the Modern Jazz Quartet, Jo Stafford, Paul Anka and Harry Belafonte. I don't know how to describe the dancing we did. It was a sort of late jive and gave no hint of rock'n'roll, twist or funky chicken.

The girls wore angular little blouses, long, flared skirts and ballerina shoes.

The boys' trousers looked like ski pants, fairly snug around the ankle, and hairstyles involved a large amount of hair cream and quiffs. One day on an impulse I had a crew-cut. As I stepped from the barbers' shop I felt distinctly chilly around the ears. Later I put my comb to my forehead and gave the customary heave at what had been a thick mop. The comb skidded across my scalp at such speed that it almost left a blister. In a moment of panic I feared my hair wouldn't grow again, or would grow in all directions – perhaps inwards. Half-way through the renewal process, I looked as if I were wearing a forage cap, with a tuft fore and aft. I suppose I should have used that period to experiment with beards and moustaches. It seems to me that every man should let his beard grow at some time, just to see what he's scraping away at every

Polly wants a zebra

day of his life. You can get away with that sort of thing on radio, but the in-between process is a little difficult if you have regular television commitments. A few weeks' holiday is the time to break in a moustache, I've found.

Whiskers weren't so fashionable in those days, unlike now when so many men are distinguishable only by the colour of the hair or by their fingerprints. I remained clean shaven – in fact, altogether I looked a clean, nice, wholesome little smoothie. But the restlessness that has always dogged me was at work. I moved from digs to digs, found new friends, and felt chrysalis-like, as if there were new scenes waiting to burst open.

One day in 1956 I received a telegram.

'Ring D. J. Thomas, TV Producer, at once,' it commanded. My reactions were several – amazement, delight and at the same time respect for the perception of the BBC in realizing that the time was ripe for me to take over from Richard Dimbleby. In fact the TV show in question was called 'Songs for the Asking' and my role was a brief one. I had to stroll down the aisle through the audience, wearing a paperboy's bag and shouting 'Songs for the Asking!' At least I didn't have to rehearse much – my shoulder still bore the mark of the bag from my newsround days in Chard. I wrote home at once, advising my parents that a star was born. I warned them that it would be a short but powerful performance. They tuned in at the right time, on the right channel, but missed me. At the crucial moment my mother turned to my father and said, 'Put some more coal on, Ted,' and when they looked back I had gone.

Still, it obviously made an impact with the TV chiefs in London, because in the spring of 1957 I was invited to go to London to audition as a guest TV announcer. What in fact happened was that Hywel Davies, husband of Lorraine and Welsh programme chief, had recommended me. It was obvious that my future in Cardiff was limited. I spoke no Welsh (although I had taken part in a Welsh language programme by reading the phonetic spelling of the words in my parrot fashion) and you don't get far in that part of the world if you're not a genuine Taffy. It's an extraordinary language, very old and fascinating, and when something new comes on

100

the scene, they have to invent a word or use the English phrase. I'd sit dumbfounded in the BBC canteen and listen to a stream of incomprehensible sounds with words like 'ashtray' popping up in the middle.

I made the journey to London wearing my natty sports coat and flannels and reported to the presentation editor, at the hallowed Lime Grove Studios in Shepherds Bush.

The BBC is divided, as you can imagine, into many different departments, most of them fiercely independent of the others. Presentation department ran, and still does, the 'front' of BBC TV – the announcements and trailers and general continuity. Producers who want their programmes to over-run by a few minutes will have to talk about it to the control room, part of the Presentation Empire.

The editor at the time of my audition, Clive Rawes, ran this empire from the fourth floor at Lime Grove. About fifteen years ago the whole outfit moved up the road to the then brand-new fourteen-million-pound Television Centre, a circular building where it's difficult to get lost but easy to go insane.

In 1957 the TV announcers were 'in vision', which is to say that the viewers actually saw them. Nowadays ITV employ visible announcers, but the Old Firm relies on voices only. Don't get confused between an announcer and a newsreader. In TV terms they're quite different animals, although many viewers refer to anybody who opens his mouth on the screen as 'The Announcer'.

Newsreaders (or -casters) do just that – they read or cast the news before the viewer, and don't venture into the announcer's world. He's the man who welcomes the audience, plugs all the forthcoming programmes, apologizes for delays and breakdowns, and reminds you to switch off at the end of the evening. He's not a reporter, commentator, interviewer, compere, correspondent, pundit or weatherman. He is the announcer, the one little Betty Bouncer fell in love with in Flotsam and Jetsam's song – except that that song was written many years ago when there were no TV announcers. Then, very sober gentlemen sat in dinner-suits at Broadcasting House and read the announcements in mellifluous and lofty tones.

So – I was shown into the presentation studio at Lime Grove, sat in a chair and pointed at the camera. Clive Rawes' voice came through from the control room, cheerful and re-assuring. Were the lights unbearable, would I move a bit to my left, would I let them know when I was ready to read the test script, and had I heard about the announcer who intro-duced the famous piece by Rimsky-Korsakov as the Bum of the Flightlebee? I was too nervous to laugh.

After reading the standard announcements I was asked to give an ad lib talk for a minute or two. Luckily I'd just had a fairly lengthy part in a radio play, so I gave them a quick précis of the plot and the character I'd played. It was fairly light stuff and seemed to go down reasonably well. In fact, Clive Rawes seemed quite pleased and hinted that I might be hearing something to my advantage fairly soon. I left the studios in a state of glee.

Some days later, back in Cardiff, I received a letter offering me a fortnight's stint in London as a guest announcer. If my excitement seems exaggerated, you must remember that there was no commercial TV in those days. The BBC announcers were the dinner-jacketed hosts to millions of cheerful slaves – and they were national figures. About that dinner-jacket. It was a communal garment shared by McDonald Hobley and Alex Macintosh and all us occasional visitors. Beneath it we wore grey flannel bags (our own, not shared) and in my case I wore a large clothes peg in the small of the back to gather in some of the spare material of the jacket. Otherwise I would have appeared to be wearing a dressing-gown. There were women announcers too, of course, although their time was about to pass. Sylvia Peters and Mary Malcolm were just bow-ing gracefully out from the TV scene, although they both continued to pop up in various programmes from time to time.

Friends and relatives gathered to wish me luck. Even the press showed an interest. 'The man from Nowhere Lands Plum TV job,' cried the *Daily Sketch*. Two weeks of saying 'Good Evening', 'Normal service will be resumed as soon as possible' and 'Good night' would hardly seem these days to be a job worth leaving the Labour Exchange for, especially for twenty-five pounds a week, but that's the way it was.

During most of my adult life I've been prey to various irrita-ting nervous afflictions, some of them, I'm sure, psychosomatic. On important occasions a cluster of herpes will break out on my upper lip, I will get severe backache before a particularly complicated assignment, or an attack of migraine will send flashes of light zig-zagging across my vision a few minutes before I'm due to make a recording. The neurotic side of my nature manifested itself three days before I was due to appear before the nation. A boil sprang up right on the tip of my nose. It swelled and throbbed and glowed. I looked more like W. C. Fields than a clean-limbed lad of twenty-four. I fled to the doctor who lanced the thing prematurely, with the result that it bubbled and rumbled and simmered and occasionally erupted for months to come.

At least it gave my features the character they'd been sadly lacking. Not long after my first appearance on television, that summer of 1957, a viewer wrote to ask why the BBC didn't get some people with faces. I wasn't offended. I wouldn't have employed me either. Fellows like Donald Gray (whose life was once threatened by a jealous husband whose wife used to kiss the screen when Donald was on) and McDonald Hobley looked as if they'd been around for a bit and knew a thing or two. I looked seventeen and about as interesting as a bunch of edelweiss. Someone suggested my name when a producer was looking for a compere for 'Come Dancing'. 'I don't think his mother would let him stay out so late,' was the reply.

Nevertheless, I did my fortnight and was offered another, and so began my life of commuting between Cardiff and London. My years in Wales had given me the vaguest hint of a Welsh accent on occasional vowels and I was known as the Welsh lad in London – a belief that was strengthened by my ability to get my tongue around any Welsh place-name that might pop up in the roadworks report. (Broadcasters make brave tries at Russian and Arabic titles, but give a laugh and a shrug at simple names like Ynysybwl or Pwllheli.)

I still continued as a member of the Radio Repertory Company, but became more and more aware that that side of my career – if that's not too grand a word – was moving to a close. In the autumn of 1957, regional TV news was introduced. This meant that Welsh viewers would have their own service. It would be in English, and someone would have to read it. I was given the job. One evening, in a converted chapel off the Newport Road the cameras switched on, the green light flashed, and, 'With a few nervous glances to left and right' (in the words of the *South Wales Echo*), I launched myself into the first edition of the news from Wales.

It wasn't easy. We had no telecine facilities, which meant that we weren't able to show any newsfilm from our studios. Our footage had to be rushed over to Bristol, and no-one was ever sure that it would arrive in time.

Our bulletin also interrupted the first fifteen minutes of Cliff Michelmore's 'Tonight' programme, so that at the end of the broadcast I would have to hand the viewers in Wales back to London. Now we were never sure exactly what item would be going out at that precise moment. Instead of simply handing over to the programme, our editors insisted that I explain in detail what was happening. It never worked. Night after night I would say, 'That's the news from Wales. Now we join viewers of "Tonight", who are watching a film about London's traffic problem' – and up would come a picture of a fellow in the middle of a field. Viewers probably took bets on which night I would get it right.

That first stint of television work was stimulating, nerve-racking and brought me a lot of satisfaction. It also brought me the first of many wonderful and extraordinary letters from viewers. The very first I received was from a lady who ran a pub in Glamorgan. 'Dear Michael,' she wrote, 'I think you are quite nice looking and well dressed, but what amuses me is that when you speak, your tie waggles up and down with your Adam's Apple. Come on, love – buy a tie-pin.' There's a useful bit of constructive criticism.

Another of the early bits of correspondence, unsigned, wondered what size nylons I took, and what shade lipstick I wore, and was I often chased by boys? It came on an open postcard. If everyone who worked in the public eye were to take seriously all the unpleasant things that were written, the courtyard at Television Centre would be piled high with people who'd cast themselves from the ventilator shaft. But I was young, inexperienced, and more sensitive than I cared to admit. I smiled bravely and tore up the card with trembling hands.

Another part of my life was about to take a dramatic turn. During the glorious hedonistic days of that summer of 1957, while I was earnestly catching up on all those deprived years, I met a lovely exotic-looking girl named Dian. She was a domestic science student in Cardiff, and we were introduced in the flickering gloom of a Saturday night party, where the only light came from cigarette ends and the control panel of the radiogram. We danced (a euphemism for a formless, stumbling embrace) to a new record by Paul Anka called 'Diana' which seemed to give our meeting a special significance.

The next day a group of us went down to the docks for tea on board a boat owned by a visiting Latvian family who'd been at the party. Dian came too, and looked even prettier in daylight than in the romantic gloom of the night before. She was quite small and slim with fair hair, enormous eyes and a voluptuous mouth. 'Like diving into a mound of tissue paper,' was the verdict of a friend after being greeted warmly by Dian. I found it a lot more stimulating.

We all squeezed ourselves into the boat's tiny living quarters. As we sat around the table and tucked into tea and Latvian rissoles, I felt Dian's leg resting against mine. I responded with gentle twitches of the sinews, coupled with the occasional meaningful look. She gave no acknowledgement of all the emotion that was being expressed underneath the table. 'Cool,' I thought. 'Cool – I like that in a woman.' Then, when she got up and left her leg behind, I realized that I'd been caressing part of the woodwork. It was only a small setback, and our relationship raced ahead. I took her to London to meet my parents, and four months later we were married at Brecon Cathedral. It was a quiet affair – just Dian's family and mine, most of the population of her home town, and press and television cameras. With their very own embryonic TV Personality, the local media had been quick to seize on the story, particularly, with such a pretty bride. 'The Night Mr Aspel Popped The Question' was the heading to a three-quarter-page article in the *South Wales Echo*, and my colleagues at the news studio made sure that the event was covered. At the reception, there were the usual excruciating speeches, and then Dian and I were pushed out by the guests who wanted to get on with the serious boozing. We went to Paris. It was November, and dull and cold, but we did the full tourist thing, including the Folies Bergere and the Bateaux Mouche. The Parisians, in their gay and endearing way, took all our money as quickly as they could, and after four days we came back. I'd been extremely lucky in renting the visitors' wing of a rambling sixteenth-century farmhouse just outside Cardiff which I'd often walked past and admired. It was furnished and comfortable and a marvellous place for entertaining. Although I'd cut off Dian's student days in their prime, she'd learned enough to be able to produce tasty and inventive meals. One way and another, life was good and full of promise.

I continued to commute back and forth between Cardiff and London, gradually developing confidence – in fact so much so that I even started to introduce the occasional facetious remark into my announcements – not when reading the news, of course: that was sacrosanct. I remember sitting in the tiny presentation studio one day introducing something like 'Watch With Mother' or 'This is Your Life' (Mark 1) when I became aware of a crackling, creaking sound. It grew louder and more menacing; I spoke faster so that I'd be able to make a swifter escape if the place was in fact collapsing.

I finished the announcement, the camera light went off, and a huge piece of wallpaper fell from the 'flat' behind me and wrapped itself around me. The sounds I'd heard were the paste drying in the heat of the lights, and the paper slowly detaching itself. The audience missed the spectacle – unfortunately. I've come to believe that there's nothing that delights the average viewer more than seeing someone make a fool of himself – and if that person is me, then I don't mind at all. I have a highly developed sense of the ridiculous (as my list of programmes shows) and, as a viewer, certainly would have loved every moment if the wallpaper had attacked Gilbert Harding or Peter West.

A few months later the BBC in London offered me a three-month contract as an acknowledgement of almost a year's disaster-free appearances. Most of the announcing by this time was being done by Alex MacIntosh and myself, with other guest announcers sharing the rest of the duties. Alex was, and had been from the start, a good friend, helpful and encouraging. And why shouldn't he have been? you may ask – We were all in it together. But you must remember that from being famous celebrities, TV 'hosts' were now assuming their correct importance in the scheme of things, and as a species were in danger of extinction. So, in such an insecure situation, it would hardly have been surprising if the established man regarded the new boy as something of a threat. However one thing Alex never lacked was confidence and when the empire eventually crumbled, Alex took his sharp fair good looks off to Scotland and worked on television there. He was originally a professional photographer, so had something to fall back on. His only drawback as a friend was that if you showed him family snapshots, instead of saying, 'What a lovely child,' he'd tut and sigh and say, 'You should have tried F8 at 100th of a second.' That and his judo. I once mistimed a visit to Alex's house just as he was limbering up for his black-belt exercises. 'Just the lad I want,' cried Alex as I hove into view. 'Just lie down there, will you?' and he pointed to the carpet. 'Er – how's your wife, Alex?' I asked, wondering if I'd been wrong about him all the time. But all he wanted to do was a few harmless strangleholds. 'Tap my arm if things start going black,' he said cheerfully. 'But I . . .' Too late. He was at my throat, and I was only saved by the arrival of our wives. I forgave him. After all, what's a charge of manslaughter to a man who's earned his black belt?

I suppose he's subjecting his neighbours to a spot of Kung-Fu these days.

Martin Muncaster, owner of one of the richest dark-brown voices in broadcasting, became a guest announcer at about the time I was given my three-month contract. He was working on the old two-weeks-at-a-time routine, and we discovered that I was earning about two pounds a week less than he was. Naturally I made enquiries about this anomaly and was told by the salaries department, 'It's quite fair. You have the added security of a long-term [contract.' Imagine. I could really plan for the future with that three-month agreement.

9
Over to the newsroom

This new job, although temporary, meant leaving Cardiff, so Dian and I bade farewell to friends and farmhouse, put our belongings in a red-spotted handkerchief in the boot of our new Ford Anglia, and drove to London. An era had ended, and as always at such times, the regrets almost equalled the anticipations. Almost.

The Anglia I mentioned had been a gift from Dian's parents, who ran a hairdressers-cum-leather goods shop in Brecon.

Tom and Mary Black were never less than generous, and the car was our wedding present. I was overwhelmed when Tom gave me a cheque and a bundle of notes and told me to deliver them to the local garage, where something would be waiting, to Dian's and my advantage. I only protested feebly, because Tom's was a mercurial nature, and the benevolence might turn in a moment into a murderous rage, so off I went, scattering notes in the breeze, to the garage.

The Anglia, although a wonderful gift, was an extraordinary car. It was manumatic, which meant that there was no clutch pedal. The top of the gear-stick was in fact, the clutch, so that if you inadvertently touched the stick, you went straight into neutral and out of control. It also jumped a foot or two when you stopped and lifted your foot from the brake. All in all, although a pretty little thing, it was mechanically a bit neurotic, and the manufacturers admitted that there had been 'a certain percentage' of complaints. We still had the car when Dian became pregnant, and I was afraid that the jerky nature of the car's progress might bring on an early confinement, so I asked the makers to modify the gear system and give us back three pedals. This they did, and everything went well until one day, when I tried to drive to the studios, the gear-stick (hollow because of the wires that had run through it, and consequently weak) snapped off at the bottom. I was in despair until I remembered the set of fireplace utensils we'd been given. I rushed indoors and grabbed the red-knobbed poker. It fitted perfectly into the stump of the stick, and I changed gear with the kitchen poker for the next month.

The nastiest shock of our moving to London was the difficulty in getting a flat. After being spoiled by the splendour of our bit of farmhouse (for which the rent had been minimal) we were shattered by the lack of, and price demanded for, places in London.

I rang one advertiser, who demanded a potted biography and who put the phone down when she discovered that my wife was Welsh. What could she have imagined? That Dian was fierce and hairy and wielded a man-killing leek?

Most of the other places had gone by the time we arrived, or were too dreadful to contemplate. We eventually found a place in Wimbledon, and I still colour when I think of the belligerent attitude of the landlord, and how I had to bite my lip, so desperately did we need a place. 'Remember – keep it clean !' he roared. 'If it's dirty – you're out !' We stayed there a few months and then found more amenable quarters.

For the next year or so I gradually consolidated my position, taking on whatever extra-mural work I was able to. Programmes like 'Come Dancing' and little features for deaf children came along. There was no extra payment for these. That grand old BBC phrase 'Staff NO FEE' was applied, although I wasn't, and never have been, a member of the BBC's 23,000-odd establishment. But my contract as an announcer stated that I could be put to any reasonable use within that designation. It was like being a Rank Starlet, without the champagne. I refused very little, although there was no money in it. I was keen to expand my contacts and experience beyond introducing 'The Lone Ranger' and 'The Woodentops'.

One day I was asked if I'd be interested in doing some holiday-relief newsreading. This would involve going to Alexandra Palace – dear old Ally Pally, where the world's first ever television broadcast had been made.

The idea of breaking dramatic news to waiting millions

appealed very much to the Thespian in me, and I accepted eagerly. If I was to be a parrot, I might as well have something worthwhile to repeat.

So I joined the news team, first on a part-time basis, and then as a regular member. Alexandra Palace was to be my place of work for the next eight years. Although the team varied over the years, in my early days it consisted of Robert Dougall, Kenneth Kendall, Richard Baker and myself. Bob the patriarch, Kenneth the immaculate, Dickie the resonant, and Mike the ... er ... well, 'ebullient' is the word Mr Dougall chose to describe me in his recent book. I suppose I must have come as a bit of a shock to the old-established tradition of 'gentleman' newsreaders. I could be as ponderous and formal as the occasion required, but my basic irreverence was never far below the surface, and I was the first to introduce the facetious 'pay-off' to the news – only when the last item was light enough to warrant it, of course. Dickie Baker was the nearest in age, temperament and background, to myself and over the years we've been involved in many charity concerts, cricket matches and musical evenings. He has a collection of Victorian song sheets, some of them real tear-jerkers. One in particular, 'Which Is the Way to Heaven?' told the agonizing story of two waifs whose Daddy was ill, and who were going to look for Mother who was up in Heaven ('We have no money, Sir, so we cannot go by train, but Jackie and I are walking there, to bring Mother back again.') Handkerchiefs were passed around before Dickie and I started on this one, for the use of vulnerable females and music lovers. We even performed it on BBC 2's 'Late Night Line-Up' and 'Woman's Hour', and backed it up with 'Daddy's Little Blue-Eyed Boy' and 'Little Betty Bouncer loved An Announcer Down at the BBC'.

Viewers might find it difficult to imagine their beloved newsreaders stepping out of character, but even the august Mr Dougall once dressed up as a tramp, and paraded outside Alexandra Palace picking up fag-ends and wearing sandwich boards advising 'Eat at Bob's', for a film we made for our annual children's party.

At the news desk, I was a useful tragedy-man (in spite of my tendency to giggle) because of my baggy eyes and sloping eyebrows. I would look fairly worn out by the gloom of it all, whereas in reality I *always* looked tired and the darkness of the grooves under my lower lids was significant of nothing at all. Sometimes I'd spring, tiger-like, into the studios, after nine hours' sleep, and they'd say, 'Oh, my God – he's been at it again. Can we get someone else?'

In one of our cricket matches at Luton in aid of a local charity, I was playing my usual flamboyant but useless game – falling over when I bowled, rupturing myself with wild swipes at the wicket, when the ball scudded across the grass towards where I was fielding at silly-mid-slip or cover-point gully. I raced to meet it, and put out my foot so that the ball would bounce from toe-cap to waiting hand. The ball did bounce, from toe-cap to unsuspecting right eye. There was a blinding flash and a sharp pain, and the crowd's laughter at my latest piece of buffoonery died away as they realized I was in genuine anguish.

The discomfort was only momentary, and soon I was bravely sobbing my way to the pavilion. My eye swelled and swelled until by the evening my right profile was classical Mongolian. The next day I was due to read the evening bulletins. The make-up girl was consulted. Could she disguise the damaged eye? 'I prefer it to the other one,' she said, 'the colours are quite sexy.' And, to be honest, it was quite a pretty eye, of delicate hues. Anyway, I went on and read the news.

The idea of a BBC newsreader with a shiner was too good to be true, and the papers made quite a story of it. It even made the international press. *France-Soir* carried the story, saying that I had 'an eye of black butter', and finishing with my explanation, ' *"J'ai recu une balle de cricket,"* dit-il avec dignité.'

My brother Alan, who worked at the American Embassy at the time, showed me a copy of *Time* magazine, and an item which read something like, 'Last night on BBC TV newsreader Michael Aspel read the news with his usual impeccable accent. His tie was straight, he showed just the right amount of cuff; in fact he was just what the British expect of their newsreaders – apart from one feature: he had a black eye. Even the manner in which he got it was typically British. "A cricket ball hit me," he said.'

Years later I still received letters from viewers – even from a doctor – who wrote to say that I was obviously still suffering from the effects of that blow. Nothing of the sort – the lights were coming at me from an angle, obliterating one bag and accentuating the other. My cricketing was a little inhibited afterwards, though. In any case, we only ever won a match if Corbet Woodall was playing. We newsmen were not a strong team; Kenneth Kendall had gone off to seek his fortunes elsewhere for a few years, Richard Baker could only bowl under-arm, and I was erratic to say the least. Corbet, who joined us at Alexandra Palace, was a splendid cricketer, a fine musician, and a hell of a character – tall and nonchalant, with patent-leather hair and a ready laugh. In recent years he's been afflicted with rheumatoid arthritis, but Corbet has the resilience of ten lesser men and is as good company as ever.

The years at Alexandra Palace were good ones. If I didn't find the work totally satisfying – and who could find fulfilment in reading aloud other people's words, with no hand in their preparation and no responsibility for them? – socially the life was good. Being at the centre of a communications business meant that we not only heard the latest developments in any international crisis, but that we also heard all the best and latest jokes as they arrived fresh into the country. It was a little irksome to stand on the steps at Ally Pally – waving the reporters and cameramen off on their latest world-wide assignments, and knowing that the nearest one would come to involvement in those stories would be to read a sub-editor's script as an introduction to the film our intrepid team had brought back. The BBC's thinking was that newsreaders could not be allowed to write their own stories, in case their personal feelings came into it. Well, we weren't trained journalists, true enough, but after a while we had all picked up enough of the technique and necessary jargon, to be perfectly capable of turning out a competent, well-balanced account of any event. In any case, the image of the faceless, characterless mouth-piece didn't fool all the people. Many thought they could read emotions in the reader's expression – and would sometimes invent opinions for us. At the time of one general election, an enraged viewer wrote to the Director-General, saying that if Aspel was allowed to read the news any longer, he would take it up with his MP. He complained of my 'wincing' and 'leering' when the names of certain politicians came up. He quoted three instances. The extraordinary thing is that not only was I not doing anything of the sort, but my political opinions were precisely the opposite to those I was being accused of brandishing.

There are times, of course, when the news is so startling or dreadful that it's impossible for the newsreader not to show some concern. Kennedy, Aberfan, Agadir – no wonder people have asked us why we didn't smile more often. 'Because the news is usually so bloody awful,' is the reply. My young daughter once watched Robert Dougall giving details of the latest industrial strife. 'Doesn't he look cross,' she whispered, and indeed he did. And yet, I found the words often used to pass through the mouth without touching the brain. Stories would arrive late, hastily typed or even handwritten, and I would rattle them off in the usual bland way; afterwards I would ask, 'What the hell was that all about?'

One of the most consistently helpful of the newsreaders aids is the BBC's pronunciation unit, which operates from Broadcasting House and sends out a daily sheet with all the awkward names that are likely to pop up, spelt phonetically. This sheet occasionally used to arrive ten minutes after the bulletin had ended. In such cases the name of the new Cambodian chargé d'affaires would be disguised by a well-timed cough. One of my most difficult times was when Sir Alec Douglas-Home's name was forever in the news. Home pronounced Hume – well, that's a good old British idiosyncrasy, and not too difficult to remember, I thought. Then one day another name appeared: Sir Evelyn Home – or was it Hume?

I couldn't be sure, and there wasn't time to check. When the time came, I decided simply to open my mouth and see what came out. What came out was: 'Today, Sir Evelyn Home – Hume – Hune – Hone . . . I'm sorry, I'll try that again. Today, Sir Evelyn Ho, . . . Hu, . . . Hoo, er Hern . . .' The news overran by several minutes that night.

We all recoiled when one day an African politician called Sir Abubakar Tafawa Balewa came on the world scene. Now there was a nice rhythm to his name – Abubakar Tafawa Balewa, so in fact it wasn't too difficult to get the tongue around.

I used to pace up and down the office – repeating his name like some tribal war chant.

A few weeks after his arrival on the scene, the pronunciation unit said, 'Awfully sorry. It should be Ab*u*bakar Taf*a*wa Bal*e*wa,' which threw the whole thing off balance and ruined his chances of a smooth introduction. In fact, a few weeks later, somebody shot the poor man and he was deleted from our list.

The cameras at Alexandra Palace were one-eyed, remotely-controlled creatures, and the only persons in the studio, apart from the reader, would be the floor manager who wore earphones for passing on instructions from the control room, and the teleprompter girl who operated the mechanical toilet roll which was attached to the camera. She typed the script on to this roll, and as we read, she would press a button and the paper would revolve, keeping the line we were reading at the correct eye level. We also had a normal script on the desk, which would contain the full bulletin, including the commentaries for the various bits of film.

The teleprompter used by the newsreaders was a less sophisticated machine than the one used for other programmes. Ours was a simple little black box slung just below the lens of the camera, so that if you looked carefully, you would see that the reader was looking you in the navel and not between the eyes. But it was easy to operate, and, more important, it was easy to dismantle so that the girl could add last-minute changes to her already hastily typed script. I always marked my script (the one I had on the desk before me) at certain points such as quotations or figures, the sort of things that the viewers would not have expected me to learn – assuming that they were fooled into believing that I'd learned the rest.

The aids we use in other programmes are far more impressive affairs. A glass-faced structure fits right over the camera, and the words are projected by mirrors in front of the lens so that the speaker looks right through them and deeply and sincerely into the eyes of the viewer. The teleprompter girls were often attractive, which was a bit of a distraction – and almost always efficient. They'd sometimes in their haste, leave out little words like 'not' which would affect the meaning of a report, but generally the system worked well. I always felt sorry for the floor managers, who were sent to our outpost in North London for three weeks at a time. There was so little for them to do. They simply pointed their finger at us to start, and we more or less took it from there without further assistance. Occasionally there would be an urgent message for them to pass on from above, but as often as not the producer would use the telephone in emergencies. Robert Dougall has recounted elsewhere the story of how I was halfway through the news one night when the phone rang. I murmured 'Excuse me', and reached for the receiver. It wasn't there. It kept ringing and I kept searching. Eventually I spotted it, peeping out from under the desk, where a tidy-minded floor manager had put it. The lead was trapped under the leg of the desk, and to answer the phone I had to dive out of sight. It rang several times that night, and for most of that bulletin all the viewers saw was the tip of my left ear as I had muffled conversations. A few months ago I was in a BOAC jumbo jet 39,000 feet over Winnipeg on my way to the west coast of the States and listening to their in-flight recorded entertainment when I heard John Timpson of the 'Today' programme introducing a talk on TV news. John quoted the story without identifying the victim. I wanted to tear the head-set off and shout, 'That was me, folks! That was me!' but I would probably have been clapped in irons and locked in the lavatory.

John has told me of the time he closed the 'Today' programme one Friday morning and said, 'That's all for today, Mike Aspel will be here tomorrow morning.' A few days later he had a letter from a listener asking him why he had told them that his gas bill would be arriving the next day.

John Timpson was a television reporter at the time I was reading the news. His dry humour was typical of the whole team of reporters, cameramen, sound recordists and lighting men. At first, as I've said, I was envious of their itinerant lives. We'd be having a drink in the club when the phone would ring and one of them would say, 'Sorry – can't have that beer now, I'm off to Singapore.' Or Iran. Or Greenland. And away they would go, their passports and visas ever ready, and their arms regularly pumped with vaccine to allow them instant travel to any part of the globe.

But I had no need to be envious. Those trips were at best a

chore, and often extremely dangerous. Even the most glamorous-sounding assignments involved a hasty journey, a job to be done, a few hours in a hotel room and back to the airport. Many of their jobs took them to war zones or to the scenes of riots or national disasters, and not a few of the filmed reports you've seen on your screen have been earned by the sweat of their brows, and occasionally, their blood.

But whenever they got back they'd have very little to say about it – they'd usually point out that you never did buy that drink they were going to have when they were so rudely interrupted; and of course there'd be the latest batch of dirty jokes picked up from their international colleagues.

Without exception, they were characters – a worldly, tough, imperturbable bunch of professionals. They knew all the wrinkles and all the loopholes to make life that little bit easier. They had imagination, too, as their expense sheets often showed. One of the most extraordinary characters in BBC TV news was, and still is, a cameraman named Graham Veale. Graham dark, sleek, with a suave moustache is Mr Fix-it, a born comic, con-man and citizen of the world. I've made several holiday trips to Italy with Graham and his family (his sister-in-law is Carole, one of the world's three top landladies) and I've never ceased to be amazed by the speed with which he can arrange things, from cheap meals to free entertainment. He tells the story, and denies that it's autobiographical, of a cameraman who was sent to cover the power-boat races in the Solent. He came back and presented the editor with a large sheet of expenses – including the hire of a motor launch from which to film the races. A few nights later, the editor went to his local cinema and saw, in a wide shot of the mêlée of craft, his cameraman in a rowing boat.

The next day he sent for him and asked him to explain. Graham – I mean this cameraman – reacted with the speed of light. 'I'm glad you mentioned that. To hire of rowing boat to get to motor launch – another three pounds, please.'

BBC news teams, when using their own cars for working purposes, get an allowance for the running and maintenance of the vehicle. I don't know what the figure is now, but there's an old story of a Scottish reporter who was apprehended for driving under the influence. In court, PC McTavish said, 'He was zig-zagging from side to side, your honour.' 'Is this true?' asked the judge. 'Aye, it's true,' said the reporter. 'I was zig-zagging from side to side – but only because I get nine-pence halfpenny a mile.'

10

At sea

I did get one trip abroad during my eight years as a news-reader. In 1961 the P & O liner, *Oriana*, was launched, and she went to Lisbon on a shake-down cruise, carrying a party of travel agents and journalists. The BBC decided to make a film of this event, and I was given the chance of going along. No hairy assignment, this. I was to interview members of the crew, but generally would be seen sharing a joke or a meal or a dance, or merely leaning over the rail. (I'm a good sailor, so the leaning over the rail would be for romantic purposes only.)

This trip brought me into contact with a gentleman who perhaps equals Graham Veale in the lovable rascal stakes. Reg Partington was our lighting man. His job was to point lights at things we wished to film. Reg looked every inch the producer. He was always immaculately dressed in a discreet three-piece suit, with watch-chain and expensive shoes. He took snuff, and had the looks of a degenerate eighteenth-century nobleman. He'd invented an imaginary character called 'The Major' and would enquire if 'The Major' had been in when-ever he went into a bar.

There was nearly always someone to answer Reg's vague description of 'The Major', although he made sure they weren't around before he discussed them in detail. I was with him once when he did it.

'Has the Major been in?' Reg enquired, brushing a speck of snuff from his lapel. 'The Major, sir?' said the barman. 'Yes,' said Reg, 'tall fellow with a grey . . .' 'I know him, sir!' said the barman, 'you've just missed him. It's his birthday today, you know.' 'Good God,' said Reg, 'He must be about . . .' 'Forty-five,' said the barman, and then, confidentially, 'you heard about his wife, of course.' 'There was some talk,' murmured Reg. And so it went on. He got a complete history of someone who, to him, didn't exist. We left after a few drinks, in case 'The Major' returned.

On our first day out from Southampton en route for Lisbon, I found I'd forgotten my toothpaste. I went to Reg's cabin, and he gave me a small tube. I squeezed some of the contents on to the brush and started to clean my teeth. I noticed there wasn't much lather, and the brush was beginning to wilt. The taste was vile. I looked at the tube. Brylcreem. I went back to Reg's cabin and said, 'Thanks a lot.' 'Never mind, mate,' said Reg cheerfully, 'not a tooth out of place.'

The trip was a five-day idyll. I went on deck as we came up the mouth of the Tagus and into Lisbon. It was very beautiful in the early morning light, the pinks and yellows of the buildings gleaming softly.

The whole of that voyage was without doubt a very special and happy experience, and yet I'm unable to think of it without sadness. Most of the passengers were middle-aged couples, with just a few younger people. One of them was a lovely girl who, like me, was on a working trip. She was secretary to one of the travel agents. I shall call her Jenny. Jenny agreed to take part in the programme as her work allowed. She would be seen with me on the dance floor, looking over the rail – the usual shipboard routine.

She was dark, vivacious and by general agreement quite enchanting. As the days passed and we saw more and more of each other, the inevitable happened. It was a romance without a future. I told her I was married and that effectively put an end to the blossoming affair. Our relationship became one of a wistful affection. The day we got back to London I telephoned her to tell her when the programme was to be shown, and then we said goodbye. That night I was woken by an extraordinary dream. Jenny appeared in a pale blue gown. She was surrounded by impenetrable darkness, and she was going away, looking back with an expression full of regret.

A few days later I recorded the commentary to the film we'd made, and watched as Jenny and I danced and strolled and shared jokes for the cameras. The producer and Reg Partington and the rest of the crew were there, and they seemed surprisingly sympathetic when I talked of what lovely company she had been. I had been very depressed since we'd got back, and Dian knew that something was wrong.

The next day I found a letter waiting for me at the studios. It told me what Reg and the others had known but had been unable to tell me. Jenny was dead. She had died the night we returned to London, a few hours after I'd spoken to her. The blinding headaches she'd had during the trip, but which she'd bravely smiled through, were caused by a brain tumour.

Her mother had written to me, after advising our producer what had happened, but giving permission for the film to be shown. Jenny had told her how she and I had felt, but that no harm had been done, and now her mother wanted to meet me, to find out all she could about the last few days of her daughter's life, the things she had said, and the things she had done. We met, and I told her all I could remember. It seemed to be of comfort.

A strange coincidence – call it what you will – was that the night Jenny died she had been wearing a pale blue nightdress, her mother told me, and that she had died at about the same time I had dreamt of her. Less than two weeks after we'd first met, I was standing at her grave. She was twenty years old.

This sad episode didn't directly affect my marriage. That had already begun to falter. It was simply a question of having married too soon. I wasn't, I discovered, emotionally ready to settle down, and I'd begun to suffer from the claustrophobic feeling that's familiar to countless married people. The condition of marriage, with its man-made laws and taboos is after all an unnatural thing, necessary perhaps in an ordered society but for some, intolerable.

Most couples manage to disguise their dissatisfaction, at least publicly, and a rare few are genuinely happy. I believe the numbers to be small. People who sublimate themselves and their own lives, emotions and fulfilment as human being simply for the sake of their children – staying together in misery and mutual disrespect – are denying their own reason for existence. It's a negative process and it's doubtful if the children will benefit.

I find the love game a difficult one to play, and am incapable of pretending or making do with anything less than absolute fulfilment. All right, life is full of compromise, and all right, I'm immature and grossly selfish. But nowadays I try not to make promises I can't keep, and I have acquired a reputation for being non-committal. Which is perhaps about time. Dian and I were divorced after just a few years of marriage, and she and her new husband now live with our two sons, Gregory and Richard, in Australia. We correspond regularly. The boys are now husky teenagers, flourishing in the outdoor life. They're bright, good-looking boys, and they call me Mike.

I've since been through a second marriage, and another divorce. Ann was one of the girls who operated the tele-prompter at the news studios. She was one of the distracting sort, fair haired and attractive, with intriguing 'bedroom' eyes behind her glasses. Coincidentally, although we met in London, she, like Dian, is Welsh.

The pattern was as before: an efficient, loving wife, a restless husband. We had temperamental differences, and have since proved that as friends, we have a much more successful partnership. And this is no rationalization. Our marriage lasted for about six years, during which time we rarely reached the intimate friendliness which we now have – when not arguing about domestic bills, that is. We have twins, Edward and Jane, who were born in 1964. I see them often, at least once a week, and we talk a lot on the phone. They know they're loved, and I make sure that no-one goes without material needs. I'm not the once-a-fortnight here-I-come-loaded-with-presents good-old Daddy. They get a telling-off when necessary, and greediness is not encouraged. Ann manages a full working and social life. We meet often, and it's generally a successful situation – rather like marriage, with some of the advantages and none of the drawbacks. I used to be irritated by reports of people who'd say 'I get on very well with my ex-wife/husband.' I'd think, 'If you get on so well, why the hell did you part?' I see what they mean now.

I'm delighted that the twins take after Ann's family. She has an uncle who lectures in English at Swansea university, and her father is a remarkable man. Eddie Thomas came out of the army after the war, and went to university at Bangor. Then his wife, Ann's mother, died. He left college to look after his daughter, and he became a bus driver, until his absent-mindedness made the company beg him to leave. He would stop the bus to read interesting posters, and once caused a mate of his to back his bus into a bridge. Eddie was directing him, and reading a book on the industrial revolution at the same time. Nowadays he works as a charge hand in a factory in Neath, and resolutely refuses all offers of promotion. Like all Welshmen, he's a fascinating talker. His knowledge of politics and literature is comprehensive, and people tend to sit at his feet. He likes to sip alcohol as he talks. He sips indiscriminately because his mind is on other things. It could be vodka or cooking sherry, or both. I've seen him slip gently from the chair, still talking as he hits the carpet.

Luckily, his intelligence has found its way into Edward and Jane. That apart, they're as different as could be. She is sturdy, extremely pretty and predictably full of feminine complications. Edward is wiry, with a gentle face, and most of the time he doesn't know what's hit him.

I actually insured against twins. Eddie Thomas was a twin, and it's likely to occur in alternate generations on the female side. Lloyds gave me very good odds – £4 10s down to win £100, slightly better than twenty-to-one. It bought a couple of thousand nappies. Later, the doctors could feel two heads and in the circumstances, we would have been rather disappointed if it hadn't been twins.

Jane emerged large and loud, Edward almost non-existent. His head seemed too big for his meagre body, and it took so long to assemble itself into the correct proportions that for months it looked like a gigantic hot-cross bun.

Once it was established that although scrawny he was as tough as nails, we were able to indulge in a little light relief. People, looking into the pram, would see Jane's great face and say 'How sweet'. Then they'd see Edward's pinched features at the other end of the pram and they'd say 'Oh dear'.

I have a miniature skeleton which I bought years ago for some forgotten reason. It now sits atop the bookcase, but I used to lay it on the couch with a little bonnet on its skull and a blanket around it, and say to visitors, 'Jane's very well, thanks, but Edward's not too well today.' A macabre joke, which caused Ann to beat me about the ears.

So there we are, still very much a family, I feel, although Dad has a different address. I probably see as much of my children as many a travelling salesman sees of his. Although my record as a husband may be disastrous, the alternative would have been worse. Dishonesty, deception, pretence and permanent tension are no basis for a peaceful life.

One Saturday not so long ago the four of us were skipping along Wimbledon High Street, on our way to our regular weekly lunch date at the Steakhouse. There was a long line of linked hands. An eager young man approached us with a pad in his hand. He introduced himself as the representative of a religious sect and wondered if we might answer a few questions. The first was, 'Would you agree that the family unit was the most important thing in life?' 'Quite possibly,' Ann and I agreed. 'As a matter of fact, we're divorced.' It was a little unfair, I suppose. He was stunned, and could only say, 'Oh . . . well . . . ha . . . ha . . . golly . . . well, thank you.'

So, at the time of writing, I live alone in my HBA (Humble Bachelor Apartment). And I am not lonely. Certain newspapers have flattered me by taking an interest in my solo state, and have tried to give the impression that I prowl from wall to wall, eating my heart out over something or other. Not true. I have friends and a full life. I may be more wary than most people about saying things others like to hear, and I do tend to change the subject or run from the room when I feel that familiar tightening of the chest if I suspect I'm being emotionally closed in on. Is it because of the cut-off years as a child? Hardly – lots of others went through that, yet manage to lead conventional lives. Are all Capricorns difficult? I don't believe a word of it, though blaming the Zodiac is becoming an increasingly popular way for people to rationalize the reasons for their actions. Well-meaning acquaintances have said, 'Well, all people in show-business are subject to special stresses and strains.' That's true, but I'm hardly in show-business. I've never had to go away for long stretches at a time, or work night after night on stage. Admittedly performers are a peculiar breed – even the gentle sort of programmes I've done have involved a certain amount of showing off; and I don't trust the artist who says he doesn't enjoy being recognized or asked for an autograph. Because their lives are so disjointed and unreal, many performers tend to behave in a supranormal way, chattering obsessively about the price of soap powder or the size of the potato they've just grown. Actors are desperately anxious to have their own corner of the bar of their local, and to be on first-name terms with every shopkeeper within five miles. Show-business attracts the talented, the neurotic, the insecure, the larger-than-life. Sir Ralph Richardson once remarked to me in an interview, 'I'm afraid that one day I shall wipe off the make-up and there will be no face underneath.' And because most of them don't know who they are, actors and actresses desperately look for an identity and for roots.

I have worked on the fringe of this other world, but have rarely had to play anyone but myself, whoever that may be. In real life I can get angry, on television I can't: I must not show any of the irritations, disappointments or frustrations I've known that day. Smooth, bland, relaxed – that's the image, and I'm bound to say that it's often as much a performance as if I were playing Cyrano de Bergerac.

But I can't, and don't, blame my work or its pressures and limitations for my own shortcomings as a stable and homeostatic member of society. No excuses. I'm just a rainbow-seeker.

We've made a great mess of love
since we made an ideal of it.

The moment I swear to love a woman, a certain woman, all my life,
that moment I begin to hate her.

The moment I even say to a woman: I love you! –
my love dies down considerably.

The moment love is an understood thing between us, we are sure of it,
*it's a cold egg, it isn't love any more.**

* D. H. LAWRENCE 'The Mess of Love', *Complete Poems*, Heinemann.

II
Dining out

During those long, happy, but apparently futureless days at Alexandra Palace, we were occasionally released for other programmes – and even paid a meagre fee – but they had to be the sort of programmes which wouldn't diminish our stature or clash with our respectable image; the point being that if we'd just been seen getting a pie in the face, we could hardly be accepted announcing the fact that war had been declared. As it happened, nobody wanted to push pies into anybody's face but mine, but I had to refuse all invitations to take part in comedy shows. There were delightful exceptions, but they were gentle affairs, not involving slapstick. There was the time I introduced a televised debate from the Oxford Union. The subject was '*Vive la Difference*' and the speakers could take it any way they wanted. I got a huge round of ribald applause when the make-up girl powdered my chin. One of the speakers was Frank Muir, who opened his address by saying, 'When I was invited to take part in this debate I was in Corfu, having taken three months off to finish my novel. I'm a very slow reader.' It was a cheerful affair, and didn't tarnish the image.

There was also a regional news magazine called 'Town and Around' which went out nightly to the South East of England, while other regions watched their own programmes. Richard Baker and I used to take it in turns to introduce it, and although it wasn't one of the most dynamic events of the twentieth century, it was certainly a good training-ground for later assignments. It gave us the chance to get out with the camera crews and do some reporting. We wrote our own introductions, and handled our own interviews. The sense of release was enormous.

One evening in the spring of 1967 I handed over to the weatherman after the nine o'clock news, escaped from the studio lights and made for the newsreaders' communal desk. Time for a couple of letters, then into the club for a refreshing glass of orange squash or tequila before the final bulletin.

'Mike,' said a voice from behind a pair of feet resting on the reporters' table, 'that Brigadier bloke's been on again. Says it's urgent. Would you ring him.' 'Give us a chance to get my breath back,' I replied.

I could picture the Brigadier. Puce, the veins on his neck standing out two inches, bellowing, 'Look here, Aspinall – what? – all right, Aspel – I want you to get down to this bazaar in Cheltenham. Saturday the 28th. 14.00 hours sharp.' I instinctively recoiled from the idea. But he had telephoned before, and the call must be acknowledged. My first call brought a frightened denial from an old lady in Sussex who'd never heard of the Brigadier. I checked with the operator. 'Could you try again, please – I think it's a Windsor number.' 'All right, dear – is this a personal or business call?' 'Business.' It always was.

This time a voice said, 'Windsor Castle,' in a perfect imitation of Bill Fraser's immortal Sergeant Snudge. Windsor Castle! 'Oh, may I speak to Brigadier Hardy Roberts, please?' Aspel trying to sound as if he'd never had less than three pips. 'One moment, sir!' Then a marching of feet, a short silence, and finally a crisp and pleasant voice saying, 'Good evening. How kind of you to ring back. I'm Master of the Queen's Household, and I'm instructed to invite you to lunch at Buckingham Palace with Her Majesty and Prince Philip on 17th May.'

There was another silence as I tried to work out which of BBC TV's news reporters was having me on this time. Was this Michael Sullivan or Chris Underwood doing one of their funny voices, or was the Brigadier for real? Play it cool, just in case, I thought.

'May the 17th? Well, I'm not sure – I'm doing "Town and Around" that day, you see, and I may not be able to get away.'

The voice was as urbane as before. 'Oh, pity. Well, there will be other occasions. We shall send you an invitation, just in case.'

A week or so later, a card arrived, confirming in gold script the invitation conveyed to me by the Brigadier. Now I was really confused. If it was a joke, it was getting a bit elaborate. Best to say nothing, but quietly accept.

And so, on 17 May 1967, I drove up to the gates of Buckingham Palace. The crowds of tourists parted and stared, unimpressed, at my Austin 1100. The car was dusty, but I was immaculate in gent's dark blue natty suiting with pale blue shirt and floral tie bought for 7s 6d from the girl in the office who made them from the bits left over from her cushion covers.

I was bright, shining and ready to share roast beef and two veg. with my Queen.

I was ready, but I still didn't believe it, and I was fairly certain that the huge police sergeant at the gate would wave aside my forged invitation with, 'Oh, you've had one of those too, have you? Hop it.'

But he didn't. He touched his helmet and waved me through. It was on! The invitation was genuine, and I was expected. I drove into the inner courtyard, where several limousines were drawing up close to a red-carpeted glass portico.

'Would you care to park over here?' said a young army officer, peeping over the collar of his dress uniform.

I got out of the car, and locked the door. The young officer smiled bleakly. 'I think you'll find it still here when you come out,' he said.

I climbed the red-carpeted stairway with the funny walk I always use when I'm self-conscious, and came face-to-face with the Brigadier. He wasn't puce, the veins seemed well subdued, he wasn't formidable at all. He was a slightly built man almost diffident in manner, and although for all I know he might have been a terror in battle, at that moment his moustache was the most intimidating thing about him – and that was neatly clipped.

Still dazed, I was shown into the Bow Room and introduced to my fellow guests. There was Cardinal Heenan, Jack Scamp (the industrial troubleshooter), The Hon. E. D. G. Davies (Chairman of National Carbonising Co.), Malcolm Morris, QC, S. J. L. Egerton (Chairman of Coutts Bank), Dr Maurice

Miller, MP, Muriel Powell (the Matron of a nearby hospital), and me.

The Bow Room was elegant and looked out on to the palace grounds. I was surprised to see that instead of a gleaming oak floor, there was a rather sexy fitted carpet, pink and bedroomy.

Flunkeys moved discreetly among us, dispensing drinks and cigarettes. There seemed to be about forty brands on the tray, and they were lit by an elegant brass-encased taper.

I sidled up to an attractive woman who didn't seem to be on the guest list. 'Do you come here often?' I enquired. 'Quite often – I work here. I'm a lady-in-waiting,' she said. 'Ah, perhaps you can tell me,' I said. 'How do we all come to be invited?' She smiled enigmatically. 'Names are put forward,' she murmured.

But why me ? Did they stick the Royal pin in a cross-section of names? Could it just as well have been the landlord of my local, or had I in some way earned my invitation? Certainly I hadn't read out any very pleasant news lately. In the old days, I remembered from school, bringers of grim tidings were put to death. At that rate I'd be in the Tower by teatime.

I don't know to this day why I was invited to the Palace – unless ... Some months before I'd introduced a charity show in aid of handicapped children at the London Palladium. Princess Margaret had been there. Perhaps she rushed round to see her sister afterwards and said, 'He's ever such a lad. You must have him round for a sandwich.' Somehow that wasn't convincing.

Never mind, I was there. I studied the seating plan and discovered that I was to be between Jack Scamp and Dr Miller, and opposite the Queen. What should we talk about?

This speculation was interrupted by the announcement that the Royal couple were on their way, and would we please line up as instructed.

Everyone else seemed about seven feet tall. I stood in the valley formed by two enormous figures. One last moment of panic. How should I address her? 'Your Majesty,' and thereafter 'Ma'am', I decided.

A few minutes passed, and three corgis trotted into the room. I bowed deeply. 'Not yet,' someone muttered.

And suddenly, there they were, looking just as I'd seen them on the newsreels, although the Queen was smaller than I'd expected, more petite, and a lot more attractive.

When we were introduced, my intended 'Your Majesty' to be delivered Raleigh-style, came out as 'Smissyeam'.

The man next to me cracked his nose on his knee in a flamboyant bow, and then I was being introduced to Prince Philip, who smiled cheerfully and gave me a few moments to take in the cut of his suit for future reference.

Introductions over, the line broke up and we formed into small groups around the Royal pair as they wandered amongst us. It soon became obvious that although the Queen might appear to be a solemn lady who only really relaxed when she was out with the horses and dogs, she was in reality a charming person – with a quick wit, and far more easy in her manner than any of us would have expected. Of course, all the Royal Family are professionals at putting people at their ease and at keeping up the pretence of being riveted by other people's company when in fact they must be bored out of their minds. I don't suppose we were the most scintillating lot they'd ever met, but if we didn't amuse the Queen, she certainly amused us. The day before, she had opened the new mammal house at London Zoo, a cavernous place where day was turned into night so that visitors could observe the nocturnal animals. The only trouble was that this meant there were dark passages, with obvious hazards.

'How did you like the new mammal house, Ma'am?' I ventured.

'I should think it's the perfect place for an assignation,' said the Queen.

And so it went. She told us of some friend of hers whose car had been sat on by an elephant, then mentioned a gift that Mr Kruschev, the Russian premier, had once made to Princess Anne – 'It was a bear,' she said. 'What a ridiculous present to give a child – all those claws.'

'You must get an awful lot of stuff you don't want,' I said, getting more self-confident.

'Yes we do,' said the Queen.

'What happens to it all?'

'Oh, people in the house take it. Billiard tables are difficult to get rid of.'

Just then a helicopter landed in the grounds, and Her Majesty looked a little irritated. 'I wish they wouldn't do that,' she said, 'it makes the windows so dusty.'

Luncheon was served. I'd heard that they liked plain food. We started with fresh salmon. I took much too large a portion, not through greed, but because I couldn't co-ordinate my movements with the cutlery. 'Will you have wine, orange squash or beer?' enquired a flunkey. I didn't hear him mention beer to anyone else. Some things show through even the nattiest of gent's suiting. I chose wine – a hock.

After the salmon, and after clearing up the lettuce which had slipped from my plate, they served ham and peaches.

All this time we chatted quietly amongst ourselves.

There was no shouting across the table, no cries of 'pass the salt' or 'anybody for the pickled onions'. The table was oval, and of course everything glittered and gleamed. Grandest of all, the fruit knives of solid gold, and plates decorated with gold leaf.

It seemed a pity to eat the fruit. I resisted the temptation to pocket a pear. That would have been the height of bad manners, and anyway the bulge would have been difficult to explain.

The timing of the whole operation was immaculate – perhaps the work of the Brigadier. After liqueurs, we rose from the table and returned to the Bow Room for a post-prandial chat.

Up until this point, the Duke of Edinburgh had said nothing to me. I was reassuring myself that he wouldn't let any guest go without saying *something* to them, even if to ask how the hell they'd got in there, when a voice from behind me said, 'Hello – you on tonight?' – and there was a beaming Prince Philip.

I explained that I wouldn't be reading the news that night as we hadn't had time to put up the 'By Appointment' sign over my desk. What impressed me most about the Duke was that he really seemed to be interested in what one had to say.

If he was amused, he didn't just smile politely and stroke his nose, he threw back his head and came back for more. I wasn't able to confuse him with BBC jargon either. He knew all about teleprompters and videotape and telecine and film cues. Come to think of it, he'd have made a damned good newsreader.

The lunch had been scheduled to run until three o'clock. At precisely 2.57, the guests formed into loose formation as our hosts said goodbye. One last handshake, a pleasant farewell, and we were left to collect our thoughts, compare notes, and in my case, use the lavatory. Once again it was my friend the Brigadier who directed me. It was a surprising loo. It was not, as I half expected, hidden away behind a tapestried wall. It was a large, honest lav. of the public type, with rows of stalls, enough to accommodate any number of desperate gentlemen.

The only slight pang of disappointment I felt as I climbed into my car (it *was* still there) was that there was no memento, no souvenir of the occasion. It would have been nice to have a photograph 'seen sharing a joke' or linking arms with raised glasses. But they only do that sort of thing in the real world.

12

Miss World and other things

————◆————

Two other major programmes (if judged by the size of the
audience) that I became involved with while I was still a
newsman were the Miss World contest and 'Family Favourites'
– both institutions in their own way, except that the former
provokes some wildly hostile reactions, and the latter inspires
affection, or at worst brings on slight indigestion during
Sunday lunch.

I first got involved with the Miss World contest in 1961,
when Peter West was the compere and needed help with some
of the announcements. Since then I've had an unbroken contact with the show. The girls come and go. They get younger
and younger, and I stay the same. A few years ago I remarked
to Miss Philippines that, at seventeen, she was one of the
youngest in the contest. 'And how old are you?' she asked,
'Thirty-seven,' I said, 'old enough to be your brother.' 'Ah,
but you are not *too* old,' she said. 'You are still a lion who
roars.' I bared my fangs, and she ran away.

Mecca's yearly frolic has been reviled and attacked with
consistent ferocity by the Press and various organizations
throughout the country. 'Here comes the Cattle Show!' shout
the tabloids. 'Degrading!' shriek Women's Lib. 'Banal,' yawn
the high-minded.

Perhaps it's all those things. I've worked on the show, and I
don't have to rationalize. The BBC pay me a reasonable fee for
compering the contest, and over twenty-five million people
watch it. It's a big, glittering, harmless bauble, and should not
be taken too seriously. It's an innocent affair; the girls are
guarded day and night by chaperones and mighty Mecca
musclemen (who watches the musclemen, I sometimes wonder),

and the Organization, under the redoubtable Morleys, Eric and Julia, jealously protects its protégées and its good name. 'Have you ever ...? 'Do the girls ... ? I'm asked, year after year. The answer is, 'No – not even for a "Crackerjack" pencil.'

Is it fixed? If it is, I wish they'd tell me. It would save me an awful lot of work. I have to prepare fifty-odd interviews in ten different languages – none of which I speak. I've been waiting for years to ply Miss Japan with searching questions: my little cue-card is yellow with age, but still she doesn't get to the final seven and my microphone. I wouldn't understand a word of her answer, but it would be a pretty sight. About those questions: of *course* they're silly and shallow. How the hell am I going to ask a girl about her country's industrial policy and what she thinks of Kafka when she's just learned how to say, 'I'm velly preased to be here in Rondon'? Play it for laughs is my policy, and it's the only way. And don't believe all you read about dumb broads. Many of those girls are a lot better educated than the journalists who knock them. Remember Reita Faria, the Indian Miss World, now a doctor? Study the list – you'll find a dozen or so at university, others in professional jobs or running their own businesses, as well as the models who want to 'travel, meet people and have a happy life'. They're here on a free trip. They may win a lot of money, but if not, well it's been fun, and I've seen no eyeballs on anyone's fingernails. My complaints are few. One is that the girl who sky-dives for a hobby and wants to be a brain surgeon rarely makes it to the interview stage. And the information I get is so often wrong. 'So you're a deep-sea diver.' 'No.' 'Oh – well, thank you, Miss Tibet.' But, as I say, I hope for laughs and if the laugh's on me, that's fine.

My own relationship with the girls? Non-existent, beyond a 'how's it going ?' from time to time. In the early sixties, I had a couple of dates with one of the girls during the few days she was in London after the contest. But why look further afield, with plenty of steadfast home-grown company?

Away from the Miss World contest, I have had a long and loving friendship with Jackie Molloy, who was a Miss Britain a few years ago, and who now lives in America. Otherwise, nothing.

One thing about the Miss World set-up that I've found

amusing and at the same time slightly sinister is the Mecca habit of calling all their employees by their full title – eg in a moment of stress, when the girls aren't responding to instructions and the Mecca man at the end of the cat-walk isn't being firm enough, you might hear an anguished cry from the organizer, 'Oh for Christ's sake get your finger out, Mr Philpot!' No Freds or Rons or Keiths for Mecca. Call them anything you like; threaten them with physical injury; they'll take it without a murmur – so long as you call them Mister.

You may have noticed that flunkeys are employed to hand over the crown and the other regalia at the end of the contest. These are usually out-of-work actors or fellows who make a regular living doing sales promotions in a variety of costumes. They're generally a cheerful, well-adjusted bunch of lads. I remember, though, one year when there were two flunkeys involved in helping the winner with her cloak. One of them had to step forward and fasten the cloak around her neck. After she had done her lap of honour, she returned to her throne and the other flunkey helped adjust her cloak as she sat down. I think this was the year Miss Holland won – a buxom girl. As she arrived back at the throne, she did a final twirl which brought her into sudden and close contact with the flunkey who was approaching to assist her coronation. He bent sharply at the waist and gave a little gasp. When the whole thing was over and we were all feeling relaxed, I asked him if he'd enjoyed that little encounter; most of the men there were envious. 'Oh,' he said, arching an eyebrow delicately and patting his wig, 'I never noticed a thing myself, love.' Perhaps that's why he'd got the job.

There was another amusing episode, in 1972 I think it was. One of the African contestants, an engaging extrovert, arrived with no biographical details for me to study. 'Can you tell me something about yourself?' I asked her during rehearsals. 'Come with me,' she beamed, and led me to a corner. 'I'm from the mid-west region of my country,' she said when we'd settled, 'and you've got a nice voice.' 'Thank you,' I croaked. I made a note of all the necessary background information, and we rejoined the others. She was walking slightly ahead of me when she suddenly turned and lunged at me, eyes closed and lips puckered. It was like being hit in the face with a bathroom plunger. I was wet from forehead to chin. 'Give me a ring at the hotel,' she whispered, and let my spent husk fall to the floor. Flattering though it was I didn't follow up the invitation.

Critics are sometimes, to say the least, inconsistent. What struck one woman journalist as having a 'certain wit and charm' one year was described, the following year as 'banal', even though the routine had hardly altered. 'Predictably embarrassing' announced a daily paper, five days before the event. And one of the most vehement attacks on the whole dreadful business came from a writer whose article was surrounded by photographs of near-nude models with far more leering captions than anything I'd ever said.

To illustrate my own theory about words passing through the mouth and by-passing the brain, I admit to one extraordinary bit of short-sightedness. During a pause in one contest I remarked that many viewers claimed to have better-looking girls down their street. If that was true, I said, I'd be pleased to receive details. And I did – hundreds of photographs of pretty, plain, sweet and spotty girls cascaded around my ears from all over the country.

A Miss World judge I would not be. It must be unpleasant to be introduced to a massive audience, to know that they're going to howl derisively at you within the next forty-five minutes. Nobody ever agrees with the judges – not even the judges. Miss Worlds are elected on aggregate marks. It has happened that the eventual winner hasn't been voted first by a single member of the panel, but her marks have been consistently high enough to beat everyone else's total. There were outraged cries when Miss Grenada won the year her country's prime minister was one of the judges. Nobody complained when Miss United Kingdom won with six Britons on the panel.

I was once foolish enough to agree to be the sole judge on a minor contest. I made my decision swiftly and confidently. As I rose to go I was attacked by the mother of one of the losers. She beat at me with her umbrella. 'You've got no bloody taste in women!' she shrieked. My partner was deeply offended. At a church fête the vicar's wife, the local headmaster and I unanimously chose a very pretty girl to be Queen of the Day. Her prize was the sash and about £1·50. As I sauntered around the grounds with the twins, one of the runners-up stormed across to me and snapped, 'It was a fix. The local papers will be informed. Your name will be used.' I could only say that I'd be grateful for the publicity. The size of the reward has no bearing on the girls' reaction to defeat. At an earlier contest which I helped to judge (I retired, hurt, after the brolly attack, never to judge again), a loser sought me out to enquire why she'd not won. She was most persistent. 'What was it?' she demanded. 'Am I too young? Aren't I tall enough? Was my hairstyle wrong?' I murmured excuses, and tried not to look at the huge boil on her forehead. The saddest contest I've been involved with was one organized in the north of England by a local bus company. One of the finalists was unable to attend because she was knocked down by a bus.

I was disappointed the year Women's Lib. attacked the Miss World contest and Bob Hope was a judge. I wasn't disappointed by the attack – that was fairly entertaining, and the Mecca Organization can look after themselves. Bob Hope was on the stage (cat-walk, cattle-grid, call it what you like) when the protesters struck. The Albert Hall's a tall building with many floors and from the heights fell bags of flour, stink-bombs and other abuse. Bob Hope caught a flour bag on his shoulder and looked, naturally enough, alarmed. Coming from America, he probably expected shots to ring out. But that was the extent of it. The disruption was short-lived, and the demonstrators ejected. They'd made their point. We all smacked our lips with relish as Bob Hope returned to the mike. He would now destroy all detractors with a few dead-pan Hoperies: there'd be a reference or two to Bing Crosby, perhaps, and good humour would instantly be restored. Sadly, he chose to counter-attack and bring in the drugs question and generally be querulous rather than quicksilver. But I'll not be a judge on this matter, either. He had no way of knowing what would happen next, and he had a right to be angry.

Outside the hall, security was tight to say the least. A phalanx of willing young policemen lined the short route to the girls' coach. A few members of the BBC's production team (including me) rode with them. As we moved off, a great baying and howling sound arose, and a mob of Women's Lib., Gay Lib., Ad Lib. – all the Libs were represented – surged forward.

They beat on the sides of the coach, shrieking abuse. I caught sight of banners with various obscene, misspelt slogans on them. 'It's Time Women Did What They Want to Do!' announced one, which seemed reasonable.

Vile though it may be, Miss World is purely voluntary.

The Gay Lib. element were fiercer than the others, as you might imagine. They had more to get out of their system. My God, they were ugly. Their gaudily-painted faces were distorted with rage and hatred. When the coach began to move through the crowd, several of them threw themselves in front of it. The delay was brief. Inside the coach the reaction was, in turn, bewilderment, fear, amusement and defiance. 'We shall overcome,' was sung on both sides of the windows. All in all, a lively evening, and I'm sure we all felt a lot better for it. The great international party that always follows the show had an extra gaiety – sorry, sparkle – that night.

And it's only one night of the year, although if you believe some people you would think I spent every working day in a gold lame suit, microphone ever ready to thrust at some vacuous and compliant cutie. It's a good line for journalists.

When I took over the Saturday morning edition of Radio 4's 'Today' programme from Jack de Manio, who was going on to other things, a writer in the *Daily Mail* did a piece about the beauty queen specialist taking over from the established host of a popular, intelligent series. He described me as 'diminutive' (probably because the beauty queens wore such high heels that my voice often got muffled). No mention of the years with news and current affairs.

It's usually best to shrug off these things, but I was intrigued to know what the 'diminutive' bit was about, and I telephoned the journalist. 'Why diminutive,? I asked. 'Well, it means you're less than average height,' he said, having the grace to sound diffident. 'I'm 5 ft 9½ ins,' I said. 'Oh,' he said. 'But I know what you're trying to say,' I said. 'You're trying to say that a man who is a giant in every way is being usurped by a physical and intellectual pigmy.' 'Sorry,' he said, but I knew he was wishing he'd thought of that. Television performers – particularly 'personalities' are perfect targets for the papers, and that's fair enough. Send us up, knock us down, tear us into little pieces; we expect it. It's all part of the game, and part of the game involves not being ignored.

So, although I suppose I get through several hundred

interviews a year on slightly more cerebral programmes, I am, and shall remain to many, the one who chats up the birds. I decided a year or two ago that the joke had worn thin and that it was time to call it a day, but I was persuaded to stay with the show. I should miss my annual date with producer Phil Lewis and floor manager Ronnie Pantlin, who can silence a packed Albert Hall with one bellow. 'Stand by!' roars Ronnie, and there is stillness.

Highlights over the years? Apart from the Night of the Stink Bombs, there was the time when my microphone broke down and I grabbed a spare one and left the original one swinging between my legs on its lead (that got more laughs than the interviews); the sight of Miss Guam (4 ft 10 ins) lining up with Miss Holland (5 ft 11 ins); the night when a herd of photographers galloped on to a flimsy stretch of muslin covering a five-foot drop; the discovery that one finalist had had a sex-change; and the palpitations I had when I discovered, just in time, that someone had been teaching a likely interviewee a very naughty phrase. And, after all this time, I've never once, in spite of rumours spread by Mike Yarwood, come close to winning the title myself.

When I was a teenager, I used to wait every Sunday with the rest of the family to hear a familiar voice say a familiar phrase. Then the strings of Andre Kostelanetz would fill the room with an equally familiar piece of music. The voice was Jean Metcalfe's, the tune was 'With a Song In My Heart', and the programme she was introducing: 'Two-way Family Favourites'. Jean and husband-to-be Cliff Michelmore would chat cosily between London and Cologne, swopping messages and records. I would groan, like all teenagers, when the music didn't suit my discerning taste, and Dad, like all fathers, would turn the sound down when it didn't suit his.

The same scene was being repeated in practically every home in the country. Today that same signature tune is still redolent of roast beef and Yorkshire pud.

In the autumn of 1967, I was spending a few days with some friends in Wales when I got a phone call from London. It was the BBC, offering me the job of introducing 'Family Favourites'. This was the accolade. I'd always felt that so long as dear old

FF existed, things would never get too bad. It was an institution, a part of the Great British Weekend, and now it was to be mine. 'The names and addresses game' is how Jimmy Saville affectionately refers to request programmes and I see his point. The names and addresses I was to play with ranged from Australia to Belfast, from Hong Kong to Cyprus, from Malta to New Zealand. I often wished I could be paid by the mile.

'Two-way Family Favourites' had become world wide. I established friendships with people I'd never met – Graham Webb in Sydney, Marama Martin in New Zealand, Bill Paul in Toronto. Listeners would sometimes claim they detected an edge in the voice, or a nuance that meant displeasure, but it was all in their own minds and proof that they took a keen personal interest, and looked on us all as a large family. The programme is 'live', that is, you hear it as it is broadcast. But of course there's a difference of many hours between the various countries. When it's twelve noon in Britain it's nine pm in Australia. This means that the Australians record the programme at their end, and transmit it the following Sunday morning, which sometimes makes it a little tricky to send a birthday greeting. The other segments of the programme are 'live', and heard at both ends simultaneously. Stand-by messages are recorded each Sunday before the show goes on the air. These recordings are sent to the countries who'll be linking in the next programme so that if you say, 'Come in Rod McNeil in Sydney,' and all you hear is the wind howling around the satellite, then you pop on Rod's recorded greeting and he, thirteen thousand miles away, plays the one you've sent him – with suitable apologies.

The Canadian link is always recorded. We used to do it on Friday afternoons, because they transmitted it in Canada on Saturday morning, just to make things more complicated. I got into a pleasant little Friday routine which was almost my undoing. I used to meet my old friend, Jim Healy, at a wine bar in Knightsbridge during the lunch hour, then go up to Broadcasting House and record my chat with Bill Paul in Toronto. Now you know that lunch-time drinking has far more effect than at any other time of day, and I remember getting so involved in conversation during one of these sessions that I got through a bottle of Chablis and forgot to have sandwiches or any other blotting-paper. Consequently the next Sunday when the 'live' chat with Sydney was finished and the engineer switched to Friday's tape-recording, the listeners heard me say, 'Well, it's goodbye to Australia ... and (hic) hello to Cazzaza.' Instant inebriation.

Sometimes the 'names and addresses' game must have seemed a bit boring to those who hadn't sent in requests and simply wanted us to shut up and play the records, but that was our brief. I used to ask the listeners to send in lively cards, with a few quick anecdotes, if possible. Some responded nobly but generally they fell into the 'Love you, miss you, and roll on November' category. We could have played Tom Jones's 'The Green Green Grass of Home' thirty-six times every week. It was by far the most requested song, even though it's all about a fellow who's going to be hanged.

Requests did arrive written on some very strange objects, particularly where the Services were concerned. Messages came on caps, knickers, shoes, gramophone records, flags and models of ships, and some very mischievous little messages there were too. Producer Jack Dabbs had a fascinating collection in his office.

I used to collect names. I remember with affection Lavinia Corduroy, Joyce Buglehole, three-month-old Dalton Flesh, and many others. And Bill Paul and I used to look forward to the brilliant cartoons that a listener, Cecil Curran of Isleworth, used to send us. We were usually depicted in desperate circumstances – Bill punctured with Injun arrows or staving off a rampant moose with his microphone, I was usually having trouble with some obscure name in Saskatchewan.

Kenny Everett, the mad genius, used to precede 'Family Favourites' on Radio 1, and usually devoted the dying moments of his show to sending me up. He would use recordings of my voice played at different speeds, or he'd announce that for the next two hours he was going to do his famous impression of Michael Aspirin, (or was it Mike Collapsible?).

He knew, of course, that I'd be unable to reply, because at midday the Radio 1 and 2 audiences merged for 'Family Favourites', and if I'd referred to Kenny's outrages the Radio 2 audience would have had no idea what I was talking about. I had to explain this to Dave Lee Travis, the Hairy Monster from Manchester, who took over from Kenny. Dave burst into the office one day and raised me by the lapels. As I wasn't wearing a jacket at the time, it was painful. 'Why don't you react when I take the Micky out of you, Aspirin?' he bellowed. He chuckled merrily behind his gorse bush, and dusted me down when I told him that I'd like nothing better than to fire back at him on the air, but that, although his forty-seven listeners might get the joke, the rest of 'Family Favourites' fifteen-million audience wouldn't.

Unlike Dave and Kenny and Jimmy and Tony and Terry and all the other DJs, I've never actually placed a needle on a record, professionally speaking. 'Family Favourites' was a large team effort. On one side of the glass, at the control panel, sat the producer and his technical assistant. Behind them, the gramophone operator, the tape operator, and the engineer who kept us in contact with the other side of the world. On my side of the glass, a large table littered with cards and twenty-eight pages of record titles and programme details, telephones, talk-back control for checking timings with Jack while a record was playing, a set of earphones, and me.

They all got the sounds on the air; I provided the prattle. Now your disc jockey will be hunched over his own set of controls – he'll operate his own tape-cassette machines, gramdeck, and his own microphone. The producer clutches a stopwatch and tries to keep the DJ under control. That's the difference. So you can imagine my surprise when I was awarded a gold trophy by the readers of *Reveille* for being the top Radio 2 DJ of 1970. The next year they gave me the silver award. It was all under false pretences, but I accepted them and ran.

I have them discreetly on display in a neon-lit cabinet attached to the outside wall of the house. It's interesting that however unworthy a nominee may claim to feel – even genuinely – few of us reject the accolade when it comes to it. I have a handsome trophy – as does every other newsreader, erstwhile or extant – which was kindly presented by the Royal National Institute for the Deaf. It's the 'Clearest Speaker of the Year' award. I got mine in 1965. I think Richard Baker has several of them, but he must have been mumbling that year. And in 1973 the Radio Industries Club gave me their Radio Personality Award which I accepted humbly and with difficulty.

It weighs about two tons. I hired a removals van and took it round to show to some friends. 'Feel the weight of that!' I cried, indicating the massive lead and gold sculpture. 'Yes, dear, it does look heavy,' they said. 'Hold it!' I commanded. 'Try it with one hand – just try it !' They did. The hole in their new leather chair was patched quite skilfully, but I still feel bad about it. I've introduced many awards ceremonies over the years, and used to smile cynically when actors would sigh that receiving a prize automatically meant being out of work for a long time to come. Typical theatrical superstition and over-statement, I thought. Soon after I got my Radio Award, the BBC decided to change the personnel on 'Family Favourites'. They also decided to end the run of Radio 2's 'After Seven' evening programmes, of which I was a regular compere, and in fact, since the day of the award, I have hardly been near a Radio 2 microphone. This hasn't caused more than half a dozen demonstration marches, and in any case I still have work to do on Radio 4. I enjoy my Saturday mornings with the 'Today' programme. I could do without the six am call, and Saturday nights do tend to be a bit lethargic these days, but I meet some fascinating people. The atmosphere of the office suits me perfectly, and best of all, I'm left alone to do things my way, whether it's writing introductions to items or interviewing a visiting celebrity.

But I would be less than truthful if I said I didn't miss 'Family Favourites'. For five and a half years I enjoyed that Sunday routine; buying the papers on the way into the studio, going straight to the canteen and bringing down the tray of coffee and biscuits for the team; meeting friends on the air; hoping for a little drama – 'Are you there, Marama?'; and quite unashamedly being pleased to be the catalyst, passing love along the line. I even liked some of the records. Saddest of all – no more chats with Sandi Jones. More deftly than anyone else she would catch all the pawky little darts I threw and hurl them straight back at me. Now, of course, Sandi introduces the programme, and she has all the warmth of the original lady.

On the morning of Thursday 18 April 1968, I left my home in Wooburn Green in Buckinghamshire to drive to London. It was about eleven o'clock. I had a lunch date with the journalist, Margaret Hinxman, and then I was going to record the Canadian link for 'Family Favourites'. I had asked to change the usual Friday date, because we were planning to go down to Wales for a few days. I have a note in my diary for that day. It says 'Llandrindod pm. Take dinner-suit.' There's also the word 'OFF' with an exclamation mark in the right hand corner, which confirmed that I had no newsreading duties that night.

It was a dull, damp day, and the wheels of my Morris 1800 slithered as I came out of the garage. I decided to use the M4 (our house was equidistant from that and the A40) and set off on what was normally a pleasant fifteen-minute drive through the lanes to the motorway.

My seat-belt dangled, unused, by my shoulder. I intended to clip it on before I reached the motorway.

After about four miles, the road became narrow and twisting, and once or twice I had to slow right down to manœuvre a bend. On the radio, Frankie Vaughan was singing 'Cabaret', a glitter-and-tinsel number which contrasted oddly with the drabness of the day. Nevertheless, I was singing cheerfully along with Frankie.

Another bend appeared, sharper than I remembered it. As I turned the corner, I suddenly saw a lorry and trailer coming towards me. It seemed to be occupying most of the lane, so I pushed my foot hard on to the brake and hugged the nearside hedge. The wheels locked on the mass of small wet stones at the side of the road, and the car went out of control. I was no longer close to the hedge, but keeping a straight line across the road, and heading straight for the lorry. It took quite a long time for us to meet. As I slid towards that vast radiator, I knew I was going to die. I felt no fear – merely exasperation and a certain curiosity. 'Pity I won't be able to see John and Brenda; wonder if this is going to hurt?'

I could see the lorry-driver frantically trying to take evasive action. But it was no use. I hit him fair and square, right on the maker's name.

There was a lot of noise. I felt myself fly forward, then back again. I felt no pain, but my mouth was full of something wet and warm. I opened my eyes. The car had changed shape. There was no windscreen, the steering wheel was no longer round, the dashboard tilted at an odd angle. Suddenly I couldn't breathe. 'Oh hell,' I thought. 'What a way to go. I suppose I've punctured a lung.' Fire! The word leaped into my brain. I pushed against the door, it wouldn't budge. I threw myself across the car and opened the passenger door. Then I staggered across the lane to the opposite bank. The lorry-driver came racing up. He was unhurt, protected by his lofty cabin. In a few moments I was wrapped up against shock and laid out on the grass. People began appearing from no-where; motorists who were now halted by the wreckage across the road, residents who'd heard the noise. None of them came near me. They looked at the scene and spoke quietly, then walked back past me, with the occasional sideways glance.

I could breathe easily now, and was quite comfortable. I still felt no pain, although I knew my left leg had seized up and it was difficult to talk. I seemed literally to have a plum in my mouth. An efficient gentleman bustled up, paper and pencil at the ready. 'Now,' he said, 'let's get some details.' And I mumbled my name and address while he tried to make notes. 'Clematis Cottage?' he said. 'How do you spell that?' 'CLEM . . .' I started. 'Now,' he said, his pencil describing small circles over the paper, 'CEL . . .' 'No, CLE . . .' I said. 'Sorry,' he said, 'now, CLM. . .' 'No,' I said. – 'It's CLEM, you daft bugger!' roared the lorry-driver.

Eventually the ambulance arrived and I was taken away. That was the worst part of the whole incident. It was a hair-raising drive. My sensibilities had started to return, and as the driver threw that vehicle about the road, shouting at people to get out of the way, I swayed and clung to the sides of the ambulance, wondering if I'd survived my own collision only to be a victim of his. We screeched up to the Accidents Department of the High Wycombe hospital, and I swiftly disembarked and was wheeled away to X-ray.

Amazingly, I'd sustained very little damage. I'd broken the windscreen with my head, ruined the steering wheel with my chest, and got my leg caught up in the newly-arranged instrument panel. This left me with one or two fairly deep holes and a few dents, but nothing serious. I'd bitten my lower lip quite severely and it was now jutting out belligerently. My clothes hadn't been quite so lucky; the glass from the windscreen had

showered over my head, and I'd slammed against the fragments
on my recoil. There were some inelegant stains on my jacket
and shirt. The receptionist stared at my matted golliwog hair,
the red-streaked complexion and huge lip and then down at my
name. 'Aspel?' she said 'Michael Aspel? I thought you looked
familiar.' 'Thanks,' I mumbled.

That night there was a scene reminiscent of *Reach For the Sky*.
You remember the part where Kenneth More (as Douglas
Bader) is lying in the ward after the accident which cost him his
legs? He's in a feverish state and apparently slipping away
when he hears two nurses talking. 'Don't make a noise,' says
one, 'there's a boy dying in there.' 'To hell with that,' thinks
Bader, and he rallies.

I know I was more or less intact, but my sense of drama was
as keen as ever. I lay there feeling all Battle-of-Britain heroic,
when I heard two nurses talking in the corridor outside.
'Quiet,' said one 'Michael Aspel's in there – the man who
reads the news. Smashed his car.' 'Oh dear,' breathed the
other, 'thank God it wasn't Robert Dougall.' I turned my face
to the wall.

Ann brought the twins to see me. They were very uncomfortable, and didn't like the look of me all bandaged and
plastered. They'd been shopping in High Wycombe when the
ambulance went tearing through on two wheels, but of course
had no idea I was in it. More friends and relatives poured in.
My mother had been on a bus and had spotted a newspaper
placard announcing the accident. She nearly broke a leg
getting off the bus and to the newsstand.

I was only in hospital a couple of days. I lived nearby, and
they let me go home on condition I let them know at once if
my intestines fell out. (They still weren't sure of internal
damage.)

The Healeys came to dinner one evening during my con-
valescence. Friends have an interesting attitude to one's personal
disasters. To them, you're either alive or dead – if you're alive,
fine – where's the gin? So I wasn't spoiled. Unfortunately, the
night they came I decided to go into delayed shock, and half-
way through the coq au vin, I got the DTs. I slid, twitching,
to the floor. They carried on talking. 'Do you want any rhubarb
tart?' Ann called down at me after a while, but by then

delirium had taken over. I suppose it was force of habit. I often slid under the table.

The most extraordinary and marvellous thing about the whole episode was the reaction of viewers. People I'd never met sent cards and letters from all over Britain, along with flowers and fruit and various homely gifts. In the first week I had a couple of thousand sympathetic messages, and I was, and still am, very grateful.

Getting back to work took a little more time. My leg had been twisted and now refused to straighten properly. 'Got to get it straight,' said the physiotherapist. 'How?' I said. 'Never mind that – just get it straight,' he ordered. But it took a year or two to achieve that.

Eventually, I took my place once again at the bar at Ally Pally. My lip jutted and I had a spectacular limp. Everybody bought me drinks. It was all very successful. After a while they began to notice that I was forgetting which leg I was supposed to limp with, and things went back to normal.

About three months after the crash I felt an irritation in my scalp. I scratched it, and found my finger came away bleeding. A piece of glass had worked its way out of my head. I was relieved that it had a good sense of direction. Today the only reminders of the pile-up are a slight scar across my lower lip, and an ability to predict the weather with my left knee.

It's been interesting to compare notes with other victims of crashes. Some felt pain, some had delayed shock, but most agree that they felt no fear at the time of the accident – merely a detached interest in what was about to happen. That and an agreeable sense of immortality, or perhaps a sense of the lack of importance of mortality, for quite a long time afterwards.

It didn't put me off motoring, although I've always been a bad passenger. Since the days of Scumpy Foo, my original 1932 Morris Minor, I've gone through a procession of motor cars, some of them bangers, some grand, rarely new and never too costly except in their consumption of petrol.

I've had several MGs and Peugeots, an Alvis, a Jaguar, a Rover, a BMW, an Alfa Romeo, one or two Fiats and a collection of Minis – a nice, democratic, international choice. I've lost count of the exact number. It's never been more than one at a time. At the time of writing I have a reliable economic

Mini Clubman. By the time this book is finished I would, in normal circumstances, have changed cars at least twice, but with the price of petrol the way it is, I'm sticking. Quite soon 'out for a spin' will mean driving from home to the filling station and home again. There's very little joy left.

It was while I had the Alfa Romeo 1750 Veloce that I made an interesting ornithological discovery. I was taking some friends out to dinner, and we parked outside the restaurant in a tree-lined avenue. I looked up and saw a plastic bag fluttering from the branches of the tree the car rested beneath. 'Do you see that?' I asked my friends. 'That plastic bag didn't get there accidentally. It was put there by the local council to frighten away the birds. They did it to the trees outside the "Cracker-jack" rehearsal rooms. There wasn't a bird in sight.'

After dinner we went to the car. It had changed. The clean white paint of my beloved Alfa had vanished completely, under several inches of crusty green bird-lime. There wasn't an unsullied inch of roof or bonnet. So much for plastic bags as scarecrows. But I did, as I say, make an interesting discovery. The Dodo is alive and not very well and living in Kensington.

The children take a keen interest in my cars. I always keep them in mind, of course. Will there be enough room for them; will they be able to see all right? 'I spy' games on long journeys are invaluable, so a good all-round vision is important. We were driving through Sussex not long ago, and Jane was telling us all the story of Jesus. Suddenly she spotted a large, wolflike dog trotting along the pavement. 'Look!' she cried. 'There's a Salvation!' Jane's interest in biblical matters reached a peak when I bought an old cottage in Hereford. It was called Yew Tree Cottage, but as there wasn't a yew tree in sight I thought it was a misnomer, and called for alternatives. We'd gone through 'Mon Repos', 'Y Wurry', 'Atlasta House' and 'The Ponderosa'. 'What do you think, Jane?' I asked. 'I know!' she said, 'let's call it Bethlehem.' Edward's suggestion was even better. He wanted to call it 'The Benny Hill Show'.

To him it seemed quite logical. He has that sort of mind. Some months ago, Jane was rushed to hospital with acute appendicitis. There were no complications. She was out in no time, complete with intriguing scar. (She'll have to stop show-ing it to visitors when she leaves school.) Edward was quite morose. 'It's not fair,' he grumbled. 'I haven't got a scar. Can I have my tonsils out?' I explained that a tonsillectomy didn't leave a scar, unless it was done from the outside, but I promised him that if he was very good, I'd have him circumcised. He was quite pleased until he found out what it meant.

I feel sorry for my children. Not simply because of my own inadequacies, but because having a father who's on telly is no joke. In fact, it's a stigma. The twins aren't impressed by what I do – 'It's just a job, isn't it, Daddy?' – and quite often they have better things to do than watch my programmes. They certainly don't find anything to boast about. But I'm afraid they sometimes have a hard time of it at school because of me. They're told they're 'posh and stuck-up', and that their father's very boring. Poor Edward and Jane. Sorry, kids, it's the only way I know of earning a living.

My two Australian sons came over for a visit recently. The four of them had not been together for some years. They got on marvellously, the two older protective and teasing in turns, the twins loving every minute of it.

One last child anecdote, which doesn't involve my own family. I was at a friend's house, changing into my dinner-suit for a big charity function we were to attend. I was just about to step into my trousers when his youngest daughter appeared, an enchanting little thing, aged about twenty-three. (In fact she was nearer five years old.)

'Have you got the same thing my Daddy's got?' she asked. 'Oh dear,' I thought. 'Yes, I expect so,' I said cheerfully.

'Where is it?'

'Oh – in the usual place.'

'What colour is it?'

'Oh, the – er – usual colour.'

'My Daddy's is red.'

I was just about to call for help, or draw her attention to the pattern on the wallpaper, when she said 'Yours is blue, isn't it?' and she picked up my bow-tie, just as her father came into the room. He was wearing a velvet tie. It was plum coloured.

13
Jumping off the perch

My newsreading days were drawing to a close. The restrictions were becoming irksome, and the thrill of being first to break the big story was beginning to pall. I'd been there for eight years, which for someone with my restless nature was quite long enough. My feet itched unbearably. Polly wanted to leave the cage.

At the same time, and unknown to me, plans were being laid which were to result in my career taking an entirely different direction. The BBC had been doing some research among viewers to find out who would be most acceptable to them as host of a TV chat show. My name, I was told, was high on the list. I was offered an early evening programme. It was to be called 'The Monday Show'. Coincidentally, Leslie Crowther had decided to leave that phenomenally successful children's show 'Crackerjack' introduced by Eamonn Andrews some years before and now very clearly Leslie's property. Would I like to take over? If it seems strange for a newsreader to be offered such completely different work from his usual run, you must remember I had by this time been introducing the Miss World contest for some years, I'd become established on 'Family Favourites', and I'd never been able to disguise the fact that, professionally, I was most comfortable in medium-to-lighthearted situations.

With those three major commitments before me, I didn't hesitate, terrified though I was at what I was jumping into – and, of course, out of. There was a sense of security in the news game, and they'd been undeniably happy days. My main consideration had always been the children – whether I should be able to earn enough as a freelance, unfettered by restrictions but with no financial guarantees to look after them. I decided that I must make the move. I could, after all, crawl back if it all failed, and ask for another chance.

In the summer of 1968, I read my last news bulletin. 'That's all,' I said. 'Good night, and goodbye.' No more international crises to describe, no more war-scares, no more film-star suicides ('An almost brutal sense of drama,' said one critic of my announcement of Marilyn Monroe's death), no more handing over to Bert Foord or Trevor Davies for the weather.

There was a maudlin booze-up in the club, glasses were raised, and estimates made of the fortune I was going to make. Most were agreed that I'd be back in three months. I knew I was going to feel rather as I'd felt after leaving the army. I'd been very content in the male-orientated society of Alexandra Palace. We were all lads together, happy chauvinist pigs, cheerfully buying drinks for the secretaries, but able to get in a corner on our own whenever we felt like it. It had often been difficult to believe that we were part of the BBC empire, so cut off were we in our outpost in North London, but I count it, without hesitation, as one of the happiest periods of my working life. It had everything – companionship and work full of variety, and drama. I remembered the night President Kennedy was assassinated; all four regular newsreaders were at a TV awards dinner, and a nervous stand-in had the job of breaking the story to the public; the days of the first space-flights; the general elections; wondering who would be on duty the night Sir Winston Churchill finally decided to give up the struggle; the Royal occasions, the human dramas, the dis-asters, the sporting events. From now on I'd have no inside stories. I'd have to watch the news like everybody else.

But it was an inevitable move. No matter how comfortable and secure my newsreading job might be, it didn't have the one ingredient essential to me: freedom. Freedom to do my own thing, choose my own work, use my own words, think my own thoughts aloud. Would the programmes I was about to do give me this freedom? I hoped so. Polly was ready to hop off the perch.

For months after I became a freelance, I hardly stopped to breathe. Apart from my regular commitments, I was offered so many 'one-off' appearances that Stanley Baxter was moved to

Jumping off the perch

remark in one of his sketches: 'This is a very unusual programme. It's unusual because Michael Aspel isn't in it.'

I was a guest in the 'Morecambe and Wise Show', dressed in
white tie and tails and doing a soft-shoe shuffle. Eric was my
dancing-partner, Goldie, and very desirable he was too. Did
you know that at one time Ernie was taller than Eric? It was
a long time ago. Ernie had long fat hairy legs then. They've
since been guests on various shows I've done, and are, as you'd
imagine, as good company off the screen as on. Eric, like Harry
Secombe, gives away thousands of pounds of free entertainment
every week.

My new life wasn't all joy and success. The much vaunted
'Monday Show' was a disappointment. Worse than that, it was
a disaster. The producer, Mark Patterson, and I decided that
we'd go for interesting people who had something to say, rather
than a procession of visiting filmstars. It didn't work. There
were various reasons. We didn't find the people, we didn't get
the right sort of production help and, most significant of all, I
wasn't ready for it. I had very little confidence. I wasn't able to
interrupt rude or boring people, and I simply became more and
more dispirited. What little confidence I'd originally had was
sapped by the late Tom Sloan, then head of Light Entertainment. I don't doubt his abilities as an administrator, and he
may have been an able and gifted man in other departments.
As a psychologist, he was a flop. He would stare blankly at me
if I attempted a joke, he would leave questions unacknow-
ledged. We had no point of contact at all. His research had led
him to believe I could do the job. His instinct told him nothing.

David Jacobs was struggling manfully and with immense
professionalism to keep the 'Wednesday Show' above water.
We were both suffering from the fact that the first half of our
shows were seen by the South East of England only; then we
were joined by the rest of the country. I was tempted to open
the second half by looking out of shot and saying 'Good night
Your Majesty, and thank you for coming . . .' And 6.15 in the
evening wasn't exactly the peak viewing hour. Occasionally
we'd have a winner, and there was usually one item in each
show that was worth seeing.

One of our early guests, in accordance with our policy of
having unknown but interesting people, was a dustman who

151

wrote poetry. It wasn't a very successful interview. Towards the end I asked him, desperately, what was the most unusual thing he'd ever found in a dustbin. 'I don't think I can tell you that,' he said demurely. 'Well, whisper it to me,' I said. He leaned over, and whispered in a very loud voice, 'I once found some child's afterbirth.' The camera cut at once to my face as I covered it with my hands and sank out of sight.

On the same lovely show, we had a herd of deer for some reason. I was talking to their keeper about the glory of wildlife when suddenly, and *en masse*, they emptied their bowels all over the stage. It wasn't a particularly messy process; it was the noise that was so disturbing. It sounded like distant gun fire, or torrential rain hitting a sheet of corrugated iron.

The floor was littered with dark brown ball-bearings, which acted like roller-skates under the feet of the studio attendants.

I do seem to have an extraordinary rapport, or lack of it, with animals. I remember interviewing a gigantic wolfhound during 'Town and Around'. It sat beside me, out of sight of the viewers, while I read the local news. After a few minutes it became bored and started to chew my wrist – not viciously, but with a gentle slobbering action. I read on, saliva dripping from my fingertips. I began to giggle, and what with that and the beast's heavy breathing, it must have been a confusing time for the viewers. Eventually I introduced the hound, and turned to talk to him. At that moment he decided to leave the studio. Nothing could stop him. Four strong men clung to his lead, and he took them with him. As they vanished, I could hear the producer's voice squealing through the floor manager's earphones, 'Get the dog to look at camera four!'

Another 'Monday Show' fiasco involved a dog. Another big one. A Saint Bernard, to be exact. He sat beside me on a couch, smiling gently at the audience. Then he turned to me. He liked me too. In fact, unlike the wolfhound, he didn't just want to chew my wrist, he wanted all of me. A Saint Bernard in a state of sexual excitement is an impressive sight. This time four strong men tried to keep *me* in the studio. I took them with me.

On those occasions, I was the victim. But the situation was soon to be dramatically reversed, and I became known in the animal kingdom as the Prince of Darkness.

We were recording one of several programmes from London

Jumping off the perch

Zoo. I was standing with the zoo's Education Officer, and we were talking about the new mammal house. He was wiping his glasses after an elephant had blown his trunk all over them, when I asked him, 'What about this dry moat between the animals and the public. Is it enough protection? Won't the animals fall in?' He assured me that there was no danger. Immediately there was a terrible trumpeting, and one of the elephants fell into the moat.

Then we moved indoors, and looked at the porcupines. Between them and the public was a stretch of water; no bars. 'But,' I said, 'is it enough protection? Won't the porcupines fall in?' I was assured that they recoiled instinctively from water and were quite safe. The next morning two porcupines were found floating, legs up.

Saddest of all was the case of the baby walrus. She was the first to be born and bred at the zoo for thirty-five years, and she was enchanting. I wish I could remember her name. She and her keeper were devoted to each other. (This sort of relationship is quite usual, I'm told.)

She would scuttle behind his legs when I approached with my microphone and she'd peep out with her great eyelashes fluttering. He would sit with his legs in the water and she would swim up and pull his wellingtons off with her flipper. They were a happy couple.

Tragically, a few weeks later she slipped and fell awkwardly. A rib punctured a lung and she died soon afterwards. Her keeper was desolate.

My own favourite was the Tasmanian Devil. I liked him because he was so ugly and misshapen and miserable. He had a right to be. His legs all seemed a different length, his mouth opened down to the small of his back and his nose was always running. He wasn't there when I last looked. I suppose he'd gone the way of all Aspel's animal victims – to the great zoological garden in the sky. With a history like mine, you might think that the Society would have rather I kept away from the zoo. But I think our programmes constituted useful publicity, and I was made an associate member of the Society. It means I can get in for nothing.

I was deeply depressed after the failure of the 'Monday Show', loathing myself for being so ineffectual and disliking the

153

BBC for making my big chance such a half-hearted affair. Mind you, I did get the front cover of *Radio Times* to myself, and for that journal to think of exploiting any of the Old Firm's properties was progress indeed. Today, many hundreds of programmes and interviews later, I know I could handle the chat-show format. To talk to a parade of stars is not difficult – much as I admire the style and personality of Michael Parkinson. A good production team, the right time of night, accurate research, and people behind you with confidence and the ability to spend a few shillings – with all these things, your only problem is yourself, and how you can manage the idiosyncrasies of your guests. I've taken over Pete Murray's 'Open House' programme on Radio 2 while Pete's been on holiday, and I've enjoyed it enormously. I like doing my own research, and coming up with questions and bits of information which surprise and usually please the guest, who's flattered that so much time has been spent studying him. But, although second chances in the chat-show world are hard to come by, I've sublimated that ambition through other programmes, on radio and television. Don't think, by the way, that 'stars' are putty in the hand of an experienced interviewer. They're not. They can be relaxed and charming, they can be so nervous as to be inarticulate, they can be noisy extroverts, or they can be so withdrawn as to be non-existent. I remember one well-known singer (female) who prowled into the 'Today' studio one Saturday morning. I was introduced. She turned from the ticker-tape she was inspecting and snarled. My hand dropped to my side. 'We'll be talking for about four minutes,' I told her. 'You mean I came here at this time of day just for four minutes?' she snapped. I apologized and explained that that was the usual length of interviews on such a programme; perfunctory, perhaps, but long enough to say enough. 'We thought we'd play the "A" side of your new record,' I said. ' "A" side! What's wrong with the "B" side?' she demanded. We didn't talk much more before the interview. Then she became all sweetness and light and talked about love and the brotherhood of man and what a warm, wonderful guy I was.

Sir Ralph Richardson was one of the most nervous people I've talked to. Urbane, amusing, and a fascinating conversationalist before and after the programme (it was part of the

'Personal Cinema' TV series) he was very uncomfortable as an interviewee, and insisted on 'getting out of the lights, dear chap' for a breather and a re-charge of confidence several times during the recording.

Roy Dotrice, head of that remarkable acting family, was reading a listener's request during an 'Open House' session when I noticed that the card was shaking violently. During the record I remarked that the Victoria Line trains which rumbled beneath us set up a lot of vibration. Roy smiled. 'That's very kind of you, Michael,' he said, 'it's not the trains. I'm terrified.'

Maggie Smith is another; a wonderfully flamboyant actress and lovely to be with, she was almost paralysed with nerves when our 'face to face' began.

It's been a revelation to meet many of the big names of the entertainment world, although I get more tongue-tied talking to writers and sportsmen, whose achievements are almost beyond my comprehension.

Let's drop a few more names, like Charlton Heston. His presence in a crowded room is electric. He looms, physically and in personality over everyone else. He also displays an old-world courtesy that's as anachronistic as many of the parts he's played, and by the end of our meeting I felt much the same as I did after my lunch at Buckingham Palace. Jack Lemmon was as animated as you'd expect from a man who's been described as 'acting with clenched hair'. I'd also heard that he had a special phrase, something he used to say just before a 'take', or at the beginning of a show. When we recorded our programme, I watched and waited, and sure enough, as the floor manager told us to stand by, he said it: 'Magic time'. It's his switch-on, his signal to himself to light up and give a performance. It seems to work. Lemmon's great buddy is Peter Falk, the actor who plays Columbo, the detective in the dirty raincoat. (He always reminds me of Phyllis Diller's mythical husband, Fang – the one who went to a fancy-dress ball; he put on his best suit and went as a slob.) Jack and Peter play a lot of pool together. Apparently Peter Falk is very good, and one day Jack Lemmon hired a professional pool player whom he introduced as his dentist. After he'd been soundly thrashed, Falk turned to the pro and said in that distinctive rasp, 'If you pull teeth like you play pool, you must be one hell of a dentist.'

Rock Hudson is surprisingly gentle and extremely pleasant. He's also a radio buff and had a colossal set in his dressing-room which could pick up broadcasts from the other side of the world.

Ingrid Bergman was patient while we filmed our talk three times. She knew it was a technical problem and nobody's fault. The most intimidating part for me was when Sir Michael Redgrave appeared and they embraced. They are both enormously tall people (I wonder how she got on with Humphrey Bogart?) and I got lost in their shadow. 'I'm sure we've met,' Sir Michael said to me. He'd seen me read the news.

I'm at my more apprehensive when going to meet people like Anthony Quinn – people with reputations for fretful behaviour, king-sized personalities, or mighty intellects. My fears are usually unfounded. Quinn was easy-going, co-operative and very interested in my side of the business. He looked fitter and younger than he does on the screen. I was nursing a broken right wrist at the time of our encounter (a studio accident which I'll describe later). The tape recorder wouldn't work, so abandoning all technical expertise, I raised my free arm and gave the thing a mighty blow. The light came on. Quinn laughed. 'You've still got a good left!' Then we did the interview and then he got out the wine.

David Niven was uproarious. His book *The Moon's a Balloon* must have taken him about a week to write, because the anecdotes pour out of him word for word as they appear in the book. He's told them all a million times before, but for the listener, and for him the joy is undiminished. We both cried with laughter as he recounted the story of his friend who stepped, fully dressed and laden with suitcases, into what he thought was eighteen inches of clear water and vanished into twenty fathoms. He, too, was patient as I struggled to make the tape recorder work (I have the same effect on machines as on animals).

When I went to meet the American writer Gore Vidal I was sure I would be in for a difficult time. I knew he could be viperish in confrontation, though I hoped he would realize that I meant no harm, that I was in fact the complete sycophant. He greeted me with non-committal politeness. I explained that I would be talking to him for the Radio 4 programme 'Today', and that the level of our discussion would not be profound. Mr

Vidal smiled and said, 'Then I shall be shallow.' He then proceeded to be eloquent and witty and just what every interviewer dreams of.

The fierceness of actor/writer Robert Shaw's intellect and personality gave me a few apprehensive moments, too. I'd seen him scowling at his questioners before, and had no reason to suppose that he would consider me anything but a parasite. I don't consider myself that, you understand. I believe writers and actors should be more understanding and humane than most other members of society, because their fellow men's weaknesses and idiosyncrasies are the life-blood of the creative person. If someone I was interviewing was deliberately obstructive and unpleasant I should certainly withdraw my microphone and go home.

Robert Shaw gave me a very nice interview and a very large Scotch.

It's an odd profession, talking to people you don't know and asking them searching questions. The encounter is such a glancing thing. They look you in the eye, pour out their souls and then you say goodbye and never meet again. It's a weird non-relationship, with the person asking the questions often having to subjugate his own intelligence by sitting at the feet of his interviewee, who may have nothing of the slightest interest to say. There is a certain skill, I allow, in drawing somebody out, and getting them to articulate thoughts or opinions that might not have crystallized before the question was brought up. We're as much therapists as inquisitors. One thing's certain; I don't like being interviewed. Like many of my own victims, I find a lack of empathy occurs, and the brain seizes up like rusty machinery. 'The darkening caverns of my mind,' is a phrase I once read which haunts me. In certain situations the caverns of my mind are pitch-black. I was once invited to join Joan Bakewell on BBC 2's 'Late Night Line-Up' to talk about my life as a newscaster and why I wanted to leave it. It was a trite subject for that high-brow programme, and I knew that if Joan tried to intellectualize, I'd be lost. She did, and I was. Half-way through my reply to some particularly convoluted question, I forgot what I was talking about. It was a nightmare, and when I left the studio my clothes were stuck to my body.

Polly wants a zebra

As the list of illustrious names I've encountered grows, I become a little less apprehensive, a little more assured. They're only people, I tell myself. They use the lavatory too. Prick them, do they not bleed? But I'm always ready to touch the forelock to nature's gentry, and my finger rarely leaves my forehead.

14

A question of identity

My other big job when I vacated the newsdesk was, of course, the children's TV show 'Crackerjack'. Ever since Eamonn Andrews first introduced Johnny Downes's brainchild in the 1950s, 'Crackerjack' has been a favourite with millions. Nowadays, the original audience watch while their children shout the magic word. The team has changed often over the years. The most consistent member has been Peter Glaze, who's seen producers, comperes and fellow comics come and go like puffs of wind in a colander. Peter was with the Crazy Gang at the Victoria Palace for many years, and what he didn't learn from them isn't worth mentioning. What he *did* learn from them I wouldn't dare repeat. Peter's a performer of great experience, as the make-up girls will tell you. What am I saying? He's an ideas man, full of invention, and he's the most dedicated professional I know. When I first joined in 1968, the team consisted of Peter Glaze, Rod McLennan, an Australian song and dance man whose face was a cartoonist's delight, Jill Comber, a dark beauty with extraordinary green eyes, and Christine Holmes, blonde and lissom and with a vivacious singing style. (Christine went on to join a pop group, and now, as a solo artist, is known as Kristine Sparkle – a sort of female Gary Glitter, only even prettier.)

Leslie Crowther had decided to leave the show after several years in which he'd helped to build it into a national institution. Leslie was 'Mr Crackerjack' to millions; he was indefatigable. He helped write the show, he was in every sketch and every song, he handled all the games. He and Peter were in the tradition of all the great comedy teams – Abbott and Costello, Burke and Hare, Rawicz and Landauer.

Two new men were brought in to replace Leslie – Rod McLennan and me. I was to be the straight man who occasionally got his come-uppance, usually in the form of a pie in the face. You can imagine my trepidation.

Producer Peter Whitmore, a cheerful man with a red twirly moustache (which a new make-up girl, believing he was one of the cast, tried to wrench from his face), reassured me that all would be well. The show had years of goodwill behind it, and it would take more than a twit like me to ruin that. His assistant was Brian Jones, who had been a variety performer himself. Brian, with his bright eyes and red button of a nose, looked like a McGill cartoon. He did the 'warm-ups' every week, which means that he went out front and worked the audience up into a state of frenzy. He was very good at it, so that by the time the show began, they were eating out of our hands.

What a thrill it was that first night. I stepped on to the stage at the Golders Green Hippodrome, and held my arms out. The audience erupted. I felt my eyes moisten as seven hundred and fifty Brownies yelled in unison, 'Where's Leslie Crowther?' In time they began to accept me, and by the end of the twenty-six week run we'd evolved into a happy successful team.

I used to take part in the occasional bit of nonsense, just to prove I wasn't a stuffy Uncle figure. One routine was set in a restaurant, the girls and I as customers getting soup and worse thrown all over us by Pete and Rod. How did we keep a straight face? We didn't. That night I went out for dinner at a posh London restaurant, and the head waiter murmured discreetly, 'I trust you will get better service here, sir, than you had this afternoon' – more proof that it's not only children who enjoy the show. Waiters, publicans, taxi-drivers, policemen – all those whose work involves odd hours seem to watch 'Crackerjack', and I'm asked regularly in pubs and trains if I have a spare pencil. Under Peter Whitmore's rule, nobody, but nobody could have a 'Crackerjack' pencil. They were exclusively for the participants in the games, and were more eagerly sought after than the most valuable prizes.

Speaking of policemen: I had an indignant letter from a retired copper who protested about my performance as a PC in our 'Rodney Righteous' finales. I wondered what he objected to – the stupidity of the character, the size of his boots (they were colossal and bright blue) or the fact that he never took his bicycle clips off? None of these. He wrote, 'Never, in my twenty-four years in the force, did I find it necessary to lick my pencil as often as you do. It would serve you right if it was indelible.' After that, I sucked it like a lolly.

Those 'Rodney Righteous' playlets were enormous fun. They were in Edwardian costume. The girls looked ravishing. Rod was dashing R. Righteous and Peter was the monumentally villainous Sir Jasper Foulpest. I trundled my bike on at the end and made stupid observations which I entered in my policeman's notebook.

One afternoon Peter began to feel very poorly after a suspicious chicken lunch. He got progressively worse, but being the trouper he is he went on with the show. During the recording he suddenly turned a pale green, an attractive hue on colour television, but a warning that something nasty was going to happen. Rod McLennan noticed the change and realized that Peter had better leave the stage. So he said something witty like, 'Go, Sir Jasper,' and Peter went. The amazing thing was that he smiled as he went. He got about three paces, but was mercifully out of shot when it happened. It was like a scene from *The Exorcist*. The audience loved it, and gave him a warm round of applause.

It was Rod's turn a few weeks later. We were performing a ballet routine, the three of us in tutus and tights. I was extremely uncomfortable because my tutu hadn't been adjusted properly, but the routine was getting laughs. Pete and Rod were doing strange things with a balloon, and I was simulating a *pas de deux*. As I swung round, arms flailing, I hit Rod smack in the face with full force as he was coming forward. He's a professional too. He grinned and danced on, his crossed eyes and bleeding nose the only signs of distress.

I can only imagine how frantic the programme must have been in the days when it was transmitted 'live'. Ever since I've been involved, it's been recorded, and it's never less than a mad scramble. Peter and Don and Jackie are constantly dashing in and out of the set, reappearing in different costumes and trying to get their breath back before the cameras get to them, while I'm handling the games and trying not to favour one child more than another because it will bring a flood of letters. I'm trying at the same time to remember the exact words I must use to introduce the film that follows, because at an agreed phrase the control room will be cueing the telecine machines to start running.

When the final game is over and I've introduced the finale, I wait until the camera goes off me, and then I, too, dash from the set, tearing off my radio microphone and then my clothes, so that Allen, the dresser, who's waiting calmly in my dressing-room can help me climb into this week's costume. I may be a Roman general, an Eskimo, a Neanderthal pop-singer, King Charles I or a Mexican bandit. I usually make it with seconds to spare – and rush back on to the set to say my two lines before the final song.

No wonder we go straight round to the pub next door as soon as the theatre's empty.

I do have to be very careful what I say on the show and to be absolutely impartial during the games. There's always some-one out of the eight million viewers (not all children) who is ready to cry 'foul! unfair! biased!'

I once introduced the show by saying – and I phrased it very carefully – that lots of children had written to ask me what hap-pened to the stack of prizes that weren't won each week. I said I was afraid I couldn't give them away, but if anyone cared to send me some brown paper and string, they could have Peter Glaze by return of post. A nice straightforward, if feeble, way of starting the show. When I arrived at the rehearsal rooms the following Monday, there, against the wall, was a mountain of brown paper and bales of string, all from young viewers who'd misunderstood what I'd said, and had sent in for their free prizes. A banner (also in brown paper) had been erected above the pile by our producer, Peter Whitmore. It said, 'Keep Your Bloody Mouth Shut!'

At the end of each series there is always a big family party for everyone involved in the programme, and the production staff occasionally give each other small presents. When I was about to move into a new flat, Allen, my dresser, very kindly pre-sented me with an antique potty, which he'd had glazed with a cheerful message. 'It will do nicely as a window-box,' he said, which came as a relief. I'd had a secret dread that he might want me to christen it before the assembled company.

One hilarious end of series party finished with a group of us going to a Greek restaurant in Soho where they practised the custom of throwing dinner-plates on to the floor at the feet of the cabaret artistes as a mark of appreciation. It's an ancient custom, its origins lost in the mists of time (actually I believe it started in the film *Zorba the Greek*). We were the guests of the management, whose hospitality was more than generous. The table was groaning with bottles. I'm ashamed to admit that I took advantage of their kindness to the extent that my plate-throwing became rather flamboyant. I don't remember much about it. Apparently I even threw an elegant fruit dish, as well as most of the crockery on our table, when really I should have restricted myself to the pile of inexpensive side-plates which had been provided. 'Another thing,' said Peter Glaze when we next met, 'you were supposed to throw the plates from the table to the dance-floor – not the other way round.' Apparently the whole restaurant had had to take cover. Anyway, Peter was in no position to criticize. When I'd last seen him, he was trying to climb into the boot of his car.

During a break in the series, Peter Whitmore, his secretary Joyce, Brian Jones and I went off with a camera crew to film sequences for our quiz. It was glorious summer. The days were so fine that we talked thereafter of 'Whitmore's Filming Weather'. It was, to use a word I flogged to death on that trip, idyllic – or, as the Australians say, 'i-bloody-dyllic'. We went all around Britain. We stopped at famous places and I was filmed from a great distance as I said, 'Where am I?' The camera, which began with a close-up of my face, then gradually zoomed out as I gave clues to my whereabouts. In the end, the whole scene was revealed. The idea was that, back in the studio, the children would get points for the speed with which they identified the place. It worked very well. We visited HMS *Victory*, Edinburgh Castle, Stonehenge, the Menai Bridge, St Paul's Cathedral, and lots of other places. And all the time the sun shone. I remember sitting on top of that white horse cut in the chalk of the Wiltshire hills, the camera crew many hundreds of yards away. I looked at the countryside spread out below me. It was quite still. Occasionally a car moved along a lane, or the sound of a tractor drifted up to me. It made me wonder where all the people were who were going to be standing shoulder to shoulder all over the world in a few years' time.

An enchanted couple of weeks. There were one or two embarrassments, inevitably. When we were filming at Caernarvon Castle, the camera crew were hidden on the other side of the river. I wasn't holding any equipment; a radio mike was secreted about my person. At the wave of a distant hankie, I started speaking. 'Where am I?' I shouted, and we then stopped filming while I explained to anxious tourists that I was perfectly all right, thank you. We saw such lovely sights that when we got back to London I wrote to the BBC suggesting that, as colour television had now arrived, wouldn't it be a good idea to film a series of programmes about the face of Britain that remained unchanged, that still retained its own character and peculiar ways in the face of progress, and despite the threat of extinction? My letter received no acknowledgement, but nine months later a series went out on BBC 2, all about 'the curious character of Britain' and how certain tucked-away places continued as they had for centuries. 'Pure coincidence, old boy,' was the reaction when I pointed out the interesting similarity to my idea, and of course I must accept that. It's not possible to copyright ideas, as I found when I put forward the notion of following a Morecambe and Wise sketch from its inception, through rehearsal and on to the stage. Eric and Ernie were all for it. The BBC said, 'Nice idea, afraid we just can't fit it in.' They managed to fit it in a couple of years later. They didn't mention who'd thought of it, but that, as someone keeps on saying, is show business.

'Crackerjack' was off the screen for a year or so, then it returned for a rather shaky series. Syd Little and Eddie Large, a couple of likeable cabaret performers, provided the comedy element and the mixture was as before: pretty girls, knockabout fun and music. It didn't really get off the ground. We needed the experience of seasoned performers like Peter Glaze, and valiantly as the new team tried, it was all a bit soggy. Syd and Eddie are still knocking them out in cabaret, so no harm was done.

I thought that it would generally be agreed that the show would now be laid decently to rest, but to my surprise and delight, it was resurrected and sprang back to life with re-

10 Here we go again. Just turn around once more for the judges, please girls.

12 Crackerjack: with Don McLean, Jackie Clark, and Peter Glaze. We've just been told we're going to get our very own Crackerjack pencils.

13 The keep-fit fanatic. Take the picture, for God's sake. I can't hold this thing much longer.

1 National Children's
Home, Harpenden,
Christmas morning 1972,
with Roy Castle. Okay, Mr
De Mille, ready when you
are.

4 Big Brother is watching
you! Jack Lemmon about
to be interviewed in the
'Personal Cinema' series.
Although his face looms
over my shoulder, he is in
fact sitting opposite me.
It's all done with mirrors.

5 Windsor Safari Park.
Sharing a joke with friendly
killer whale during BBC
Outside Broadcast.

16 Devonshire Park Theatre, Eastbourne, February 1974. *Private Lives*, Act I. Elizabeth Power willing me to remember my lines.

newed vigour. Peter Glaze returned, Don McLean became his comedy partner, joined by Jackie Clark, and myself as front man. What a team!

Pete and Don are every bit as successful as the Pete and Leslie combo. Don with his elastic mouth and gleaming horse's teeth, always ready with a different characterization and an ad lib in time of trouble, Pete the perpetually put-upon little lump, glaring with outrage through his contact lenses. (He wears glasses always, though on the show they are empty frames – it's safer that way.) Pete, too, is a man of many parts and a bewildering selection of facial expressions, all numbered. ('After No. 14 I start to bleed.') And I'm a devoted fan of Jackie Clark, one of those rare creatures who can be extremely funny and sexy too, although perhaps not at the same time. When she slips into a scanty dancing-girl costume there are appreciative cries from the Cubs in the audience, which she dispels with a quick crossing of the eyes and a mad laugh. Over the months, I've made Jackie a bit self-conscious of her attempts at dialect, which do occasionally wander a little. I must admit she did a very good South American accent in one sketch. She was playing a Scottish charlady at the time. Our latest series was directed on alternate weeks by the two Bills – Bill Ersser and Bill Wilson, who'd both done spells as floor managers at Alexandra Palace, pointing their fingers at the newsreaders, so I was in familiar, friendly company. The overall producer was Robin Nash, who is a boon to any performer. He's large and impressive, with a laugh to match. His joyful braying has drowned the children's laughter on many a recording. The show is recorded early on Tuesday evenings from the BBC TV Theatre at Shepherds Bush, and the children sit patiently peering through the maze of cameras and studio equipment between them and us while we tape the various items bit by bit, with occasional false starts and re-takes. A quick shout of 'Crackerjack', with its deafening response, usually restores flagging spirits. The 'warm-up' sessions I mentioned are changeless. With a different audience each week, why vary the routine? That's the theory – anyway. I stand there and I warn the grown-ups there's to be no mucking about or they'll have to leave. I tell them I'd like to sing a song but I've got a bad leg (joke stolen from Harry Secombe), then I introduce Don and Pete, who bound on stage and go through a noisy routine, ending with a little ditty that goes:

PETE: I wish I were a raven
And on my bench I'd sit
I wish I were a raven . . .
DON: . . . instead of a ravin' twit!

Hoots of laughter, the floor manager says, 'Stand by please, a minute to go', and we take our places. The routine doesn't vary, although we did for a time have trouble from a lad who somehow managed to get into the theatre every week. He'd lean over the balcony shouting the punch-lines to all the jokes. Eventually I invited him to visit us at the stage door for a quick strangle, and he took the hint.

All very different from newsreading, and all very enjoyable. Except, perhaps, for the finale to the 1973 series. It had gone very well, and Frankie Howerd had accepted our invitation to join us for the final sketch. He was there, ostensibly, to present us with a cake or custard pie from 'Thing' (the Director-General) as a token of his appreciation for a successful series.

The cake was in fact a twelve-foot swimming pool, which was to be filled with crazy foam. We were to mount a dais, Frankie would give me a huge knife to cut the cake with, and then I was to be pushed in – everyone else to follow.

A nice idea, but impossible to rehearse. ('Count the numbers going in,' I said. 'We don't want to lose anybody.') At the end of the show we all climbed the dais several feet above the floor. Frankie made his speech on behalf of 'Thing', and I took the mighty knife. 'I'm looking forward to this,' I said. 'Are you going to have a slice?' asked Frankie. 'I certainly am.' 'Right then – you can have the lot!' That was the signal for me to be pushed into the pie. Unknown to Frankie Howerd or to me, the children on the dais had decided to give me a big send-off, and I was pushed with great force by several small hands. I went through the air like a dart, flying foamwards at an angle of forty-five degrees. I had no way of judging exactly where the floor was, and crazy foam has no resistance. I whistled through it and crashed on to the hard floor beneath. My head, shoulder and right wrist took the impact. I was stunned for a few seconds. It was quite easy to breathe in the foam, and I was in no hurry to get up. Then it occurred to me that dying was no way to end a children's series, so I struggled to my feet, and was greeted by gales of laughter as I emerged from the foam. Soon the whole pie was full of soapy bodies, and the closing credits were shown over scenes of hilarity.

'That was fine!' said the director. 'You stayed under so long – it was very funny.'

At the party that followed, I found it easier to raise my glass with my left hand. My right wrist seemed to have seized up. Driving home was a delicate, finger-tip operation. The next morning when I was in the 'Today' office at Broadcasting House, somebody said 'What have you done to your hand?' It certainly looked odd. My fingers had become white and blue sausages. I was advised to see Matron, who took one look and then sat down and wrote a letter. 'Take this,' she said, straightening my tie and tidying my hair, 'to the Middlesex Hospital – and no stopping on the way.' At the hospital I was taken to the X-ray room, where they confirmed that my wrist was broken. The best part was when the receptionist took down the details – 'Pushed into twelve-foot custard pie,' she typed, without a blink or smile. I had a few smiles of my own, however. When I was shown into the waiting-room, the only other person there was a gentleman in an airline pilot's uniform. He looked very dashing – pale blue uniform, gold rings up to his elbow, tie dead straight, hair immaculate, cap under his arm, and no trousers. We had a drink afterwards and bored each other with how we got our injuries. He'd hurt his leg in a motoring accident, I believe. He said it didn't interfere with his work. It must have been very reassuring for the passengers to see him limping up to the plane.

When I went back to Broadcasting House in my virgin plaster and sling I met, of all people, the director of 'Crackerjack'. 'My God!' he exclaimed, 'that isn't – you didn't—?' 'Yes,' I said, my lip trembling, 'I did.' 'Oh, my God!' he cried again, and he clapped his hand to his forehead. 'This is terrible! This is awful!' 'Oh, it's not too bad,' I said, 'it only hurts when I—' 'Think of all the accident reports I shall have to make out,' he moaned 'all that paperwork . . .', and off he went, shaking his head.

I don't know if you've ever lost the use of a hand, but it's

167

only when it's out of action that you realize quite how much you rely on it. Shaving, doing up buttons, writing, driving – they all become monumental tasks. Mine wasn't a spectacular fracture – my hand wasn't dangling by a thread – but the inconvenience was enormous, and it was useless for several weeks. I managed a primitive and laborious form of handwriting with my left hand. And I grew a moustache. Its life was short – only a few weeks – but during that time I recorded a number of programmes for Yorkshire Television (as a freelance I can work for anybody). They were part of the 'Jokers Wild' series, a panel game in which two teams of comics, plus guests, listen to Les Dawson tell funny stories. They always *are* funny, so it was no hardship. I did about fifteen of the programmes, three of them with the moustache and plastered wrist. The television company stockpiled the shows, and showed them months later, but out of sequence. As a result, I popped up one week with a hairy lip and a broken wrist, the next week clean-shaven and whole, and the week after that again with a moustache and plaster. How accident-prone can you get?

If it seems odd for me to appear on a programme which is introduced by an announcer shouting 'Two teams of the nation's top comedians fight it out . . .' then I can only say it seemed odd to me too. But no-one expected the guests (who were usually actors or 'personalities') to be really funny, and I doubt if the resident comics would have been too pleased if they had. It's extremely difficult to think of jokes which can be told in public, especially three per programme for fifteen programmes. I used to turn up each week with a copy of Michael Kilgarriff's *Make 'Em Laugh* (a comedian's handbook) plus all the latest bromides that Jane and Edward had brought home from school – although not all of *those* were fit for public hearing. Jane is a clever raconteur. She gets the accents right and does a nice line in characterization. 'I say, I say!' she says, as she rushes in, dropping her school books. 'What do you get if you cross a sheep with a kangaroo?' 'I don't know – what do you get if you cross a sheep with a kangaroo?' (I've heard it all ready, but I daren't say so.) 'A woolly jumper! Boom – boom!' 'All right, then – what do you get if you cross a parrot with a lion?' 'We've heard that before Daddy, and it's not very funny, is it?'

A question of identity

Perversely, I've enjoyed doing 'Jokers Wild'. Les Dawson is always encouraging without being patronizing, and ready to laugh if it's worth it. And the dinner-parties afterwards, with Les and chairman Barry Cryer and Jack Douglas and Clive Dunn and whoever's on the panel that week, are memorable occasions. Oh, the pain.

I was once invited to do a cabaret spot. It was at one of the London airport hotels and was for a group of gentlemen in the licensed victualler's business. I can't remember how it came about; it may have been because I'd gone through a few of my favourite jokes after recording a film commentary for one of their trade shows.

The idea was attractive and yet unthinkable. Attractive because I'd never done it before, and because they were willing to pay a handsome fee; unthinkable because I'd never done it before, and the handsome fee might not cover my hospital bills.

By yet another of those extraordinary coincidences, I was due to fly to Malta the next morning to declare open the new British Forces Broadcasting Services Studios, and as the cabaret was to be held at the airport hotel, well . . .

I got hold of one of the conference folders and stuck two pages of closely-written headlines to the inside. This was necessary because I knew I'd never remember more than two jokes before their sullen silence drove the rest from my mind. Also, I thought, it was quite a clever gimmick. They might even think I was David Frost.

Came the night. I changed my underclothes for the eighth time and braced myself. The chairman gave me a fulsome introduction (Star of television . . . familiar face . . . popular personality . . .) – I could sense the buzz of anticipation. They were obviously hoping that Judith Chalmers was going to spring out wearing a piece of string and two tassels. Then he got to my name. I felt sorry for them really. They tried hard not to make their shock and disappointment too audible, but they were clearly puzzled. I launched straight into my prepared pattern before they had time to stampede for the bar.

I gave them the one about newsreaders not wearing trousers, I told them the Bank Manager's, 'You work at Harwell?' story. I got in early with a few Welsh stories, the one about the two mountaineers, and then a couple of Guinness stories, and suddenly I realized I'd got them. They were really laughing. It was a beautiful sound. I threw in a few topical references and dropped a few executives' names and they responded like an audience at 'Worker's Playtime'. When I'd finished they actually called for more, and I managed to dredge up a few salacious stories to round off the evening. Afterwards their chief thanked me so warmly that I began to wonder if they weren't going to pay me. I went to bed tired and extremely happy.

There is a belief among certain people that those of us who speak for a living want to do it all the time. They will invite us to dinner – 'Just a few friends. It'll be quite informal. I'm sure you'll enjoy it.' Then, just as we're about to fork the chicken and chippolata into our face, they'll lean over and whisper. 'It's OK. I've arranged for you to say a few words after dinner,' and then expect us to shower them with thanks. Now I'll accept an invitation to speak, if it's made well in advance. I'll think about what I'm going to say, I'll write it out, I'll commit it to memory, I'll throw it away, and I'll give a performance. But I won't enjoy the meal. I'll scribble frantic last-minute notes on the menu, I'll glance around at the faces, trying to anticipate their reception, I'll feel my appetite and confidence slipping away, and I'll wish it was tomorrow. I seem to spend a great deal of my life wishing it away, willing the time to pass so that the next batch of dinners or prize-givings will be over and I can relax, however briefly.

When I have an after-dinner speech to make, I often arrange an invitation for my good friends Eddie and Mary Ramonde ('The Blancmanges', as Jane calls them). Eddie is a founder-member of Rentalaugh. I open my mouth and say 'Good evening', and Eddie guffaws. I say 'Unaccustomed as I am', and he falls off his chair. He has – they both have – a remarkable gift for responsive listening, whether it's to the latest joke or another, 'what-do-you-think-happened-to-me-today' saga. I've bent their communal ear a good deal over the past few years, and I've never found the door bolted against me yet.

Mary, attractive, with a wide dimpled smile, invariably hits it off with the lady I bring to dinner and Eddie, bearded, bespectacled and slightly manic, greets everybody with instant warmth and familiarity – especially the ladies I bring to dinner. He is, however, a total convert to a belief about which I'm, to say the least, cynical. He believes, as many do, that an accident of birth can and does affect our every action. He believes that because he and I were born under the same star sign – Capricorn – our destinies are inescapably interwoven. What happens to me he believes will happen to him within three months. If it doesn't, he'll invent something. About a fortnight after I broke my wrist, their beloved cat, Bumface, bit Eddie's hand. Eddie was overjoyed. Destiny had struck again. He bandaged himself to the armpit. In the face of a passionate conviction on their part, I steadfastly refuse to accept that I am what I am because I was born on 12 January. In any case, Capricorns, according to the Zodiacal description, are about the worthiest (and the dullest) people to plod this earth: determined, unswerving, heavy-handed, utterly reliable; all the things I patently am not. These things can always be rationalized by the believers. 'It depends if your ruling planet was in the ascendant!' they cry. 'You were born on the cusp.' No thanks. I'll make a mess of things my way. I don't need help from the stars. It's an amusing game to play, but I'm sad to see so many people apparently becoming dependent on mystical omens for their motivations.

Magazines dealing with the occult are springing up daily. Their popularity is attributed to people's disillusionment with the materialism of modern life. I think it's more sinister than that. There are academic journals who take the ancient sciences seriously, but I think many of these magazines are cashing in on a great wave of self-indulgence. They appeal to the dark corners of human nature; although they'd claim that they're opening the doors to self-knowledge and ultimate serenity, the lurid covers and sensational articles (shrewdly punctuated by the occasional scholarly piece) prove that they're really in the business of selling cheap thrills. I think a good deal of erotic literature is marvellously stimulating; I hope I'll never cease to admire a lovely body; and I'm interested to know what makes me tick. But I don't want to bend my mind completely out of shape in the process.

Some years ago I decided that I wouldn't commit myself any longer to a sincere belief in God. I felt there was weakness and dishonesty in throwing oneself and one's ultimate responsibility in the lap of someone or something else. I felt the need all right. That was inbred. But it seemed to me an easy way out.

Polly wants a zebra

In a television programme (it was one of the 'Monday Shows'),
I once had Bernard Miles as a guest. We were talking about the
remarkable radio series he'd done on the life of Jesus, all in his
best Hertfordshire accent. I said that it had been very moving,
even for those of us who didn't necessarily believe in a Divine
presence. I received many letters about that, most of them
extremely angry. A typical letter said: 'How dare you say such
a thing? Don't you realize the responsibility you have towards
the youth of this country?' I was astounded by the hypocrisy of
it all. Was I expected to lie? Had I urged others to lose faith?
Were they so weak that a word from me would send them
into despair? And if the angry brigade themselves believed in
God, wouldn't they expect him to forgive a transgressor like
me?

It is, of course, a basic human instinct to worship. But is God
a Catholic? A Muslim? A Mormon? A Seventh-Day Adven-
tist? I can never understand how people can commit themselves to a particular sect, unless, of course, they've tried every
one in the world. I admire their supreme confidence, but not
their imagination. And it must be wrong to instil a certain
dogma in the mind of an infant, thereby closing it forever.
Sadly, but significantly, religion is all too often a bolt-hole for
the socially inadequate, the sexually repressed, the mentally
unhinged, and those who are about to die. It's also a source of
joy and comfort to many millions of perfectly normal, useful
people. That must be nice.

I do find the trappings of religion attractive – the ritual, the
music, the beautiful objects, and the magnificence of many of
the buildings. I can benefit as well as the devout from the
atmosphere of an old church. In a television discussion on religion, the panel were asked to suggest ways of bringing people
back to the Church. 'Build more old churches,' said one, and
he wasn't trying to be facetious. I'm afraid the faith has eluded
me. I have to rely on good, day-to-day human relationships. I
don't want to go upstairs for help, and I don't want to start
digging either. One thing I'll acknowledge – and I believe in
the existence of the man as an historical character – Jesus was a
Capricorn.

Where was I? Yes, I was telling you about my friends the
Ramondes. In the past few years, we've been making cassettes

for the children's market. We started with historical subjects, went on to natural history, and lately, a series of fairy stories. One of our major titles was the story of Lord Baden Powell, the founder of the Scout movement, a special copy of which was presented to Sir William Gladstone, the Chief Scout. These recordings have also been produced as long-playing records. It's amusing to listen to them and remember the circumstances of their production. Eddie has his own very small studio; from the outside of the building there is no sign of it. Although the dramatized episodes sometimes sound as if they have a cast of thousands, it's usually Eddie and Mary and me and the bloke upstairs. I'd disappear into the building carrying a briefcase and looking like a brisk young executive, and minutes later there'd be shouts and screams and animal noises as we'd record the relief of Mafeking, or Pinocchio being turned into a donkey. Some very dark rumours began to spread among the neighbours.

When we were doing the Baden Powell story, I needed the voices of two or three teenage boys for a re-enactment of an incident from B. P.'s days at Charterhouse. I contacted a stage school, and they sent some lads along to Eddie. I listened to the recording. It was unusable. Instead of the sons of gentlemen romping on the playing fields of a venerable public school at the turn of the century (cries of 'spiffing!' 'top-hole!' and 'cavey, chaps!'), they sounded like a bunch of layabouts having a Saturday night punch-up outside the *palais de danse*. One line in particular was a problem. One boy has to say to another in a cultured drawl, 'There's a method in his madness, don't you think?' Eddie had a solution. 'The lads upstairs will do it,' he said 'they're a nice family.' And so they were. What he didn't tell me was that they were Irish. So we now had two versions of the line. One was, 'There's a mefod in 'is madness, doncha fink?' The other went: 'Dere's a metod in his madness, don't ye tink?' I toyed with the idea of changing the title to 'The brutal story of B. P. – Basher Powell', or 'B. P. – Brendan O'Powell of the Ballymurphy Troop'. Or scrap the whole idea. In the end I did the line myself. To get the right timbre of voice I grasped myself in a delicate spot and spoke quickly. We recorded it in one take.

I spend a good deal of time at the Ramondes'. Long sessions of listening to records, watching their collection of W. C. Fields

movies, or doing our own Goonish tape recordings of im-
promptu dramas or spoof interviews, which we send out as
Christmas presents to people who've never done us any harm.
Or Eddie will try to catch me out with a specially compiled
series of clips from movie sound-tracks. 'Who's this, then?'
'Elisha Cook Jr.' 'Swine! I'll get you yet!'

We were all down at Brighton one evening – it's not rare to
motor down to Wheeler's for dinner – and were having a drink
in one of the hotels. At the bar was a man in evening dress who
rubbed his hands together in managerial fashion and said,
'Good evening, Mr Aspel. Nice to see you. What will you have?'
I was flattered to be recognized, and I airily ordered two large
gin and tonics and a couple of brandies. The waiter brought
them to our table. I went to pay him, and he said, 'No need,
Sir – it's on the other gentleman.' The man I'd taken to be the
manager was a guest like ourselves. There was no sign of him.

I was still blushing over the incident when a shadow fell over
the table. A man stood, swaying gently, and staring at me.
'Danger Man!' he accused. I suppose there could, in certain
circumstances – such as a very dark room – be a vague resem-
blance between Patrick McGoohan and myself. The man
seemed so sure that I was Danger Man that I thought it best
to smile nicely and say yes, and he'd go away happy. I gave a
modest nod.

'Didn't reckon your last series,' said the man.

'Sorry,' I said, hoping he wouldn't say any more.

'Never mind, a lot of people get pleasure from it,' he said,
burping. 'What are you doing now?'

'Well,' I said, 'I've just done a film with Charlton Heston,
and I'm off to buy some property in Hollywood.'

'Good luck,' he said, and turned away. As he went he told
the people at a nearby table, 'I've just been talking to Roger
Moore.' They looked surprised.

I usually enter strange bars a little warily, particularly if it's
fairly late in the evening. It's not so much that I'm afraid of
flying glass, but people do tend to get a bit outspoken with a
few drinks inside them, and I'm not always sure I'm going to
like what they say. A woman may nudge her husband and
point me out, and he may react by saying, 'Who? – Oh, him.
Isn't he nice? Hello, Michael' – and he'll start blowing kisses

and generally asking for a mouthful of signet rings while I wish *a*) I was wearing a false moustache and *b*) that he wasn't quite so big. I tell my partner to drink up. Once, in a crowded bar, I was forced into conversation with two ladies who were so disappointed with me that they got quite angry. 'What a let-down!' said one. 'Sorry,' I said, 'not as tall as you expected?' 'No!' she shouted. 'Not as good looking?' 'You're nothing *like* him!' the other one snapped, and we stood there, together, running me down, for about ten minutes.

I went to Torquay one summer to open a hospital fête. It was a glorious day, and we were driven to the grounds in an open Rolls – a Silver Ghost, I think it was. On the way we met a funeral cortège. The hearse went by – and then I was spotted by one of the mourners, who sprang to the window and waved her hankie. Within seconds there were people at the windows of every limousine, laughing and shouting, and as they finally disappeared I could still hear the cries of 'Crackerjack!' and, 'Wish I had your job!'

There are, as I've explained, occasional cases of mistaken identity. I was once out walking with my first wife, Dian, when a woman came up to us with an autograph book. I reached for my pen, but she ignored me, and said to Dian, 'Can I have your autograph, please – you *are* Judith Chalmers, aren't you?'

During a break in rehearsals for one of the many awards ceremonies I've compered, I was having a drink with floor manager Ronnie Pantlin and several of his team, at one of the bars at the Cafe Royal. Suddenly an old man detached himself from a group of people at the other side of the room and came towards us, his hand outstretched. 'I've been watching you!' he grinned, and he tottered nearer. 'Excuse me, lads,' I said, wiping my palm on my sleeve. As the old man drew level, I put out my hand. 'Get out of it!' he snapped, and pushed past me. The barman, it transpired, was a long lost pal of his. Ronnie and the others were very sympathetic. They just pointed at me and howled with laughter.

I really don't mind too much if the joke's on me, I'm quite happy to spend most Saturdays during the summer at various charity functions, but I do not like being used.

Being asked down for a quiet weekend and finding my name on the hoardings as the fête-opener was one experience I didn't enjoy. All they had to do was ask. A colleague did ask me once, as he passed me in the corridor, if I'd like to come to his wedding. 'Fine,' I said. 'Will you be best man?' he said. I was a bit taken aback, but agreed. On the wedding day he was holding his head and nudging his chums about the wild night they'd had. As I'd not been invited to that, I had to conclude that I was there as a professional. I waived my normal fee as a wedding present.

Bazaars and garden parties are usually quite enjoyable, even if the letter that invited you said, 'We've tried everybody, we're desperate, will you help?' The children always come home laden with plunder, and we see some pretty places. School speech-days I shy away from, not just because I don't like making speeches, but because the whole idea strikes me as presumptuous. By standing there in front of hundreds of bright young people, I imply that they too, if they're extraordinarily gifted, and ready to work hard, can be like me. Cricket matches are best. I love the game, although its skills elude me. It's therapeutic to stand out there, breathing fresh air, hoping the ball won't come your way, crossing slowly back and forth at the end of each over, occasionally sprinting towards the boundary in a vain chase, anticipating the taste of the beer when the stumps are finally pulled. It's a great honour to be allowed to play on such hallowed turfs as the Oval and Lords. 'Throw me a few easy ones,' you whisper to the demon professional bowler as you go in to bat. 'I'm only a learner.' So he does, and you hit them hard, and he then pins you against the sight-screen for being cocky.

Andy Williams played cricket at the Oval a year or two ago in a benefit match. 'A sparkling twenty-eight runs', was how his score was described in the press. He made them baseball style, standing at the wicket with his legs apart, bat raised above his shoulder. Later, he gently worked his way to an exit near a distant boundary, where a fast car was waiting to whisk him away from the clutches of his fans. When I went out to bat I made some wild flailing movements without the leather contacting the willow. In short, I missed every ball. 'Bring back Andy Williams!' shouted a wag in the crowd. 'Bring back *Emlyn* Williams!' shouted another. I was bowled before they got to Bransby.

A question of identity

The unpredictability of people's reactions makes a television performer very light on his toes. One moment you'll be doing someone the greatest honour in the world by writing your name on a bit of paper, the next you'll be fighting for your life with some irate viewer who wants to hammer you personally for all the crap he has to endure on the screen.

I had a bitter-sweet experience not so long ago when I bought various bits and pieces in a department store and went to their cashier to pay for the lot. 'Oh!' gasped the woman behind the counter, 'I shall have to have your autograph.' So I wrote a cheerful message for her. The word spread around the office that someone from the telly was out front, and dozens of pieces of paper were sent out for me to sign. It was a moment of supreme glory. Eventually I turned to the lady who'd started it all, and wrote out the cheque for the stuff I'd bought. Her manner changed instantly. She squinted at the cheque and snapped 'Have you got some means of identification?'

The most magnificent put-down of them all, and quite un-cappable, didn't have anything to do with me. It happened at the reception desk at Broadcasting House. Apparently there was a programme about monarchs who'd been unfrocked or decomposed or whatever it is that happens to them when they lose their crowns and go into exile. Quite a number were turning up at the BBC, and the harassed receptionist was heard to say, as she reported the arrival of yet another, 'I'm sorry – where did you say you were king of?'

15
California here I come!

As the programmes I do become more and more diversified, my 'image' becomes less and less clearly defined, which bothers me not at all. I am in no sense a specialist, and never could be – although I do seem to be firmly established in many people's minds as a children's entertainer. I have a television programme (an occasional, rather than regular series) on BBC 1 in which I show clips from shows that were particularly enjoyable or spectacular, and I have star guests who answer questions the viewers have sent in. It's called 'Ask Aspel' and ask me they do. The children want to see the Osmonds or David Cassidy or Chelsea's winning goal. The adults think I'm some sort of Ombudsman, another Bernard Braden. They ask me to re-arrange the television schedules, to banish certain people, and to send them locks of hair from others. By the number of letters we get, it seems to be a popular programme. On holiday in Italy a small boy came up to me and said, 'Hello Ask.' That was one of my favourite encounters, and that's how I'm now known in the 'Ask Aspel' office.

I think I might be a little less popular with some of the girls who watch 'Ask' if they knew that I've never actually met David Cassidy, although he was one of my guests.

When David was available for filming his spot in the programme, I was not, so my producer, Frances Whitaker, sat opposite him and put the questions while the camera stayed on his face.

He played along with the idea very well, and even called her 'Michael' every now and then to add verisimilitude. Afterwards I went along and recorded the questions. My voice was added to the sound-track in place of Frances's, and the net result was that David Cassidy was interviewed by an invisible 'Ask'.

I once had the idea of compiling a slim volume from all the unusual letters I've received over the years – the whimsical, the outrageous, the pathetic, the hilarious. It would probably get a bit boring. But there have been some beauties since the lady in Wales pointed out my waggling Adam's Apple.

When I left Wales, a viewer wrote a warm farewell and offered me best wishes for the future, ending with the affectionate reminder: 'We'll keep a Welshman in the hillside.'

We all seem to have heard from the lady who apologized for sitting too close to the screen. She hoped it wasn't putting us off, but her eyes were bad.

One letter expressed a doubt that seems to have been in the minds of many viewers over the years. 'I've not been in this country very long time,' he wrote, 'but I'm wishing to know where you buy your wig.' May I please scotch that rumour for ever. My hair is my own. It grows fast and plentiful. There's an abundance of grey creeping into it, but every strand grows directly out of my head. The short, Italian-style haircut I used to favour made it look so set as to be unreal, and the legend has persisted. There was once a report in a newspaper that a certain newscaster wore a toupee. Perhaps – but it wasn't me.

'May I have a photograph of you in bathing trunks and *all* your measurements?' wrote a viewer who I hope was female. I couldn't supply either, though I was tempted to invent some mammoth dimensions just to disturb her.

A letter I treasure is from a lady who wrote to me when I left Alexandra Palace. 'I'm sorry to learn that you will not be reading the news any more,' she wrote, 'but I would like you to know how much pleasure I have had over the years from your projection.'

I gave a little less pleasure to a certain ex-colleague of mine when I was quoted in the press as saying that newsreading was not a full-time job for a grown man. He wrote to me and pointed out that it wasn't the first time I'd knocked my old job. I replied that of course I hadn't been quoted fully: nothing had been said about the happy times I'd had, or the exciting moments, but at the same time I felt bound to point out that it had seemed to me then, as it did now, that any job that required one to do a few hours' work for a couple of days a week, with no responsibility other than opening one's mouth, was not a job at all, but a sinecure.

There was one time, about ten years ago, perhaps more, when I thought my career was about to take a dramatic turn. The film producer, Hal Roach, a famous name from the past, came to London and sent for me. 'Young man,' he said, 'before your time I used to make movies with a feller called Harold Lloyd. Now I've been sent over here by MGM to make some new movies. I've seen you on TV and I think you're the man.' He outlined the stories he meant to film, and talked about the sort of money I would make, which was a lot. My agent, Bagenal Harvey, hadn't come into my life then, so nothing was committed to paper, no agreements were signed. The talks continued for six weeks or so, then there was silence. The films were never made, and I didn't see Mr Roach again. But the idea was nice while it lasted.

I think one of the most exciting developments for me has been the amount of travelling I've done in recent years. I'll never notch up the mileage of the news and documentary teams, but I've been around. Most of the journeys have been privately arranged and therefore paid for by me, but there have been some worthwhile working trips. When the Common Market arrived there was a good deal of to-ing and fro-ing between the member countries for various programmes. I've broadcast from Belgium, Holland, and Gibraltar. I've brought back recordings from the West Indies and America as well as popping across to the Channel Isles to introduce programmes.

My trip to Malta for the British Forces Broadcasting Service was memorable. I'd been invited to declare open their new studios, which I'd assumed meant a quick 'God Bless Her and all who fluff in her', and then round to the mess for a quick g. and t., ice and slice. (I now favour gin, having found that my previous favourite, whisky, was beginning to make me morose.) But no. It was a full military operation, the duties being shared between the Army Commander in Malta, and myself. At 18.27 hours precisely, the staff car collected me from my hotel, and we headed for Floriana and the ceremony.

It was a dinner-jacketed affair. One of the studio staff eyed my blue velvet tie. 'The Brigadier won't like that,' he whispered. 'What do you mean?' I said, getting indignant. 'Well, he likes to wear them himself,' he said. The Brigadier arrived. We were introduced. He was wearing a blue velvet tie, and he glared at my throat. After the speeches and tape-cutting we all had cocktails and then I was whisked back to the Commander's residence for dinner. When I got there, the Brigadier had changed into a white tuxedo and was wearing a pink bow tie. What's more, he was carrying a multi-coloured bunch of spares to show me what he could have worn if he'd felt like it.

It was a splendid evening. The air was balmy. The ladies were elegant, the atmosphere was very Noël Coward.

After dinner, the Brigadier handed out shawls to the ladies and dismissed them while we men passed the port. There were several generals there, and they all looked like advertisements for VP wine.

The next day the navy gave us an invigorating ride around the harbour in a powerful gunboat, the RAF entertained us for drinks and I finally had a few in the squaddies' mess before being flown home.

Italy has always been a magnet for me; even more so for Ann. She fell in love with the country at first sight, and goes back every year. She's even taken her GCE in the language. I was put on to a particular region of the country by an Italiophile friend whose wife is herself Italian. She becomes embarrassed by his lack of inhibition. I've been with them on holiday, and he strides about the place singing snatches of opera and embracing everyone he meets. The part he favours, and I've grown to love, is the top left-hand coast, just south of Genoa and La Spezia. It's known as the Bay of Poets because, as my friend Frank says, 'Byron, Shelley, Thackeray – all the lads used to come here!' It's the bay where Shelley was drowned, in fact. It has a castle at each end of the bay, a small beach, and a fishing village.

Frank tells me there's a monastery not far away with a notice on the outer wall. It means to proclaim that the monks will take care of anyone in need, whatever their trouble, and regardless of their denomination. What it actually says, in English, is, 'The brothers within have all diseases and do not care about religion.' I don't believe him.

A few years ago I determined to have a change. The following summer I wouldn't chase the sun, I'd go to Ireland and wallow in the lush greenery of that enchanted land. It was the day after Boxing Day that I made up my mind. I was seeing off the last of the Christmas drinks, and I was in a euphoric state. I telephoned this hotel in Kerry, a hotel which had been strongly recommended in various books. The line was atrocious. They were obviously celebrating at the other end too. I finally managed to explain that I wanted a couple of rooms next June. 'That's grand, sor, that's grand!' said the distant voice. A week later I received an enormous envelope which was about an inch thick and designed to look like an old oak chest. I creaked the lid open, and found all sorts of bits and pieces inside.

'Dear Sir,' said the covering note, 'We thank you for your enquiry. We enclose our tariff and details of all the local goings-on at that time, which we're sure you'll find most interesting. We assure you of our best attention at all times. By the way, we don't have any rooms vacant. Yours, etc.' It made me all the more determined to go. I found rooms at a gigantic, soulless modern hotel in Killarney and as soon as possible after our arrival we went off in search of the original hotel. It was cosy and attractive. The owner was mortified to find he'd had to disappoint us, and to prove his sincerity he invited us to lunch the next day. We started that lunch at 1.15 and finished at four the next morning. He brought us each a lobster that was so big it must have fought off fifteen men, he got out his own personal stock of wine, and the party continued through the day and into the night. At the end of it all, he wouldn't take a penny. Perhaps what he actually said was that he *couldn't* take a penny; he was incapable of holding his hand out. It was a marvellous holiday. It rained every day; the ponies we hired turned back half-way to the beauty-spot, just as they'd been trained to. One even threw me off. I described a very slow arc over his head and landed on my base with arms and legs in the air. Very painful, and very amusing for the others.

They were still filming *Ryan's Daughter* nearby. David Lean used to come into the hotel for dinner every night. I put on my best suit and paused by his table every night reciting lines from *Lawrence of Arabia*, but he took no notice. Maurice Jarre was bashing out the music for the film in the rooms below mine, so I felt a certain affinity with it when it was finally released.

Ever since I was a very small boy, I have wanted to go to

California here I come!

America. At first it was simply because of what I saw in the pictures: skyscrapers and cowboys. Then we got our own skyscrapers and I lost interest in cowboys, but the desire to go to the States remained. In fact it grew, and after three attempts to visit the place, all of which had to be cancelled because of work, it had become a jinx which I had to beat, a need that had to be fulfilled.

I had to wait until I was forty years old before I finally got my chance. I had just started making the tape cassettes. Someone pointed out that there were six million Scouts in America, and that one person in every five was in some way involved in the movement. My business partner at that time, whose name I shall not mention because it gives me pain, suggested that we go to New York to meet the local representative of the cassette producers and pay a visit to Scout Headquarters. They would surely be interested in our life-story of their beloved leader, Lord Baden Powell.

So in January 1973, my dream came true. I climbed aboard a Boeing 747 at Heathrow and within hours we were flying over America. I couldn't believe it. When the pilot announced that the lights of Boston were visible below, I dropped my earphones and magazines and rushed to the other side of the plane. I no longer cared if I upset the balance.

The streets of New York were bleak, grey, and bitterly cold. My hotel room was the same; but I was too excited to sleep. I stared and stared at those lights and those battered yellow taxis. As soon as possible I booked a seat on a sight-seeing bus trip. We did the town. 'Look up through the glass roof of the bus,' said the commentator in a flat voice. We looked up, but we could see nothing. All was condensation. The rain bounced off the glass roof of the bus and cascaded down the windows; the Statue of Liberty was barely visible; from the top of the Empire State Building, instead of the sight of ships at sea forty miles away as promised, there was a fine view of fog. I loved every minute. I suffered slightly from claustrophobia in the taxis. They have built bulwarks between the driver and the passenger. You speak through a wire mesh, and put your fare into a metal tray which swivels round to the driver's side. Human contact is at a minimum. I saw no mugging in the streets, but I believe there was plenty. The hotel telephone operator was a delight. She had precisely the same voice as the girl in the 'Laugh-In' sketches. 'Your number plee -erse,' she would coo, 'one moment plee -erse.' I loved the sound of the telephones. They had that single mellow ring – just as they did in the movies!

I bought a pair of shoes on Broadway, just to be able to tell people. The negro assistant was a cheery soul.

'You got it!' he shouted as he gave me my change, 'right on, baby!'

Jackie Molloy had by this time joined her mother, who'd gone to live in America. They were out on the West Coast, as far from New York as New York is from London. But it seemed to be silly to be on the same continent and not meet. So Jackie flew east, I flew west, and we met in Chicago, which is hardly half-way, but saved me a long trip. We had a couple of days together, strolling along the shores of Lake Michigan, visiting the splendid art gallery and thinking how very different it was from Rainham in Essex, where we'd last met. Then I went back to New York, Jackie went back to California. A few days later I was back in London. I'd fulfilled an ambition, and was itching to go back and see more. The business trip? That was a flop. The Scouts gave us their Gold Seal of approval, but I don't think we've sold any cassettes over there. Business isn't my scene. I merely produce the stuff; it's up to others to market it. My lack of business sense has cost me a great deal. One thing I have learned is that I haven't learned a thing.

In spite of the availability of several attractive companions, I always seemed to end up thinking about Jackie. Ours had been a fairly stormy relationship, but a lot of fun, and I missed her. So I was more than ready to take up the invitation to go out to California for a holiday the following summer.

I carefully laid my plans, arranging what work I could around the dates I wanted to be free. I booked my flight well in advance. There were a few last-minute heart failures and near cancellations, but in mid-June I was back at Heathrow and climbing aboard a plane for Los Angeles. It was a long, long trip. I spent the night (the American night – the English night had passed during the journey) – in Los Angeles, then flew up to Oakland, about three hundred and fifty miles north. There Jackie met me, looking bronzed and her hair sun bleached, and there began a wonderful three weeks. She lived a twenty-minute drive from San Francisco which, like Paris, is a city that does not disappoint. It's just like the songs say, with the cable cars and hills where *Bullitt* and every other movie car chase was filmed. Alcatraz sits, unoccupied now, out in the bay. The magnificent Golden Gate Bridge glows redly in the sun or peeps through the mist, while the Bay Bridge opposite carries traffic to and from Oakland and beyond. Chinatown, Fisherman's Wharf, all the colourful spots are there as you've read about them.

Jackie's mother had shrewdly written to the local broadcasting station to let them know that a great international TV star was arriving from England. She must have made some extravagant claims, because I was invited to go on an afternoon radio phone-in show run by a man called Jim Easton. When I turned up I was amazed and delighted to see a familiar face. Gay Byrne of Dublin's RTE was also a guest. I'd last seen Gay when I'd been a guest on his own TV spectacular, 'The Late Late Show', in Dublin, a few years earlier. Gay explained to Jim Easton that his name was short for Gabriel, and that point cleared up, we went on to spend most of the afternoon on the radio show, answering queries from listeners about British and Irish broadcasting, and about the way of life in the Old Country. One caller was embarrassingly fulsome in her welcome to me, and expressed the hope that I'd be appearing on coast-to-coast TV while I was in the States. I confessed to Gay afterwards that I'd recognized the voice. It was Kay – Jackie's mother, always the opportunist. Afterwards we drove over the Golden Gate Bridge as the sun was sinking, and had dinner at Sauselito, a fishing village across the bay.

That whole trip was a dream. We drove down to Monterey, where I posed for photographs by the 'Cannery Row' street sign, near the Steinbeck Theatre. Then along the magnificent Seventeen-Mile Drive – a wild stretch of coastline dotted with expensive houses and containing the Del Monte Lodge, where the Bing Crosby Pro-Am golf tournaments are held. Just south of there is the village of Carmel, neat and pretty. Clint Eastwood owns a restaurant there. The dishes are named after his movies – you can get a 'Few Dollars More' sandwich and a slice of 'Dirty Harry' Pie.

Polly wants a zebra

We also took a weekend trip north to the Sierra Nevada – huntin' and fishin' country. I caught no fish, but Kay's American husband, Chuck, loaned me his ·38 special and I had a fine time shooting beer cans off rocks. He had a large selection of firearms. (Every American family has a phone, a fridge, and a gun.)

One of the most astounding sights of America is the number of fat people, really gross creatures, whole families of them waddling into restaurants and tucking into ham 'n' eggs, hash browns, and flapjacks with maple syrup – and that's just for breakfast.

You see them cruising around the car parks at supermarkets, trying to get that little bit closer to the front door and so save walking a few paces; for the Great American Dream is never to leave your car. It's hardly necessary anyway. You can cash a cheque, buy food, eat it, and go home without your feet touching the ground.

I've read a lot over the years about the savagery of American barmen and shop assistants, and I've heard one or two first-hand accounts of astounding rudeness. But I was lucky – I met with unrelenting politeness just about everywhere. Perhaps they're a bit nicer on the West Coast. Every waitress, every shop assistant approached us with a big smile and a 'How are *you* today?', and when we left they always called, 'Have a nice day'.

I don't suppose they would have cared for a moment if our wheels had fallen off, but at least they *pretend*.

So often you go into a shop at home and are greeted with tight lips, raised eyebrows and a jerk of the head, to which I always respond with a corresponding jerk so that we go on like a couple of marionettes until one of us cracks.

If you stop for petrol on an American freeway, your windscreen is washed as part of the service. Our garages don't seem to carry the necessary equipment.

To many Americans, the world ceases to exist beyond the US coastguard stations. I was staggered by some of the questions I was asked about life in Britain. Do our mothers use pushchairs? Do we still have public executions?

But it's not possible to take offence at such open and warmhearted people. They may not know a thing about our country, but they insist that you enjoy and want to return to theirs.

California here I come!

I was the perfect tourist over there – gaping, taking pictures, buying mementos and all, of course, without being recognized by a soul. No autograph books, no cries of 'Crackerjack!' no Miss World nudges. I was too excited to know if I missed it.

Best of all – Hollywood and Disneyland, greatest wonder of the world. I put my feet in the footprints of the stars outside Grauman's Chinese Restaurant. I found that John Wayne's feet are tiny, and that Humphrey Bogart's were the same size as mine (a manly nine). We toured Universal Studios, saw a house that burns all the year round. We saw the house where Antony Perkins did those terrible things in *Psycho*, and the house where Gregory Peck lived in *To Kill a Mocking Bird*. We saw Mexican towns, Vietnamese villages, and a demonstration of the parting of the Red Sea all in a temperature of 108°. Snapshots show me as a wizened old man with sunken eyes. We were shown Lucille Ball's dressing-room, which was a complete house, furnished like a Georgian mansion.

Television in America is a non-stop, low-grade affair. Silence is a crime; while the credits of one show are rolling, a voice advertises something else. The audiences at American quiz shows make the 'Golden Shot' congregation seem like Trappist monks. They scream and jump up and down and clap their hands and keep on screaming. No words, just the endless shriek.

There's a news channel in San Francisco where all the team wear blazers and ties with the station's emblem. They do very jokey news bulletins, and the weatherman leans on the desk and laughs throughout. He finishes his forecast by saying, 'Bye now. Take care of yourselves. We love you and we want you back.'

Disneyland is wonderful. My only complaint is that there were rather too many children there. It's the most professional, efficiently run, imaginative and ingenious set of attractions I've ever seen. It overwhelms all one's critical faculties. It's clean, too. No endless acres of empty cartons and wrappers. It's divided into different Lands – Storyland, Tomorrowland, Frontierland, Fantasyland. You can go down in a submarine, and watch almost-real divers fighting monsters from the deep, whiz through the treetops in a monorail, go in the Haunted Mansion where the floor sinks and lures you into a freaky world of back-projected films and special spooky effects. You can take a ride in a boat through subterranean passages to see 'The Pirates of the Caribbean' – lifelike figures fighting and yo-ho-hoing on full-scale model ships. It's vast, stunning. And every evening Mickey Mouse and Snow White lead the whole cast of Disney characters up the Main Street for the big parade. When I'm a big boy I'm going again.

Back in England, I had startling news. A week or so after Gay Byrne and I had appeared on Jim Easton's radio show in San Francisco, they had had a real-life drama. The studio is on the ground floor, with windows on to the street. Passersby wave and mouth greetings. One afternoon there had been a banging at the window. Everyone in the studio had turned to see a man emptying his revolver at them. The glass was of course soundproof and heavy enough to protect them, but the gunman ran round to the front door, where he was met by an executive of the company who tried to remonstrate with him and was shot dead. A secretary was shot and wounded, and then the man turned the gun on himself. The inquiry revealed that the dead man believed himself to be consumed by radio waves and that he must destroy the station and the broadcasters. I suppose it could happen anywhere. Mental illness isn't a prerogative of the United States.

16
Moving target

My only little piece of England, my blessed plot in Hereford
that the children had thought of such quaint names for, was not
to be mine for long. A few years ago I thought the time had
come to get involved in something other than broadcasting, to
find a business interest which could become my mainstay if I
lost my voice. I found the very thing. I was asked to record
some commentaries for a company who were going to market
a new teaching aid. It consisted of a series of slides and tape
recordings, plus responder-units with buttons marked A, B, C,
D, which the pupils would press in response to certain questions. Their answers would show on a console on the teacher's
desk. The teacher could see who had answered correctly and
who had not. He could stop the lesson at any time. The company had acquired a massive mathematics programme, and
they wanted me to record the lessons. I would have no idea
what I was talking about, but I had been a radio actor, so I
could probably disguise my confusion.

It all seemed to me such a nice, clean, worthwhile business,
and the independent assessment of its value by education ex-
perts was so encouraging that I suggested that I took no fee but
accepted shares in the company instead. The company in turn
suggested I might like to buy a directorship. I thought about
it for a while – for a very short while – and agreed. With all my
savings (and quite a lot of the bank's) I became a director, and
set about employing colleagues and other well-known voices to
record the hundreds of lessons in the maths course. I did a large
number myself, of course.

I don't know what went wrong. People did try to explain.
Phrases like 'cash flow' were used. There wasn't any, it seemed,

and to stay in business it seemed reasonable that cash had to flow. It was a matter of timing, I think. The education authorities approved of the system, but none was ready to buy. Our independent researchers had been wildly over-optimistic. People began to drift away and withdraw support. I was confused, depressed. Everything seemed to have gone. I had insisted all along that the 'voices' were paid as they made the recordings, but had taken no payment for myself. That would have been pointless. Nevertheless I was led to believe that all would be well. We were about to be bought up by a large concern who would take over the company's present debts, which were considerable. On the basis of this information I signed a guarantee. The buyers changed their minds. We were not taken over, and I was left with a ruined company and responsibility for its debts. I began to pay.

The cottage in Hereford was complete by this time, and very pretty it was too. I had had high hopes for it as a summer home, and perhaps as a permanent base. It had to go, and I was left with rented accommodation.

I have now paid off the entire debt, and it has not been easy.

And yet I can't get very emotional about it. Friends and other sensible people get angry on my behalf and exasperated at my foolishness, and my agent has now forbidden me to lick a stamp without his approval. I've never been accustomed to having a great deal of money, and losing all I had simply made me shrug my shoulders and try to think about other things. I get quite heated if I'm delayed by traffic lights, but when things are really tough – well, *c'est la vie*. Perhaps I should do what one of Spike Milligan's characters did in 'Puckoon'; he had the faces of his enemies inlaid in his lavatory bowl. There might be some satisfaction in that.

My losses didn't stop me travelling. Broadcasting is a spasmodic affair, and in the gaps I like to keep on the move, even if it's only a trip to the nearest river bank.

I did a series of presentations for one of the big package-tour operators, going around the country and introducing their new schedules to travel agents. At the end of the series, they suggested I join them on one of their trips. It wasn't entirely free, but the price wasn't exorbitant. We went to Jamaica. It was a long, long trip with one stop-off. As we flew into Bermuda, the pilot gave us a chatty description of what we would see, and finished by saying, 'As we make our final approach, ladies and gentlemen, you will notice that there are, scattered about, one or two very lovely cuh-cuh-cuh-coral islands.' I was busy recording this and all the announcements for possible programme use, and the stammering came as a shock. 'If *he's* nervous,' I thought, 'how are *we* supposed to feel.'

In fact it was, as I discovered later, only a very occasional impediment, and the pilot was as cool and efficient as they come. He and his wife were taking a holiday too, and I got to know them.

'Roy's stammer can be a bit embarrassing at times,' his wife told me cheerfully. She remembered the time when he'd introduced her to one of the company's air hostesses. He said, 'I'd like you to meet Jean. She's one of the first girls I ever fuh-fuh-fuh-flew with.'

When we arrived at Montego Bay at eleven o'clock at night, the heat was stifling. A cameraman approached me at the airport. 'Where's your wife?' he demanded. 'I haven't got one,' I said. 'But you're supposed to be on honeymoon,' he said petulantly. 'Sorry,' I said, 'you must be thinking of two other people.' 'Your car awaits, milord,' said a set of teeth, which flashed in the darkness, and a carload of us was whisked away in the cool of an air-conditioned limousine on the sixty-mile journey to our hotel.

Jamaica was certainly different. Not a single blade of vegetation was like anything I'd ever seen before, and there were more beautiful people in one place than I'd ever seen. The hotel was superb, I was shown into a suite with ankle-deep carpets, two enormous white leather couches, primitive paintings on every wall (one of which was entirely of glass and led on to the verandah, with the sea ten paces away). There were flowers and buckets of champagne.

A bedroom contained two full-sized four-poster canopied beds; there was another bedroom with bathroom en suite, and a kitchen with fully-stocked fridge. And me. 'It's all a mistake!' I shouted, popping the corks. The next day I scotched the honeymoon rumour and asked to be moved to less grandiose quarters.

Unfortunately, although the hotel and its setting were so

marvellous, the weather wasn't. It rained torrentially for the first four days, swelling the river that flowed into the bay and turning the blue Caribbean into a Southend brown.

There was an uneasy atmosphere about the island. Some of the locals were charming, others surly and unco-operative. The hotel staff were not keen to work. Of course we understood why; we were the exploiters, the colonizers and plunderers of their land. The English were particularly unpopular. Ironically, the chef was a Spaniard, and popular with the staff, I was told. The fact that the Spaniards had killed every living member of the original Arawak tribe had been forgiven. Prices were gauged to the American market, and very high. Service was poor. One afternoon a group of us ordered some drinks and sandwiches. After a very long time they arrived. The waiter was immaculately dressed, and the crockery and linen of the finest quality. As he laid the table, he dropped a plate. He stared down at the fragments. 'Oh, shit,' he apologized.

I have no complaints about the social life. I had a very nice time, although I was disappointed in my hope of getting to talk to any of the local beauties. That was quite taboo. But it is a glorious place – lush vegetation, glorious beaches – there's even a waterfall that cascades and tumbles over layers of rocks, right down to the sand.

I knew that the water teemed with life; I'd heard that a marlin weighing 610 pounds had been hauled from the bay not long before. A group of us took a boat for five hours. We went fifteen miles out, and caught nothing. We had more excitement from a trip round the bay in a glass-bottomed boat. There were wondrous things to be seen – fish of every shape and hue, fantastic coral, and sudden, breathtaking canyons dropping away for hundreds of feet.

One lazy day I was lying on a raft with half a dozen others about a hundred yards from shore when a diver broke the surface and hauled himself aboard. He tore his mask off and lay gasping on the boards. His face was white – I mean he was deathly pale. He had just come face to face with a barracuda, one of the deadliest creatures of the sea, consisting mainly of a mouthful of cruel teeth. It's one of the few predators that will attack without provocation. He had remembered that the thing to do in such circumstances was to swim towards the creature.

Not an easy thing to do, but he steeled himself, and after circling him a few times, the barracuda swam away. When he'd recovered his breath and composure, he glanced at his inches-thick underwater watch and said, 'Twenty-past five. Time to get back.' Actually it was ten-past six. His watch had stopped. The shock must have been enormous.

Now came the problem. We all had to get back to land – but where was the barracuda? It was unusual for them to be so close inshore, and it was probably back in the deep, but we couldn't be certain. 'Only one thing for it,' I said, 'we'll have to go back in a shoal. One-two-three!' And in we all went. I spent the first ten seconds threshing wildly with arms and legs, about eighteen inches above the surface like a Tom and Jerry Cartoon, but when I hit the water I moved through the others like a torpedo.

As we lay recovering on the sand, the lifeguard came shambling along. Lifeguard! – it took him twenty minutes to uncross his legs. 'You don't swim in the sea,' said our diver. 'Are you afraid of the barracuda?'

'Listen, man,' said the lifeguard – indicating the water, 'don't let no-one tell you no different. Dat's dere house – I don't live dere.'

One other curious thing happened during that trip – at least, it had curious results. An American woman I'd had a few conversations with said, just before I left, 'I think you might find this book interesting,' and she gave me a paperback. She said no more than that. I found it more than interesting. It was compelling and disturbing. I finished it at home, and have to admit that for the first time in my adult life I had to sleep with the light on.

Shortly after I got back I went to lunch with Joyce Hopkirk, then editor of the new magazine *Cosmopolitan*. 'No, I don't think I'll pose nude for your centre spread,' I said. 'Let's change the subject. Have you read . . .' – and I told her about this extraordinary book. Now I only learned very recently that as a result of my recommendation, Joyce Hopkirk did read the book; she ran it in her magazine; it was picked up by the American edition of *Cosmopolitan*, and read by film director William Friedkin, who then made *The Exorcist*. This story may be quite untrue, but it's the way I heard it. Of course the book

would have been filmed anyway. I must say I don't want to
see it.

Another film I didn't see was *The Devils*, not because I'm
especially squeamish (I sat through Kubrick's *Clockwork Orange*
in stunned, admiring silence) or because I don't admire the
cinematic skills of Ken Russell. But I don't enjoy being party
to another person's self-indulgence, and it saddens me to see
actors and actresses degrading themselves to gratify the whims
of the director and so obviously without any idea of what
they're supposed to be doing. (I've spoken to some of the people
who were involved and I know that most of them got no
pleasure from their public self-abuse; they needed the money.)

Among the various jobs that come along from time to time
– non-broadcasting jobs, I mean – was an invitation to help
judge BEA's Personality Girl contest. This was no Miss World
in miniature. The girls didn't parade in swimsuits; they
appeared in uniform and were interviewed individually by a
panel of people involved in the airline business, plus myself to
represent the travelling public (and to present the prizes). The
winner would have a year's hard work of public relations
duties ahead of her.

I was pleased to accept. 'We don't propose to offer you a
fee,' said BEA, 'but we'd like you to accept two first-class
return tickets to any place we fly to.' That's my idea of a very
nice fee.

I didn't take advantage of the tickets immediately. The
time had to be right. Eventually I gave one to Ann so that she
could spend Easter in Rome with her Italian friends.

When BEA and BOAC became British Airways, I was still
holding my one remaining ticket. 'Suppose,' I said, 'I wanted to
go to Cyprus. Wouldn't a first-class return ticket for Cyprus be
about the same as a working-class trip to the West Coast of
America?' 'Well, roughly,' they said. And so I once again
plotted and planned my working routine to fit in with another
lightning trip to the States. Only this time it was Las Vegas.

More than any other place on that bizarre continent, Las
Vegas is somewhere you loathe or are knocked out by, or both.
Barry Norman wrote a piece about it in the *Guardian*. He said,
'It was a shrewd decision by the National Funeral Directors'
Association of America to hold their convention in Las Vegas

For my last trick

Some of the comments from the audience were quite audible, too. On the first matinee, every time Elizabeth Power pranced on to cause more mischief, an old gentleman cried, 'Oh my God! here she comes again!'

At the end of Act 1 she and I elope. We were once married to each other, and meet again while honeymooning with our new spouses. We realize we're still in love, and make our escape. As we rushed off together at the end of Act 1, we heard a lady in the front row say to her companion, 'Oh, dear. I do hope they're not going to be unfaithful.'

And now I sit waiting for the phone to ring, trying to decide where to eat tonight, wondering whether to accept the offer of another stage play. It's tempting, but it would mean a long time away from radio and television, and there are small mouths to be fed. I also think ahead to my next trip abroad. I must keep moving. There's much to be done, many old ambitions unfulfilled. I have yet to star in a Western, write the definitive novel, share a keyboard with Erroll Garner, win Wimbledon, and feel the spotlight beat down on me at Caesar's Palace. But the night is young. If I needed a sub-title to this book, it might be, 'My Old Man Said Follow The Band, But Don't Dilettante On The Way'. At least Polly's learnt a few words of his own, and I hope to be allowed to squawk on until they have to sellotape me to the perch.

Then I'll take out an advertisement in the personal column:

'For sale: One cross-bred parrot. Suitable pet for retired Customs and Excise Man.'

Index

―――――◆―――――

Index

Index

Index

Index

Index

Index

Company 80, 84, 94–5, 103; *see also* place names
Walsh, Michael 61
Wandsworth, London, childhood in 3–5, 8, 23, 24–5, 32–7; school 27–32
War, Second World: outbreak of 7; evacuation of children 8–23, 26; end of 25
War Office Selection Board 49
wartime evacuation 8–23, 26
'warm-up' sessions 160, 165–6
Waterloo station 23, 52
Webb, Graham 139
'Wednesday Show, The' 151
West, Peter 132
Western Mail 81
Whitaker, Frances 178
White, Eddie (uncle) 34
White, Phoebe (aunt) 34

Whitmore, Peter 160, 162, 163
Williams, Andy, at the Oval 176
Williams, Arthur 94
Williams, Prysor 78–9
Wilson, Bill 165
Wilson, Manning 97–8
Wiltshire, White horse of 163–4
Wimbledon 109, 123; tennis 99
Winchester, army camp near 47–53, 64–5
Wise, Ernie 97, 151, 164
'Woman's Hour' 110
Women's Lib 132, 136–7
Woodall, Corbet 112
Wooburn Green, Bucks 142–3

Yorkshire TV 168

Zodiac, signs of the 123, 171
Zoo *see* London Zoo